100 THINGS
PEARL JAM FANS
SHOULD KNOW & DO
BEFORE THEY DIE

Greg Prato

TRIUMPH
BOOKS

Library of Congress Cataloging-in-Publication Data

Names: Prato, Greg, author.
Title: 100 things Pearl Jam fans should know and do before they die / Greg Prato.
Other titles: One hundred things Pearl Jam fans should know and do before they die
Description: Chicago, Illinois : Triumph Books, [2018]
Identifiers: LCCN 2018000459 | ISBN 9781629375403
Subjects: LCSH: Pearl Jam (Musical group)—Miscellanea.
Classification: LCC ML421.P43 P73 2018 | DDC 782.42166092/2—dc23
LC record available at https://lccn.loc.gov/2018000459

This book is available in quantity at special discounts for your group or organization. For further information, contact:

Triumph Books LLC
814 North Franklin Street
Chicago, Illinois 60610
(312) 337-0747
www.triumphbooks.com

Printed in U.S.A.
ISBN: 978-1-62937-540-3
Design by Patricia Frey

To Eddie, Stone, Mike, Jeff, Matt, Boom, Jack, Dave, Matt, and Dave. Thank you for the amazingly inspiring music and for consistently fighting the good fight.

Contents

Foreword

At the time of the release of *Ten*, I was doing fill-ins at MTV. I was also running WHTG, a radio station up at the Jersey shore and one of the 13 original alternative rock stations. Radio hadn't really caught on to Pearl Jam yet but we gave them a chance. It wasn't really until "Even Flow" that most rock stations went back and started playing "Alive." And then the Mark Pellington video [for "Jeremy"] just put the band over the top. That was like ground zero for the band—even though they were already getting played on stations by people like me and being championed by people in radio programming. They just exploded. They struck a nerve that really hit with the youth of America, as far as I was concerned. People related to that feeling of alienation, but at the same time, that feeling of hope. I think that's the thing that really is so important about the band and that period of time.

As they were exploding through radio and MTV, they were coming onstage early in the day at Lollapalooza, and people were going *bananas.* They would hear the beginning of a Pearl Jam song and they would run from wherever they were and go crazy in front of the stage. And Eddie would do what Bono had done during the *War* tour—climbing up the structure of the stage—and people of course loved that. So that record became such an important part of that time, and people couldn't get enough of them.

When it came time to release *Vs.*, they wanted to figure out a way to slow down the train. They decided to take things slower, because it was just getting way out of their hands. Eddie had a really bad reaction to Kurt Cobain's suicide—he was very, very upset. I remember they ran a story in *NME* about him, and there's a picture of him, and he looks just so distraught. So, they ended up deciding not to make videos for a long time—not until the animated video for "Do the Evolution" off *Yield*.

We've had many personal interactions over the years. I remember during the Tibetan Freedom Concert at Downing Stadium in 1997, Eddie and Mike were playing acoustic songs in the afternoon. Eddie walked offstage and said to me, "Hey Matt, I've been wanting to meet you." The thing was, we had met, back when they were Mookie Blaylock.

But how could he remember that? We met in San Francisco when they were playing this pool hall. People would play all over town—it was like South by Southwest—and any place could become a venue. And there was a poster that said, TONIGHT: MOOKIE BLAYLOCK. FORMER MEMBERS OF MOTHER LOVE BONE. It was a handwritten poster! So, I was there in this pool hall, and it was pretty amazing.

So, years later, Eddie didn't know it was me, but he knew me from TV. He said, "I want you to know I heard you're a great guy from the Soundgarden guys. They said you were the real deal. I just want to apologize that we're not making videos anymore, or I would have loved to do something with you."

We did end up doing something years later, because at the time they were doing *Storytellers* on VH1 in 2006, they demanded that I do the actual interviews, even though I was off-camera. But they wanted me to do it, so we did it at the old Limelight in New York—which was still in the shape of a venue at the time. I did the interviews backstage with the band, and it was really incredible.

But getting back to *Vs.*—it's my favorite Pearl Jam album, because I felt it was a really important album and I thought that the things that they did around that time were very cool and ballsy. They put out "Go" as the first single—they could have released *anything* and it would have gotten airplay. But "Go" opens the album, and it's a great, powerful thrasher of a song.

Some people like to say, "Oh, it's a setup track for the radio hit." But no, not in the band's eyes. In the band's eyes, it's another one of their babies—like anything else. And "Go" was a great track to lead off with. And then of course, the singles started to come from the record, and radio was playing songs like "Glorified G," "Daughter," "Dissident," and my favorite Pearl Jam song of all-time, "Elderly Woman Behind the Counter in a Small Town." I love so many of their songs—I love "I Am Mine," too.

One of the things that I would recommend you do is check out as many of the covers that the guys have done as you can get your hands on. And it's really easy today, with YouTube and so many people being an active part of the Pearl Jam community. One of the greatest things were the Christmas singles that they came out with every year. Like, one year it would be "Angel," but my favorite was when they covered "Sonic Reducer" by the Dead Boys, because it's one of my all-time favorite punk songs. Now, when Stone and Jeff were in Green River, they covered "Ain't Nothin' to Do" by the Dead Boys—punk was as important as metal or hard rock and just melodic music to the guys in Pearl Jam.

They've done some incredible covers. Recently, I found a version of "Timeless Melody" by the La's that Eddie did with Ben Gibbard from Death Cab for Cutie—another guy from Seattle. It was just great. I love the fact that Pearl Jam has never shied away from doing cool covers—they love to play other people's songs. And obviously, Eddie is one of the biggest Pete Townshend and Who fans ever, which is why he's done a number of Who songs over the years.

I think Pearl Jam is one of the most important bands in the world. I also think the decisions they've made over the years turned out great for the band, because they became what I consider to be the Grateful Dead of the '90s alt/grunge era. In other words, they are like road warriors, and they are unbelievable. Now, Pearl Jam is not necessarily a jam band, but they change their sets, they change their songs. They've settled into that position—a ferocious live band with lifelong fans. It makes them really special. I love them.

Matt Pinfield is one of the most knowledgeable and well-known music personalities in the industry. His career began in radio, and he is most widely known as a VJ on MTV and VH1. He's currently the host of Flashback, *a syndicated classic rock radio show airing on more than 200 radio stations across the United States, and the 2* Hours with Matt Pinfield *podcast. Follow him on Twitter @MattPinfield.*

Introduction

During my lifetime, I honestly cannot think of another rock band that has consistently looked out for their fans as much as Pearl Jam has. As David Letterman so eloquently put it during his speech inducting the band into the Rock and Roll Hall of Fame, they "recognize injustice and they would stand up for it." Prior to Pearl Jam, it seemed like whenever I discovered a new rock band to get behind, it was only a matter of time until disappointment was in order, when the inevitable obvious maneuvers would be made to cash in on their sudden fame or win over as many new fans as possible, whatever the cost.

Not Pearl Jam. As Eddie Vedder once sang, "This is *not* for you." Before Pearl Jam, can you think of a band that purposefully *did not* issue a song as a single off their debut album that had "smash hit" written all over it? Or what about abruptly abandoning music videos during an era when MTV's exposure was crucial to a group's success? And what about using their popularity to stand up against business practices they did not feel were fair, voice their political views, or seemingly work overtime for causes they felt were worthwhile?

As a result, when Pearl Jam became the biggest rock band in the U.S. around the release of *Vs.*, I did not feel let down as I had in the past, when a band I had discovered pre-fame had become famous. This was something else entirely—a band that had made it on their own terms and was doing what was right, time and time again, and not what was "expected" by the music industry.

As someone who was lucky enough to witness the changing of the tides in rock music in late 1991, I can say that with each passing year that experience looks more and more like a once-in-a-lifetime event. All of a sudden, there was a musical style that felt so organic and natural that it made everything else sound less authentic, and it was being created by people who could have been your friends or in a local band. The only difference was the whole world was seemingly listening to their music, copying their look and sound, and hanging on their every word...or riff.

One personal measuring stick of how popular Pearl Jam was at the time: attending college in the early '90s and living in a dormitory, the music I heard most often blaring out of open windows or into hallways was undoubtedly Pearl Jam. Something else I could never understand was the whole "Nirvana vs. Pearl Jam" feud that the press seemed fixated on during that era. Out of all my fellow music-loving friends, I cannot think of a single one who did not enjoy the music of *both* bands.

Besides Pearl Jam's music providing the soundtrack to certain stages of my life, the band is responsible for one of my top concert memories: their performance at Jones Beach Theater in August 1992, and witnessing Mr. Vedder defy death (something he seemed to be doing on a nightly basis that year).

Having told part of the Pearl Jam story in my earlier book, *Grunge Is Dead: The Oral History of Seattle Rock Music*, I simply couldn't pass up the opportunity to write about them again. By doing so, I had the opportunity to rediscover music and video footage that I had not heard or viewed in quite some time (and in a few cases, ever). My final thoughts after all the research, listening, viewing, and writing? Pearl Jam is—without question—one of the greatest rock 'n' roll bands. *Ever.*

1 Who Is Pearl Jam?

So, who exactly is Pearl Jam, you ask? Anyone with a passing knowledge of rock music post-1991 will know them as one of the most popular, important, and enduring rock bands of modern times, with a lineup featuring singer Eddie Vedder, guitarists Stone Gossard and Mike McCready, bassist Jeff Ament, and several drummers over the years (in chronological order: Dave Krusen, Matt Chamberlain, Dave Abbruzzese, Jack Irons, and Matt Cameron). And although Pearl Jam will forever be associated with Seattle as one of the leading bands of the early '90s "grunge movement," some of the members originally hailed from other locales.

Eddie Vedder was born Edward Louis Severson, on December 23, 1964, in Evanston, Illinois, to Karen Lee Vedder and Edward Louis Severson Jr., an organist/violinist who sang in restaurants and was the leader of the group Eddie Severson & Hollyridge. The couple divorced in 1965, and Karen would eventually remarry to Peter Mueller. She worked as a waitress while Peter attended law school, and the couple ran a group home, serving as foster parents. As a child, Eddie was led to believe that Mueller was his father and that Severson was merely a friend of the family; Eddie would meet his real father only a handful of times during his life before Severson passed away in 1981 from multiple sclerosis. Eddie also has three brothers that have been previously mentioned in articles as being either half-brothers *or* step-brothers—Jason, Michael, and Chris.

Eddie's first instrument was a ukulele. An uncle introduced him to the sounds of the Beatles and the Rolling Stones, and also took him to his first concert: Bruce Springsteen and the E Street

1

Band at the Auditorium Theatre in Chicago in 1977. During the '70s, Eddie and his family relocated to San Diego, California, and by high school, Eddie was listening to the likes of the Who, Public Image Limited, and Springsteen, and playing in bands himself. By the late '80s, Vedder was surfing, singing in such local bands as Bad Radio, working as a roadie at a local club, the Bacchanal, as well as working a midnight shift as a security guard. It was around this time that he befriended Red Hot Chili Peppers drummer Jack Irons, who would be crucial to the formation of Pearl Jam—he was the one who passed a tape of original tunes from Jeff Ament, Stone Gossard, and Mike McCready to Vedder. Between 1994 and 2000, Vedder was married to Beth Liebling (aka Sadie 7 from space rockers Hovercraft), and since 2010, he has been married to former model Jill McCormick. The couple have two daughters—Harper and Olivia.

Stone Carpenter Gossard was born on July 20, 1966, in Seattle. His father, David Gossard, was an attorney, and his mother, Carolyn Gossard, worked in the city government. He has two sisters, Shelly and Star. At the suggestion of eventual Green River/Mudhoney guitarist Steve Turner, Gossard first picked up a bass before settling in on the six-string, with early musical influences being Led Zeppelin, Simon & Garfunkel, and Iggy and the Stooges. Along with Turner, Gossard formed the Ducky Boys before crossing paths with Jeff Ament, who had just recently relocated to Washington from Montana. At first, the pair didn't exactly hit it off; Ament found Gossard to be a tad too sarcastic for his liking and considered punching him...until Mudhoney's Mark Arm intervened. But the two obviously found common ground, as they've been bandmates in four bands spanning several decades— Green River, Mother Love Bone, Temple of the Dog, and, of course, Pearl Jam. Gossard and his first wife, Liz, had a daughter named Viv; he and his current wife, Vivien, have two children of their own, Marlowe and Faye.

The members of Pearl Jam: Mike McCready, Matt Cameron, Eddie Vedder, Jeff Ament, and Stone Gossard. (AP Images)

Michael David McCready was born on April 5, 1966, in Pensacola, Florida, to Roy McCready and Louise McCready. The family relocated soon after to San Diego before settling down in Seattle. His first guitar was a black Les Paul copy, and by the age of 12 he played well enough to join such local bands as Warrior and Shadow; his early influences included Kiss, Jimi Hendrix, and local rockers TKO. For a spell during the '80s, McCready moved to Los Angeles with Shadow in a valiant attempt to "make it" on the Sunset Strip during an era when such homegrown hair metal bands as Quiet Riot, Mötley Crüe, and Ratt were ruling the roost. It was also during this sojourn that McCready was diagnosed with Crohn's disease. By the dawn of the '90s, the guitarist had returned to the Pacific Northwest—which proved to be a smart move, as he would soon receive an invite from an old schoolmate, Stone Gossard, about forming a new band. McCready has also disclosed that he struggled with alcoholism and/or drug addiction at various points during his life. McCready is married to Ashley O'Connor, and is the father of three children whose names—to the best of my knowledge—have never been made public.

Jeffrey Allen Ament was born on March 10, 1963, in Havre, Montana, to Penny Ament and her husband, George, who worked as a barber and also served as the mayor for the town of Big Sandy. Jeff has a brother named Barry. After beginning on piano and then moving over to drums, Jeff was inspired to pick up the bass by the late, great Dee Dee Ramone—which led to being equally influenced by '70s-era heavy metal (Kiss, Aerosmith, Ted Nugent) and punk rock and new wave (the Ramones, the Clash, Devo). After dropping out of the University of Montana in 1983, Jeff and his bandmates in the local punk band Deranged Diction packed up and headed to Seattle. Before long, he crossed paths with Gossard. Ament and his wife, Pandora Andre-Beatty, married in 2016.

And what about the drummers' stories? Patience, patience, patience—you will be reading about them soon!

2 Get to Know the Emerald City

For a spell during the early '90s, it seemed like you couldn't turn on your TV/radio or open a magazine without seeing, hearing, or reading about Seattle, Washington. And while it may seem like the rest of the world was finally taking note of this city located in the Pacific Northwest, it has long been a location rich with history and the birthplace of some of the world's most renowned entertainers as well as successful companies.

Seattle was incorporated in 1869, and named after a Suquamish Tribe and Dkhw'Duw'Absh chief who forged a friendship with Doc Maynard, one of the city's main founders. The chief, referred to over the years as Seattle, Sealth, Seathle, Seathl, or See-ahth, once gave a speech or penned a letter—it has never been definitively proven which—that dealt with ecology and respecting Native American rights which was later used by Soundgarden in a cover of Black Sabbath's "Into the Void." By the early 20th century, the city's logging, fishing, and maritime industries were thriving. One of the city's most renowned brands, the Boeing Company, was founded in 1916.

But by the early '70s, Boeing had cut 60,000 jobs and the unemployment rate in Seattle reached an alarming 13 percent, more than double the national average at the time. (A billboard was raised near Seattle-Tacoma International Airport which read, WILL THE LAST PERSON LEAVING SEATTLE TURN OUT THE LIGHTS) Thankfully, things eventually picked up, including the emergence of global giants Microsoft, Starbucks, and Amazon.com. Boeing, on the other hand, relocated its corporate offices from Seattle to Chicago in 2001.

Seattle has given us some of the best-known names in the world of entertainment, including the legendary Jimi Hendrix (born in Seattle on November 27, 1942, and buried at Greenwood Memorial Park, in Renton), Bruce Lee (who moved to Seattle at the age of 18 and is buried at Lake View Cemetery), producer/songwriter Quincy Jones, and many more. And, of course, Seattle gave birth to the grunge movement in the 1990s, spearheaded by the likes of Soundgarden, Nirvana, Alice in Chains, and Pearl Jam, as well as the Sub Pop record label, which is located at 2013 4th Avenue.

If you are thinking of visiting Seattle, don't miss out on its abundance of music venues, such as the Showbox (located at 1426

1st Avenue), the Crocodile Café (2200 2nd Avenue), the Moore Theatre (1932 2nd Avenue), the Paramount Theatre (9th Avenue and Pine Street), and the KeyArena (305 Harrison Street). If you're looking to broaden your musical horizons a bit, consider enjoying a performance by the Grammy Award–winning Seattle Symphony, which regularly performs at Benaroya Hall, located at 200 University Street. (The symphony also has legitimate ties to grunge, as it took part in a Mad Season reunion with Chris Cornell on vocals in 2015, later issued as the album *Sonic Evolution/January 30, 2015/Benaroya Hall.*)

While we're on the subject of music, Seattle has a number of great record stores, including Easy Street Records (4559 California Avenue SW), Sonic Boom Records (located at 2209 N.W. Market Street), and Bop Street Records (2220 N.W. Market Street), among others. Additionally, drop by the Museum of Pop Culture (formerly "Experience Music Project") located at 325 5th Avenue N, which contains all sorts of entertainment-based exhibits.

The Godfathers of Grunge

Considering the level of popularity grunge achieved in the 1990s, fans can be excused for assuming those crunchy riffs and personal lyrics were invented by Pearl Jam, Nirvana, and their peers. But grunge's roots run deep, and while a few of the names that belong in the "grunge godfathers" category may be familiar to the casual fan, the majority of them are rather obscure but proved to be influential and important to the formation of the genre. So here they are, with a short description about just what made them so darn special (plus a recommended album):

The Sonics

One of the greatest garage rock bands of all-time, it's baffling that the Sonics did not break out in a big way nationwide. They were quite popular back in the 1960s in the Seattle-Tacoma area. Just give a listen to their classic original, "The Witch," to hear an obvious influence on such subsequent grunge bands as Mudhoney.

Required Listening: *Here Are the Sonics* **(compilation, 1999)**

The Wailers

I bet just about any article written about this band after the 1970s has started with the disclaimer, "Not to be confused with the reggae group from Jamaica of the same name, best known for their work with Bob Marley…" So I'll borrow it for the beginning of this entry, as well! Along with the Sonics, the Wailers (who also go by "the Fabulous Wailers") were a great garage rock band and one of the first to cover Richard Berry's "Louie Louie" (in 1961), although another local band, the Kingsmen, would score a hit with virtually the same version of the tune two years later.

Required Listening: *At the Castle / The Wailers and Co.* **(compilation, 2003)**

The Blackouts

Although not much grunge can be detected in the Blackouts' sound, the band was unquestionably cutting-edge and original, and at times approached industrial rock territory—many, many years before the likes of Ministry and Nine Inch Nails perfected and popularized it. That makes sense—Ministry's head honcho, Al Jourgensen, would produce the Blackouts' final recording (1985's *Lost Souls Club*), before two members of the band (Paul Barker and Bill Rieflin) would become full-fledged members of Ministry.

Required Listening: *History in Reverse* **(compilation, 2004)**

The U-Men

Led by larger-than-life frontman John Bigley, the U-Men lasted for much of the 1980s, and were known for an unpredictable live show that would sometimes see its members performing in odd-yet-coordinated outfits on stage. Musically, the band sounded comparable at times to Jesus Lizard, years before David Yow and company were in business.

Required Listening: *Solid Action* **(compilation, 2000)**

The Fastbacks

Not all the Seattle rock bands were dudes—as evidenced by pop-punkers the Fastbacks, who included two ladies (Kim Warnick and Lulu Gargiulo) in their lineup. It turns out that none other than Pearl Jam were admirers of the group—the Fastbacks opened on much of the *No Code* tour in 1996.

Required Listening: *...And His Orchestra* **(1987)**

Mr. Epp and the Calculations

This Flipper-sounding group proved to be an important grunge pre-cursor for one simple reason: it was singer Mark Arm's first band—the same Mark Arm who would later be a key member of Green River (alongside Stone Gossard and Jeff Ament), as well as Mudhoney.

Required Listening: *Sleepless in Seattle: The Birth of Grunge* **(compilation, 2006: only one song included, "Mohawk Man")**

The Accüsed

Were they punk? Were they metal? It's impossible to pinpoint exactly what style the Accüsed truly aligned themselves with, but they were one of the first bands to merge the two together. And the band also had one of the gnarliest—and seemingly most danger-ous—mascots of them all, Martha Splatterhead.

Required Listening: *The Return of Martha Splatterhead* **(1986)**

The Fartz

This awesomely named band was Seattle's answer to the burgeoning hardcore-punk movement that was sweeping the underground during the early '80s. The band included a pre-pre-pre-Guns N' Roses' Duff McKagan in their lineup for a spell (on drums, not bass).

Required Listening: *Because This Fuckin' World Still Stinks* **(compilation, 1998)**

10 Minute Warning

The Fartz would morph into 10 Minute Warning, who somehow seemed to find a way to kick the intensity level up a few more notches. Duff McKagan would move from behind the drum kit over to rhythm guitar, while another chap with some crystal-clear ties to Pearl Jam's history—eventual Mother Love Bone drummer Greg Gilmore—kept the beat.

Required Listening: *Survival of the Fittest* **(1982)**

The Melvins

The band often credited with inspiring Kurt Cobain to form his own band has been led from the beginning by Buzz Osborne on growls and guitar. It's one of the first bands credited with slowing down punk rock's rapid-fire pace to a snail's crawl.

Required Listening: *26 Songs* **(compilation, 2015)**

Malfunkshun

Malfunkshun is how many members of the Seattle rock underground were introduced to Andrew Wood (then known as L'Andrew the Love Child). With Wood playing bass and handling lead vocals, Malfunkshun certainly leaned more toward the metal side of things (Andrew's brother, Kevin, was a flat-out six-string shredder) and were unafraid to flaunt their love of '70s-era Kiss (as seen by Andy's fondness for performing in whiteface makeup (à la Ace, Gene, Paul, and Peter).

Required Listening: *Return to Olympus* (compilation, 1995)

Green River

While I will explore Green River at greater length, they belong on this list as they included eventual members of Mudhoney, Mother Love Bone, and Pearl Jam. Furthermore, they turned out to be quite the musical petri dish, merging punk, metal, and '70s glam.

Required Listening: *Rehab Doll* (1988)

Screaming Trees

Screaming Trees would eventually enjoy a bit of commercial success during grunge's heyday (namely the tune "Nearly Lost You" on the *Singles* soundtrack), but their roots stretched back all the way to the mid-'80s, and is where much-heralded singer and future Queens of the Stone Age member Mark Lanegan got his start.

Required Listening: *Clairvoyance* (1986)

Soundgarden

Again, I will explore them at greater length later on, but of all the bands listed, Soundgarden was the best at merging metal and punk together, and early on even amalgamated psychedelic and goth elements into their dark and brooding sonic blend.

Required Listening: *Screaming Life* (1987)

Skin Yard

Prog-grungers Skin Yard could be included on this list based solely on their pedigree—seemingly all of their members went on to leave their mark on the music biz elsewhere. Guitarist Jack Endino went on to produce countless acts, including Nirvana and Soundgarden; singer Ben McMillan would front Gruntruck; bassist Daniel House ran C/Z Records; and seemingly all of their drummers found grand gigs outside SY (including Matt Cameron, who joined Soundgarden and Pearl Jam).

Required Listening: *Skin Yard* (1987)

4 Green River

What would you get if you united a group of young musicians during the mid- to late-'80s whose record collections ran the gamut from Kiss and Venom to the Stooges and the Ramones? The answer is simple: Green River.

Formed in Seattle in 1984 and originally comprised of singer Mark Arm, guitarists Stone Gossard and Steve Turner (the latter replaced by Bruce Fairweather in 1985), bassist Jeff Ament, and drummer Alex Vincent, the band tastelessly took their name from the serial killer known as the Green River Killer (aka Gary Ridgway).

Despite being a hip band to name check post-1991, Green River only managed a handful of releases during their brief run together, including a pair of EPs (1985's *Come on Down* and 1987's *Dry as a Bone*) and a single full-length album (1988's *Rehab Doll*)—although truth be told, *Rehab Doll* is less than a minute longer than *Come on Down* (28:40 vs. 27:43), so should it truly count as a full-length? Regardless, Green River made a name for themselves locally with an unpredictable live show, in which Arm would try and out-Iggy Iggy (he once hid a smelly dead fish down his trousers, before hurling it into the audience). Additionally, Soundgarden covered a GR original, "Swallow My Pride," on their 1988 EP *Fopp*.

By 1988, however, the band was finished—the final nail in the coffin supposedly involving a disagreement over the music of

Jane's Addiction (Ament and Gossard were smitten; Arm was not impressed), resulting in Ament, Gossard, and Fairweather going off to form Mother Love Bone, and Arm reuniting with Turner to form Mudhoney. A compilation that combined *Dry as a Bone* and *Rehab Doll* was issued in 1990 by Sub Pop.

Ultimately, Green River was better in theory than in actual execution, as future Presidents of the United States of America guitarist Dave Dederer explained to me in the book *Grunge Is Dead: The Oral History of Seattle Rock Music*: "That whole thing was starting then—people wanted to have bands that were the New York Dolls meets Pere Ubu meets Def Leppard. [Laughs] Stone was listening to *Pyromania*, Kiss, and the New York Dolls. They started to put it all together, and it didn't work very well. [Laughs] Green River is an example of that—'Hey, let's mash all this stuff together and see if it works!' People figured out how to make it work [later]. Alice in Chains and Soundgarden figured out how to make it be something that was new that sounded good."

While Green River's split was supposedly not all that rosy, by 1993, the hatchet was officially buried when Mudhoney was invited by Pearl Jam to open shows (which they have done numerous times subsequently), and a one-off Green River reunion took place on November 30, 1993, in Las Vegas, which saw Arm, Turner, Gossard, and Ament share the stage with drummer Chuck Treece (Vincent was unavailable) at the conclusion of a Pearl Jam performance, before reuniting again several more times (with Vincent back in place) during the early 21st century.

5 Mother Love Bone

Glam and grunge are considered to be at the complete opposite ends of the musical spectrum. After all, it was grunge and alt-rock that helped exterminate glam/hair metal (thankfully) in the early '90s. But one of the few bands that managed to combine glam and grunge successfully was the one that served as a precursor to Pearl Jam: Mother Love Bone.

To be clear, the kind of glam that MLB drew inspiration from was not of the Poison variety but rather earlier glam icons such as T. Rex, Elton John, and Queen. In fact, the presence of a piano on several MLB songs was a clear divider between them and the rest of the '80s glam pack, who were content to instead use synthesizers and keyboards to sweeten their sound.

Formed in 1987, Mother Love Bone was the union of members from three different/popular/influential Seattle-area club bands—Malfunkshun (singer/keyboardist Andrew Wood), Green River (bassist Jeff Ament, guitarists Stone Gossard and Bruce Fairweather), and 10 Minute Warning (Greg Gilmore). And while most singers of Seattle acts at the time were busy embracing the eventual back-to-basic "grunge uniform," the larger-than-life Wood had more in common with Marc Bolan's and Freddie Mercury's flamboyant wardrobes, which were provided by his designer girlfriend, Xana La Fuente.

And the musical results were quite impressive—so much so, that along with Soundgarden, Mother Love Bone was one of the first Seattle grunge bands to sign with a major label (in MLB's case, Mercury Records), resulting in the 1989 EP *Shine* and the 1990 full-length *Apple*. And as evidenced by such tunes as "Stardog Champion," "Stargazer," and especially "Crown of Thorns," MLB

Apple, *Mother Love Bone,
1990.* (Stardog/Mercury)

sounded like they were on a path to creating a truly unique spin
on hard rock.

As Wood explained about some of the album's standout tunes
in 1990 to *Rip Magazine*: "'Stardog Champion' is a kinda...fake,
kinda patriotic rock anthem of sorts. That's gonna be the first
single and video. When I wrote 'Holy Roller,' I didn't even know
what a holy roller was. I just thought it was a cool term. Actually,
I was thinking of a Paul McCartney and Wings song, 'Let Me Roll
It.' I don't know why it made me think of holy rollers. 'Captain
High-Top' is just a total rock propaganda kinda thing. I kinda see
'Heartshine' as our 'Achilles Last Stand' of the album. It's long and
real powerful. I was kinda depressed about leaving Malfunkshun
for a long time. Still am, kinda. I feel like, you know, I left them
stranded. I've got a brother besides Kevin who, ah, is kinda insane
in a way, and he makes the whole family worry about him, so
'Heartshine' is a little about both of my brothers."

Tragically, MLB's potential was snuffed out prematurely when
Wood died as a result of a heroin overdose on March 19, 1990.
With Wood proving to be irreplaceable, MLB opted to pack it in
rather than attempt to carry on with a new singer, AC/DC-style.
This eventually led to Ament and Gossard deciding to form a new

band, receiving a suggestion from Jack Irons about a singer friend of his, and...well, I'm sure you know the rest of the story.

In the wake of Wood's passing (*Apple* would be released several months later, on July 19), MLB seemingly almost immediately developed a cultish following, thanks to the aforementioned feature in *Rip Magazine*, a combined feature with other Seattle bands in *Rolling Stone*, as well as Wood's onetime housemate, Chris Cornell, writing several tunes in tribute to his friend, which resulted in the formation of Temple of the Dog.

Eventually, MLB received some serious MTV airplay, via their "Stardog Champion" clip, when both of their releases were reissued together as a compilation, *Mother Love Bone*, in the wake of Pearl Jam mania on September 22, 1992; the song peaked at No. 77 on the Billboard 200. (A year later, a home video surfaced, *The Love Bone Earth Affair*, as well.) Interest in Wood has remained strong throughout the years, as evidenced by a compilation of Malfunkshun material, *Return to Olympus*, being issued via Stone Gossard's Loosegroove label in 1995, as well as a must-see documentary of his life and career, 2005's *Malfunkshun: The Andrew Wood Story*, and another comp in 2016 via Monkeywrench Records, *On Earth As It Is: The Complete Works*.

6 Momma-Son

Just about any musician in a rock band has at some point had to go through the arduous process of listening to tapes or viewing videos of potential bandmates. And usually, it seems like it's a hopeful musician who is woefully off the mark. So, imagine the situation that Stone Gossard and Jeff Ament were in when they decided to soldier on and try to form a new band in the wake of Andy Wood's tragic death and the abrupt end of Mother Love Bone.

Luckily, Ament had a solid contact in Jack Irons, former drummer for the Red Hot Chili Peppers, who suggested that a friend in San Diego may be a good fit behind the microphone. A cassette of three originals that Gossard, Ament, and Mike McCready had recorded with Matt Cameron, on loan from Soundgarden, made its way to Irons, who then handed it off to a mysterious fellow named Eddie Vedder.

Speaking to Vedder for *Grunge Is Dead*, he recalled receiving what would be referred to as the *Momma-Son* tape: "When I got to Jack's house in L.A., he gave [the tape] to me—I played it on the way home to San Diego. Then I'm sure I went right to work. I was a glorified security guard / gas station attendant doing midnight shifts. I had been doing midnight shifts for quite a while—maybe five or six years. I'd also work three shifts at this club called the Bacchanal. I had the music in my head. I went out for a bit of a surf in the morning, and then wrote the songs in this shack that I had a four-track sitting in. I sent the tape off that day—my version of three songs. Two days later, I saw a little article in *Rolling Stone* that had a picture. I think it was Bruce [Fairweather], Stone, and Jeff. It was the first time I could put a face to it."

Vedder used Wite-Out across the top of the cassette and wrote FOR STONE + JEFF over it, then sent it back to Seattle. While Iron's recommendation of Vedder may have raised their hopes, it's safe to say the expectations of Gossard, Ament, and McCready were not Space Needle–high as they awaited a response from the unknown singer. So, imagine the sense of excitement they must have experienced when they heard Vedder's voice for the first time, as well as the original lyrics he had fit to three songs—"Alive," "Once," and "Footsteps." Needless to say, the recipients of the tape were blown away, and Vedder soon was invited to visit Seattle for a week to see if there was chemistry between the musicians.

Listening to those versions of the songs today, it's incredible how close "Alive" is to the track that appeared on *Ten*—the lyrics and music are all virtually identical. The demo of "Once," on the other hand, has a funkier vibe and different verses than the album version. "Footsteps" is similar musically to the song that would appear under the title "Times of Trouble" on Temple of the Dog's self-titled debut, but lyrically it is completely different. Of the trio of tunes, "Footsteps" was the only one to not make the *Ten* cut; it would be rerecorded (on a May 11, 1992, *Rockline* appearance) as a stark acoustic version and serve as a B-side for the "Jeremy" single.

So, why was the cassette referred to as *Momma-Son*? The reason is that Vedder tied all three songs together as a mini "rock opera" (borrowing a page right out of the handbook of his favorite band, the Who) that tells a disturbing tale of a killer and how he became deranged. At a Pearl Jam show on June 18, 1992, in Zürich, Switzerland (later issued as a bootleg, *Five Alive*), all three songs were performed back-to-back-to-back, and Vedder offered the following noteworthy tidbit: "I don't wanna ruin any interpretations of the songs that you have, but it's about incest and it's about murder and all those good things. And if you can picture it in your mind, the third song takes place in a jail cell—so this is our own little mini-opera."

That would not be the last PJ fans would hear about the tape. In a charming scene in the *Pearl Jam Twenty* documentary, director Cameron Crowe presents Vedder with what is purportedly the actual *Momma-Son* cassette. Fans who wanted their own personal copy of the *Momma-Son* tape got their wish in 2009; the release of a "super deluxe" version of *Ten* contained a faithful replica of the cassette. That said, the more alert PJ fans will notice that the cassette Crowe gives to Vedder in *PJ 20* looks different than the one included in the *Ten* reissue. Perhaps it's fitting that such an iconic artifact remain somewhat shrouded in mystery.

7 Temple of the Dog

One oft-repeated axiom about songwriting is that great music is borne from tragedy. While this certainly isn't always the case (I bet "Macarena" was not the result of pain and suffering), it is true in the case of Temple of the Dog. Still reeling from the tragic death of Andy Wood and the abrupt end of Mother Love Bone, Chris Cornell penned a pair of songs in tribute to his late friend/house-mate, "Say Hello 2 Heaven" and "Reach Down."

As Cornell explained during an interview on Seattle's KISW on April 14, 1991: "Actually, when he died I was on tour or, actually, I had got back the day he died. And then like about five days later I went to Europe for another tour, and I figured it would be this great thing, because I would be away from home and I wouldn't have to look at places where I saw him or see things that would remind me of him and I thought it would be really great. But it was awful because I couldn't talk to anybody. So I started writing songs—that was the only thing I could really think of to do. The songs I wrote weren't really stylistically like something my band Soundgarden would be used to playing or be natural for us to do, but it was material that Andy really would have liked, so I didn't really want to just throw it out the window or put it away in a box, y'know, put the tape away and never listen to it again. So I thought it would be good to make a single, and I thought it would be really great to record it with these guys, Stone and Jeff, because they were in his band and I just thought it would be a really fun thing to do...I was getting to be friends with these guys before he died, actually, and it just seemed like maybe it was a good idea. At first I thought about it and then I thought maybe they would think it was horrible and that I was an asshole..."

Suffice it to say, they did not, and with Cornell, Gossard, and Ament on board, the idea soon expanded from a single to a full album—with Soundgarden's Matt Cameron providing drums and Pearl Jam's Mike McCready rounding out the lineup on guitar. (For its name, the nascent band borrowed a line from the Mother Love Bone track "Man of Golden Words.") During a band rehearsal of the material, none other than Eddie Vedder was a spectator, and when he saw Cornell struggling to pull off a tricky vocal part for the song that would become "Hunger Strike," he sauntered up to a mic and provided some assistance. The result was so outstanding that Vedder was invited to make his major-label debut on the record (*Ten* was still a ways off), even singing lead on certain parts of the song (as well as providing backup on three other tracks, "Pushin' Forward Back," "Your Saviour," and "Four Walled World").

The 10-track album was recorded at London Bridge (where PJ had just wrapped up work on *Ten*) and included all the afore-mentioned tracks, as well as "Call Me a Dog," "Times of Trouble" (which was basically the early Pearl Jam tune "Footsteps" but with different lyrics), "Wooden Jesus," and "All Night Thing." It was co-produced between Rick Parashar (who had also just worked on *Ten*) and issued on April 16, 1991, via Soundgarden's label, A&M.

To say the album was released with little fanfare is an under-statement—aside from a feature interview in *Rip Magazine*, a video for "Hunger Strike," and a handful of live performances, the album was barely promoted, and only found its way into the hands of the hardest of hardcore Soundgarden and Mother Love Bone fans at the time.

Fast-forward to the summer of 1992: grunge had stormed the world, with both Pearl Jam and Soundgarden seemingly being fea-tured nonstop on MTV and in the press, as well as performing to the masses as part of Lollapalooza. It didn't take a genius to realize that the marketplace would be a lot more welcoming to TOTD, so the wise folks at A&M finally decided to properly promote the album. Soon, the "Hunger Strike" video was being heavily rotated on MTV, and the song became a rock radio hit (peaking at No. 4 on the Billboard Mainstream Rock Tracks chart and No. 7 on the Billboard Modern Rock Tracks chart), while the album would reach No. 5 on the Billboard 200 and be certified platinum.

Since both Pearl Jam and Soundgarden were touring together that summer as part of Lollapalooza, a buzz surrounded the festival concerning the potential of TOTD performances. And on two of the dates (August 14 in Reston, Virginia, and September 13 in Irvine, California), the fans' wishes were granted, when "Hunger Strike" was performed (on the latter date, "Reach Down" was also played).

Fans could be forgiven for assuming that would be the last anyone would ever hear from Temple of the Dog, as years went by without a peep about the supergroup. But beginning in 2003, there would be sporadic/surprise/one-off TOTD reunions, and the band did end up in the press once again during the early 21st century, when it became known that there was a battle going on behind the scenes between London Bridge Studio and A&M Records concerning who owned the album's master tapes. To fans' delight, Chris Cornell tweeted a photo of six separate boxes of master tapes on May 24, 2016, with the message, "Temple of the Dog masters returned today. History made whole 25 years later!"

TOTD celebrated the resolution of the dispute by releasing an expanded 25th anniversary edition of the album issued in four configurations, the most expansive being a four-disc "Super Deluxe" version that was newly mixed by producer Brendan O'Brien, and included 48 unreleased tracks and/or mixes, as well as a 180 gram, 2-LP vinyl edition of the original remastered with gatefold jacket, lenticular cover, and download code. To promote the release, a November mini-tour was announced (sans Vedder), and saw the band perform classics from their lone album, as well as covers by Led Zeppelin ("Achilles Last Stand"), David Bowie ("Quicksand"),

Black Sabbath ("War Pigs"), the Cure ("Fascination Street"), and Syd Barrett ("Baby Lemonade"), among others, as well as Mother Love Bone tunes ("Stardog Champion," "Stargazer," etc.).

The odds of the band making new music seemed promising, as Cornell told *Rolling Stone* in September 2016, "There's always a chance [we'll record more songs]. Just from my perspective, it would have to feel great. It's a scary thing. I don't want to say it would have to live up to the [first] album, but I wouldn't want to take away from it. That's the issue with me. I don't want to detract from what happened before."

Unfortunately, the possibility of further TOTD shows or new music was extinguished on May 18, 2017, with the sudden and tragic death of Cornell.

Relive the First Shows

As with most successful veteran rock artists, Pearl Jam's career has been chock full of memorable performances—Drop in the Park, Wrigley Field, their many visits to Madison Square Garden, etc. But it was their earliest performances that were probably their most important; not only were they figuring out what their sound would be, they were also finding out whether there was chemistry between its members on stage.

Pearl Jam's first public performance took place on October 22, 1990, at the Off Ramp Café in Seattle, when the band was still going by the name Mookie Blaylock and included original drummer Dave Krusen in its lineup. Opening for a pair of bands—Green Apple Quick Step (who were then named Inspector Luv and the Ride Me Babys) and Bathtub Gin—the Vedder-Gossard-McCready-Ament-Krusen

Pearl Jam performing at the Limelight in New York City, 1992.
(Steven J. Messina)

lineup offered a set that featured embryonic versions of songs that would eventually appear on *Ten* ("Release," "Alive," "Once," "Even Flow," and "Black"), as well as tunes that would eventually appear elsewhere ("Alone," "Breath," and "Just a Girl"). Luckily, an extraordinarily wise-minded individual filmed this historic show, and you can find the footage on YouTube. Vedder's ensemble for the live debut? A backward baseball cap, cargo shorts, and a blue jacket, quite reminiscent of the one he wore often during the *Vs.* era.

After playing a show at the Vogue on December 19, Mookie Blaylock opened for Alice in Chains at the Moore Theater on

December 22 (Alice in Chains filmed the show, portions of which would be issued the following year on their *Live Facelift* home video). A snippet of "Alive" from this show was included on the *Pearl Jam Twenty* doc, which sees Vedder dressed in quite a baggy blazer, trousers that resemble pajama bottoms, and a white Cramps T-shirt.

By early 1991, MB/PJ would have the good fortune of supporting Alice in Chains on a swing of West Coast dates throughout February (video of a performance on February 11 at Club with No Name, in Hollywood, shows the group beginning to sonically resemble the Pearl Jam we all know and love). They also did a show supporting goof-rockers Green Jellö (best known for their best-forgotten 1993 novelty hit, "Three Little Pigs").

In the *Pearl Jam Twenty* doc, Gossard had this to say about those early performances: "In the early years, we had those transcendent shows where it was just like, everybody was drunk and just the 'lose your mind shows'—everybody lose your mind at once."

As evidenced by this early video/audio footage, the band was already taking the necessary steps toward becoming the world-class live band they would soon become, resulting in quite a few "lose your mind shows."

Ten

For many of us, *Ten* is the album that provided the gateway to the wondrous world of Pearl Jam (myself included). And while the album would go on to be the best-selling of their career and spawned the largest number of classic tracks in the PJ catalog, what is often forgotten is that the album built momentum relatively slowly. That is in contrast to the album that *Ten* is often compared to, Nirvana's *Nevermind*, which skyrocketed up the charts seemingly right out of the gate.

The material that comprises *Ten* is a bit of a hodgepodge, with the tracks coming from a variety of sources: "Alive" began life as a tune called "Dollar Short" circa 1989, compositions from the *Momma-Son* tape ("Once"), a song that appeared to be largely penned by Vedder but was ultimately credited to all five members ("Release"), and so on.

Recorded between March 27 and April 26, 1991, at London Bridge Studios in Seattle, and co-produced by both Rick Parashar and the band, the results were stellar. Although purists have criticized the album's sonics for sounding a bit dated (i.e., heavy on the reverb), *Ten* is undoubtedly one of the greatest debut recordings by a rock band ever, and certainly one of the most consistent. A total of four singles were plucked from the disc ("Alive," "Even Flow," "Jeremy," and "Oceans"), but there really is not a single stinker in the bunch. Highlights include the fiercely rocking "Porch," the meditative "Garden," the slide-guitar-propelled "Deep," and arguably the album's best song, "Black."

The album cover's now-iconic image features the five members of the band (including Dave Krusen) striking a one-for-all pose, with their arms pointing skyward, in front of a humongous wooden cutout which partially spells out a reddish PEARL JAM (on the CD booklet, a smaller, grayish PEARL JAM is placed near their hands). Once unfolded, the CD booklet was similar in size to a vinyl album cover, something the band (who were vinyl supporters years before it became fashionable again) did on purpose.

Released on August 27, 1991, via Epic Records, *Ten* took its sweet time climbing up the Billboard 200, eventually reaching its peak of No. 2 almost exactly a year after its initial release (August 22, 1992). It would linger on the charts for four and a half years, its last appearance coming at No. 186 during the week of October

Ten, *Pearl Jam, 1991.* (Epic)

12, 1996. But perhaps most impressive is how steadily the album sold between 1992 and 2009—certified gold on February 25, 1992, platinum on May 5, 5x platinum on June 8, 1993, and 10x platinum (aka Diamond certification) on November 27, 1996. At last count, *Ten* is sitting pretty at 13x platinum, but this certification was made on March 31, 2009, which makes it a bit baffling as to why the RIAA (Recording Industry Association of America) was so eager to regularly report how much the album was selling up until 2009, before clamming up about any certification updates ever since. *Ten* would also come in at an impressive No. 14 on Billboard's "decade-end chart" for the 1990s.

Due to its colossal popularity, *Ten* has been issued in quite a few different editions over the years. One of the first would be in 1992, when the UK branch of PJ's label issued a picture disc that resembled an orange basketball on the first side (simply stating Pearl Jam in script and then Official beneath it), while its second side had a black background with a bunch of purple figures (referred to as "Alive guy" or "Stickman" by fans) in varying sizes spotted all over it. However, an actual vinyl release of *Ten* would not rear its head stateside until November 22, 1994 (the same day that the vinyl edition of *Vitalogy* was unveiled). Another picture disc was spotted in Brazil in 2008.

But apart from its initial release, the most satisfying and appealing version of *Ten* was the expanded and reissued edition from 2009, which contains a variety of goodies. The biggest story was the inclusion of an item dubbed *Ten Redux*, which was essentially a new remix of the album courtesy of Brendan O'Brien (which scrubbed away all that dastardly reverb), as well as six extra tracks: "Brother" (with vocals), "Just a Girl," "Breath and a Scream" (a demo of the tune best known as simply "Breath"), "State of Love and Trust," "2,000 Mile Blues," and "Evil Little Goat" (rehearsal studio outtake). A "deluxe edition" included a DVD of the band's 1992 appearance on *MTV Unplugged* (including previously unaired performances of "Oceans" and Neil Young's "Rockin' in the Free World"), while the "super deluxe" edition contained vinyl versions of the album and the band's September 20, 1992, concert at Magnuson Park in Seattle (also known as Drop in the Park), a replica of the original *Momma-Son* demo cassette, and a reproduction of Vedder's composition notebook containing personal notes and mementos.

10 The Great Grunge Gold Rush of 1991

By 1991, mainstream rock music had become completely predictable, played out, and stale—especially within the realm of hard rock and heavy metal. It seemed like if you enjoyed loud 'n' proud rock, you were split into either one of two factions—glam/hair metal (Guns N' Roses, Bon Jovi, Mötley Crüe, Poison, etc.) or thrash metal (Metallica, Megadeth, Slayer, Anthrax, etc.). But to listeners of college radio and viewers of the MTV program *120 Minutes*, there was something bubbling under the surface of the mainstream—bands that had obviously studied their Sabbath and Zeppelin records, but were open to a variety of other styles, especially punk rock.

Looking back, it's easy to say, "One day, Warrant, Slaughter, and Winger were the top dogs of rock. The next day it was Nirvana, Pearl Jam, and Soundgarden." Not the case, dear readers. To wit—the Red Hot Chili Peppers, Fishbone, Faith No More, Pixies, Jane's Addiction, Living Colour, Primus, Ministry, Nine Inch Nails, and Smashing Pumpkins, among others, all helped pave the way for the great grunge gold rush of 1991. Then, if you were looking for rock 'n' roll that wasn't as predictable as what mainstream radio and MTV were peddling, there were other options available if you dug a bit deeper.

So, with those bands having blazed the trail, the stage was now set and the spotlight ready. A precursor of things to come occurred during the summer of 1991, when Seattle's own Alice in Chains broke big on MTV with their dark anthem "Man in the Box." The single made their nearly year-old album *Facelift* almost slither inside the top 40 (peaking at No. 42 on the Billboard 200), eventually obtain platinum certification, and thanks to tours opening for a multi-bill featuring Slayer, Megadeth, and Anthrax (as part of the Clash of the Titans tour) and Van Halen, it introduced the little-band-that-could to a massive audience.

By the fall of 1991, it seemed as though a new, interesting, and original rock artist was being discovered each week. Amongst the artists leading the charge were three bands from the Pacific Northwest—Nirvana, with *Nevermind*; Pearl Jam, with *Ten*; and Soundgarden, with *Badmotorfinger*. Comparable to such past musical movements as hippie/psychedelia in the 1960s and punk rock in the 1970s, the grunge uprising showed once more that when multiple artists share the same ideals and approach in a natural and organic way (while not afraid to speak their mind nor forfeiting originality) they can reach far beyond just music—they can influence society. In other words, they can cause an adjustment in fashion, other forms of art, and even political views and opinions.

But just as with the other aforementioned musical movements, once the initial wave of bands broke through commercially, major labels soon swooped in and started signing bands that were pale imitations of the originators. And with the emergence of Nirvana, Pearl Jam, Soundgarden, and Alice in Chains came what can be described as the "grunge uniform," featuring a combination of flannel shirts, ripped jeans, Chuck Taylor sneakers, cargo shorts, Dr. Martens boots, and thrift store–worthy jackets. Many of the top fashion designers and clothing stores took notice.

When will the next group of artists who are so fed up with the mainstream that they decide to take a stand, unite, and come up with new and original approaches that reflect their own personalities and the region they hail from? As of this book's release, we are still waiting patiently...

 **Vs.**

"Sophomore slump" is one of the most dreaded phrases you can mutter to a musical artist trying to follow up a hit debut. But avoiding a critical and commercial step backward was exactly what Pearl Jam needed to do while writing and recording what would become their second full-length album, *Vs.* Interview footage with the band recorded during the touring cycle for *Ten* implied they were eager to return to the studio to record new music. But due to the slow-building and massive success of their debut, PJ remained on tour probably far longer than initially anticipated, especially if we were to mark Dave Abbruzzese's live debut with the band, August 23, 1991, at the Mural Amphitheater in Seattle as the tour's first date, and a performance on September 27, 1992, at the War Memorial Gymnasium in Maui as its last.

Thankfully, as the best bands often do, Pearl Jam somehow found a way. Hooking up with producer Brendan O'Brien (fresh off the success of producing Stone Temple Pilots' *Core*), the band made a conscious effort to make the album sound more like the way they sounded onstage. And they certainly succeeded, as *Vs.* is sonically much more aggressive than its predecessor. The album was recorded between March and May of 1993 at two different studios, the Site in Nicasio, California, and Potatohead Studio in Seattle.

Eddie Vedder recalled in *Grunge Is Dead* that recording *Vs.* was not all milk and cookies: "I had a hard time. I hadn't finished all the lyrics by any means, and I remember thinking, being in some kind of idyllic place was exactly not where I wanted...I wasn't going to be getting inspiration from the trees. I had this Toyota truck, and had a shell in the back, so I had a sleeping bag. Just going to the park up the street in San Francisco, in skid row, and trying to get inspiration from the conversations of crack addicts walking by or something. I remember it being really difficult—it felt like we were still on tour, and now we're making decisions which to me were more important than 'Where's the next show going to be?' It was, 'Do we cut out the bridge or lengthen the chorus?' The first record we made not thinking anybody was going to hear it. Now, it's a little different—'Millions of people heard that last thing. I wish we would have changed it then and I'm not going to let that happen again.' And everyone's probably feeling that way on different things. We weren't allowing ourselves space."

Despite the writing and recording being somewhat challenging for Vedder, the end result made it all worthwhile. The material that comprised *Vs.* was not as easily digestible as the songs on *Ten*, which was made instantly clear when the band opted to kick off the album with two explosive rockers back-to-back ("Go" and "Animal"). The rocking "Leash" had been written years earlier, as it was being performed in concert as early as November 1991. But it was not all abrasive, as PJ got surprisingly groovy in certain spots (namely "Rats" and the experimental "W.M.A."). The song that would eventually become the acoustic ballad "Daughter" had been fleshed out while on the Lollapalooza tour (video footage of Eddie Vedder and Stone Gossard working on the song—then going by the working title of "Brother"—can be found in the *Pearl Jam Twenty* doc).

Vs. also offered several tunes that probably had MTV salivating over the possibility of receiving the music videos—the rocking-yet-melodic "Rearviewmirror," plus a pair of acoustic tunes—"Elderly Woman Behind the Counter in a Small Town" and the aforementioned "Daughter." And the album's closing tune—the mood-shifting "Indifference"—has gone on to become a concert favorite. The late, great Jeff Buckley once performed a rendition of the song for Vedder, which the PJ singer called "one of the most memorable moments of my life" on *Monkeywrench Radio*.

The CD and cassette cover of *Vs.* featured a photo that Jeff Ament snapped of two goats in his home state of Montana, with one showing off its choppers and snout. Inside the CD booklet, fans found photos of the group, as well as handwritten lyrics and sketches by Vedder. At one point, the album was supposedly going to be titled *Five Against One* (a line yanked from "Animal"), and early printings of the cassette actually said *Five Against One* on the tape, while the early CDs simply stated *Pearl Jam* on the cover and the spine of the case. Regardless of the title snafu, *Vs.* was released to much fanfare on October 19, 1993, less than a month after another hotly anticipated rock album arrived, Nirvana's *In Utero*, on September 21.

Vs., *Pearl Jam, 1993*. (Epic)

Vs. sold a whopping 950,378 copies in just its first five days of release. To give you an idea of how in demand PJ and *Vs.* was around this time, the album's first certification took place on January 6, 1994, when it was certified 5x platinum. Sales did slow down eventually—at last count (May 24, 2000), *Vs.* had made it to 7x platinum, but since the RIAA certifiers seem to be as slow as a slug to update certifications nowadays, additional certifications could potentially easily be tacked on. As far as chart placements, *Vs.* takes the cake for the highest-charting PJ album worldwide, hitting No. 1 on the Australian, Canadian, Dutch, Irish, New Zealand, Norwegian, Swedish, and U.S. album charts. But the album sold the strongest in the band's homeland, where it topped the Billboard 200 for an impressive five straight weeks. For some time, *Vs.* held the record for most copies sold of an album in a single week (eventually unseated by Garth Brooks' *Double Live* in 1998).

A total of four singles would be issued from *Vs.* ("Go," "Daughter," "Animal," and "Dissident"), and there was a conscious decision made by the band to not film any music videos, which undoubtedly left MTV fuming. A vinyl version of the album was issued on the same day as the CD; the cover featured a different photo, a profile of a single goat. It was the first PJ album to be simultaneously issued on CD (available as both a Digipak and regular plastic case release), cassette, and vinyl. And on March 29, 2011, *Vs.* was reissued and expanded (along with 1994's *Vitalogy*) as a box set containing three rarities ("Hold On," "Cready Stomp," and a cover of Victoria Williams' "Crazy Mary"), as well as a third CD documenting one of PJ's best shows, titled *Live at the Orpheum Theatre: April 12, 1994.*

12 See Pearl Jam in Concert

At the time of this book's writing, Pearl Jam is the only band remaining from grunge's "Big 4" with most of its original lineup still intact. But as fans of the era, we're in luck: it just so happens that Pearl Jam was the top live band of the bunch, and they continue to regularly tour and put on exceptional performances. While Eddie Vedder may not be doing onstage stunts like Evel Knievel anymore, he is still in fine voice and the band sounds as vibrant as ever.

To score prime seats to a Pearl Jam show, you should most certainly consider joining the band's fan club, known as the Ten Club, which offers members the chance to purchase tickets before the general public—and those pesky scalpers—get their turn. But be forewarned, it's not a free-for-all when it comes to purchasing tickets via the Ten Club; presale tickets are only available online through a drawing, and only available in pairs. There is no such thing as guaranteed tickets, no matter how long you've been a member of the Ten Club. But all that said, the best seats for Pearl Jam shows are reserved for Ten Club members, and the band and its staff do their best to accommodate everyone.

With an increasing number of performers relying on tapes, loops, and other behind-the-scenes trickery in concert, you can always count on Pearl Jam to deliver the real deal live—no gimmicks, no tricks. And since the band never relied on choreography, pyrotechnics, or extravagant light shows, they have the ability to switch their setlist up from night to night, perfectly mixing up the old and the new with the well-known and the obscure. As a result, Pearl Jam remains one of the world's top live rock acts, and have gained a well-deserved Deadhead-like following, with fans traveling far and wide to attend as many PJ concerts as possible.

13 Kurt Cobain

Along with Eddie Vedder, the clear figurehead of the early '90s grunge movement was Nirvana's Kurt Cobain. An unlikely icon—Kurt was somewhat diminutive in size, especially when he stood next to Nirvana bassist Krist Novoselic; fashion-wise, he was equal parts thrift store model, gas station attendant, and Jeffrey Lebowski. The enormous shadow he has cast on pop culture ever since "Smells Like Teen Spirit" and *Nevermind* changed the direction of mainstream rock music is undeniable.

Born Kurt Donald Cobain on February 20, 1967, in Aberdeen, Washington, Cobain's parents divorced early in his life, and according to past interviews and articles, he was an outcast in high school before dropping out just short of graduation. It was during his high school days that he was first exposed to punk rock, via a *Creem* magazine article documenting the Sex Pistols' short-but-sweet U.S. tour in 1978, as well as befriending Buzz Osborne and becoming a major fan of his band, the Melvins. Uniting with another local in Novoselic, Nirvana was formed in 1987, going through several drummers before hooking up with Chad Channing in 1988 and issuing their debut full-length, *Bleach*, on June 15, 1989 (via Sub Pop Records and produced by Jack Endino).

By 1990, a then-unknown Dave Grohl had replaced Channing behind the kit, and the release of the glorious *Nevermind* (on September 24, 1991, via DGC Records, produced by Butch Vig) proved to be a true game-changer—getting rock fans' focus back to the importance of songwriting and lyrical message rather than how fast you could shred on your overpriced/pointy guitar. The album was a watershed moment in music, spawning such eventual classics as the aforementioned "Teen Spirit," plus "Come As You Are," "Lithium," and "In Bloom." And like Pearl Jam, what made Cobain and Nirvana so unique was their unwillingness to compromise. For example, they turned down an invite to open a summer 1992 stadium co-headlining tour with Guns N' Roses and Metallica, and did not launch a substantial U.S. headlining tour in the wake of *Nevermind*'s massive success. Nevertheless, *Nevermind* eventually hit No. 1 on the Billboard 200 and earned Diamond certification (for sales of 10 million copies sold in the U.S. alone) in 1999.

It was also around this time that the press began focusing on a supposed feud between Nirvana and Pearl Jam. In the April 16, 1992, issue of *Rolling Stone* (with Nirvana serving as cover boys), in an article penned by Michael Azerrad, it was pointed out that Cobain had previously accused Pearl Jam of specializing in a "corporate, alternative, and cock-rock fusion." Cobain added, "Every article I see written about them, they mention us, and they're baiting that fact. I would love to be erased from my association with that band and other corporate bands like the Nymphs and a few other felons. I do feel a duty to warn the kids of false music that's claiming to be underground or alternative. They're jumping on the alternative bandwagon."

Azerrad then contacted the Pearl Jam camp and quoted Ament as responding, "I don't know what I did to him; if he has a personal vendetta against us, he should come to us. To have that sort of pent-up frustration, the guy obviously must have some really deep insecurities about himself. Does he think we're riding his band-wagon? We could turn around and say that Nirvana put out records on money we made for Sub Pop when we were in Green River—if we were that stupid about it."

When I interviewed Ament for the *Grunge Is Dead* book years after the fact, he was unhappy with how he was portrayed in the *RS* article: "The guy that did that interview, Michael Azerrad, called and buttered me up, and then got me to say some things. I'm sure he turned that back around and said something to Kurt. Michael is who I think about every time we play 'Blood.' *Fucker.* If I would have seen him on the street at any point over that next 10 years, I would have kicked his ass."

Around the time of the *RS* article, Cobain had married Courtney Love and was battling a painful yet mysterious stomach ailment that doctors could not properly diagnose, and became addicted to heroin. But Nirvana managed to soldier on for another album—the rawer *In Utero*, released on September 21, 1993 (produced by Steve Albini). The album was another success, albeit on a smaller scale, topping the charts and spawning the hits "Heart Shaped Box" and "All Apologies," and was supported by Nirvana's first true U.S. headlining tour post–mega success. However, despite Cobain telling interviewers he was fine (and that his infant daughter, Frances Bean Cobain, had brought him happiness), he was still battling addiction as well as depression, and on April 5, 1994, he committed suicide at his home, at the age of 27. (His body was not discovered until April 8.)

Pearl Jam was still on tour in support of *Vs.* when the news of Cobain's death broke, and Vedder immediately heaped praise upon

Nirvana's late leader. At a show that night at the Patriot Center in Fairfax, Virginia, he told the crowd, "I don't think any of us would be in this room if it weren't for Kurt Cobain." And during PJ's performance on *Saturday Night Live* just a few days later (April 16), Vedder quoted a line from Neil Young's classic "Hey Hey, My My (Into the Black)" at the end of their rendition of "Daughter"—a supposed nod to the fact that Cobain quoted the song in his suicide note. And at the very end of the program, when the entire cast came out to offer farewells, Vedder opened his jacket to show a "K" scrawled on his shirt.

In an interview with *Spin* magazine later that year, Vedder discussed Cobain further: "I wish that Kurt and I had been able to, like, sit in the basement a few nights and just play stupid songs together, and relate to some of this. That might've helped us to understand each other, that he wasn't the only one, or that I wasn't the only one. We kind of knew that in the back of our heads, but we certainly never…I mean, we had a conversation on the phone, but we didn't really address that. Courtney told me later that he was so excited about a song he'd written with Pat Smear about beans. And that was exactly where I was coming from at the time. I don't want anything to do with this larger-than-life bullshit."

14 Ticketmaster

Ticketmaster is certainly a puzzling entity. On the one hand, it's super convenient to purchase tickets via your computer or hand-held device, eliminating the need to sleep overnight in the freezing cold outside a venue's box office like you had to in the good old days.

Jeff Ament and Stone Gossard testifying before a Congressional subcommittee looking into the ticketing industry, 1994. (AP Images)

But on the other hand, the company's fondness for tacking on mysterious service and convenience fees on top of a ticket's face value can inflate its purchase price in the blink of an eye. It can get to the point that many have to give serious thought about the affordability of those third-row tickets to see Billy Joel...or if they'd rather put that monetary amount toward paying their mortgage for the next two months.

So you have to give credit where credit is due—while for years artists were shrugging their shoulders and/or turning a blind eye to Ticketmaster, its robust fees, and its seemingly nefarious maneuvers, Pearl Jam was the first major band to take a stand and publicly question Ticketmaster's practices, a move that came after

PJ wanted to lower ticket prices on their *Vs.* tour and was met with resistance from the company.

Eventually, this led to the band opting to not tour after April 1994. At the request of the Justice Department, Jeff Ament and Stone Gossard testified before a Congressional subcommittee looking into the ticketing industry that June. As evidenced by vintage footage featured in *Pearl Jam Twenty*, it was obvious that the members of Congress were utterly out of touch and from another generation (that still had no clue what to make of touring rock bands) and did not take it entirely seriously—one member went so far as to call the two members "darling guys." As a result, the investigation did not go further concerning the mysterious fees and the monopoly that Ticketmaster had created.

As a result, Pearl Jam attempted to tour in non-Ticketmaster venues in 1995, which turned out to be a Herculean effort, one that did not go all that well. As a result, the band was eventually left with no choice but to go the Ticketmaster route to sell their concert tickets.

Really, isn't that the perfect sign of a monopoly?

15 The Roskilde Tragedy

While attending concerts is one of the most joyous events in a rock music fan's life, there have been instances throughout the course of history when tragedy has struck. Case in point: 11 people were killed when a stampede ensued going into Riverfront Coliseum in Cincinnati, Ohio, for a Who concert (December 3, 1979); two concert attendees were crushed to death during a Guns N' Roses performance at the Monsters of Rock Festival in Donington Park,

People gather the morning after eight people were crushed to death and others were injured during a Pearl Jam performance at the annual Roskilde Festival in Denmark, 2000. (AP Images)

England (August 20, 1988); and three people were crushed to death, at an AC/DC concert in Salt Lake City, Utah (January 18, 1991), among other catastrophes.

And sadly, there was another similar incident on June 30, 2000, at the Roskilde Festival in Denmark, during a Pearl Jam performance, when nine people were crushed to death. In a *Rolling Stone* article penned by David Fricke around the time, attendee Tomas Miller described what he experienced that horrific evening: "It was tight even before the music started—people were stumbling left and right. Half an hour in, I knew it was life and death. I couldn't lift my arms. It was difficult to breathe. I lifted my head to feel clean air. I was scared for my life."

To the band's credit, the music stopped as soon as they were notified that people may be hurt in the audience (it was unclear at that point that people had actually died), with Eddie Vedder offering the following plea: "What will happen in the next five minutes has nothing to do with music. But it is important. Imagine that I am your friend and that you must step back so as not to hurt me. You all have friends up front. I will now count to three, and you will all take three steps back. All who agree say 'Yes' now." Obviously, the band opted not to continue with their performance; they played a total of 12 songs that night, the final of which was "Daughter."

In an interview with *Rolling Stone* in 2003, Vedder recalled the disturbing events he witnessed that fateful evening: "The second they were pulled over the front [wall]. It was chaos. Some people were yelling, 'Thank you!' Others, who weren't in bad shape, were running up and saying hi [shakes his head in disbelief]. Then someone was pulled over, laid out, and they were blue. We knew immediately it had gone to that other level. There were still 40,000 people out there; they were ready for the show to start again. They started singing, 'I'm still alive.' 'Alive' was going to be the next song. That was when my brain clicked a switch. I knew I would never be the same."

Once it had been confirmed there were fatalities, Pearl Jam issued the following statement:

This is so painful...I think we are waiting for someone to wake us and say it was just a horrible nightmare...And there are absolutely no words to express our anguish in regard to the parents and loved ones of these precious lives that were lost. We have not yet been told what actually occurred, but it seemed random and sickeningly quick... it doesn't make sense. When you agree to play a festival of this size and reputation, it is impossible to imagine such a heart-wrenching scenario. Our lives will never be the same, but we know that is nothing compared to the grief of the families and friends of those involved. It is so tragic...there are no words.

Devastated,

Pearl Jam

After the Roskilde tragedy, festivals began taking more security measures to improve audience safety—barriers are often set up to corral the audience into several smaller "sections," with a large pathway cleared in the middle. That brings up an obvious question: why did it take so many deaths over the years for promoters and security planners to finally investigate and come up with solutions?

It later became known that Pearl Jam came close to breaking up in the wake of the Roskilde tragedy, and on the next PJ album, 2002's *Riot Act*, two songs contained lyrics referencing or motivated by the tragedy: "I Am Mine" and "Love Boat Captain."

16 Pearl Jam's Activism and Philanthropy

Another thing that differentiated the grunge bands of the early '90s from most of the '80s hard rockers/heavy metallists was a willingness to voice their political opinions and get involved in causes they believed in. Pearl Jam is a fine example of this, as the band has used their popularity and celebrity status to try and raise awareness for a variety of causes.

One of the most obvious instances of this was when Pearl Jam donated all the proceeds of their popular song "Last Kiss" to aid refugees of the Kosovo War. The song was issued as a single and also included on the charity compilation, *No Boundaries: A Benefit for the Kosovar Refugees.*

They've also raised awareness about Crohn's disease (which Mike McCready suffers from). Eddie Vedder has been photographed wearing shirts with the Rock for Choice logo, from a series of concerts that supported the pro-choice movement. And who can forget the shirt he wore for the performance of "Porch" during PJ's first-ever appearance on *Saturday Night Live*, featuring a coat hanger, another pro-choice symbol, on the front and NO BUSH '92 on the back? Earlier, he'd used his own body to get his point across—writing PRO-CHOICE!!! on his left arm with a black marker during Pearl Jam's performance of "Porch" on their *MTV Unplugged* appearance.

PJ has also found the time to play shows aiding specific organizations, including headlining a Seattle concert in 2001 supporting FAO (the UN's Food and Agriculture Organization), playing a show at the Chicago House of Blues in 2005 to help victims of Hurricane Katrina (with the proceeds donated to Habitat For Humanity, the American Red Cross, and the Jazz Foundation of America), and appearing multiple times at Neil Young's Bridge School Benefit concerts (a school that aids children with severe physical impairments).

Additionally, Vedder was vocal about supporting the release of the West Memphis Three (Damien Echols, Jessie Misskelley Jr., and Jason Baldwin), who many felt were wrongly accused of the horrific murders of three young boys in West Memphis, Arkansas, in 1993. Undoubtedly thanks in part to celebrities like Vedder speaking out on their behalf (as well as three documentaries that were part of a series called *Paradise Lost*), the three were eventually freed from prison in 2011, with Echols co-writing the lyrics to the PJ song, "Army Reserve." Sadly, the murder of those three boys has never been solved.

Politically, the band has never backed down from voicing their anti-Republican stance—Vedder openly criticizing both Bush administrations (father George, and his son, George W.) and supported candidates Ralph Nader, John Kerry, Barack Obama, and Hillary Clinton. Pearl Jam was also named 2011 Planet Defenders by Rock the Earth (for their environmental activism), while Vedder has an EARTH FIRST! tattoo on his right calf (Earth First! is an environmental advocacy group that often uses extreme measures to get its point across), and has supported the Surfrider Foundation.

17 Neil Young

If there was another artist who has been as uncompromising and intent on fighting the good fight as Pearl Jam, it would have to be Neil Young. So it would make perfect sense that both NY and PJ would collaborate and cross paths countless times over the years.

Born Neil Percival Young on November 12, 1945, in Toronto, Canada, the man who also sometimes goes by the alias "Bernard Shakey" has touched upon a variety of styles over the years (psychedelic, folk, country, garage rock, proto-punk, proto-grunge, electronic, rockabilly, etc.) as both a solo artist and as a member of such bands as Buffalo Springfield; Crosby, Stills, Nash & Young; and Neil Young & Crazy Horse, among others.

Along the way, Young has penned some of the greatest songs of all time—"Cinnamon Girl," "Down by the River," "Ohio," "Heart of Gold," "Old Man," "Tonight's the Night," "Like a Hurricane," "Rockin' in the Free World," and "Harvest Moon," to name but a handful. What has made Young so special is that just when you think you have his next move figured out, he often completely swerves in the opposite direction—at one point, exchanging lawsuits with his '80s-era record company, Geffen, which felt he was delivering albums that were "unrepresentative" of the Neil we all know and love.

And like Pearl Jam, Neil Young is unafraid to write about what's on his mind, regardless of what others may think; the aforementioned "Ohio" dealt with the horrific Kent State shootings, "Southern Man" and "Alabama" took on racism, "This Note's for You" fired back at a time when every major music artist seemed eager to embrace corporate sponsorship, *Living with War* criticized then–U.S. president George W. Bush, etc.

The first sign of Pearl Jam's admiration of the Godfather of Grunge came when they started covering "Rockin' in the Free World" during the *Ten* era (March 9, 1992, in Berlin, Germany, marked its first appearance in the set list). Later that year, PJ performed for the first time at Young's annual Bridge School Benefit (they returned for performances time and time again, including in 1994, 1996, 1999, 2001, 2003, 2006, 2010, and 2014; Vedder performed solo in 2004, 2011, and 2012).

During the summer of 1993, Young invited Pearl Jam to open a string of European shows and a handful of North American dates, and they united again to offer the undisputed highlight of the 1993 MTV Video Music Awards—a rip-roaring rendition of "Rockin' in the Free World," which they had been performing together at select dates during the summer. PJ added another NY song to their live repertoire, "Fuckin' Up," which would be included as part of the bonus *Live at the Orpheum Theatre* album, with the *Vs./Vitalogy* reissue in 2011.

In 1995, Vedder was chosen to introduce Young at his Rock and Roll Hall of Fame induction and gave a memorable speech, offering such praise as, "He's taught us a lot as a band about dignity and commitment and playing in the moment." Mere days later, Young, Pearl Jam, L7, and Lisa Germano performed at Constitution Hall

Eddie Vedder, Mike McCready, and Neil Young perform during the MTV Video Music Awards, 1993. (AP Images)

in Washington, D.C., as part of a Voters for Choice Benefit (on January 14 and 15). Young also came to PJ's aid at a show that year on June 24 at Golden Gate Park in San Francisco, when Vedder fell ill and couldn't continue the show—resulting in Young joining the band for the rest of the set.

But the biggest PJ/NY merger occurred later that year, when Young enlisted the band to back him on his 22nd studio album, *Mirror Ball*. Released on June 27, the mostly rocking album proved once and for all how similar both artists were, resulting in such standouts as "Song X," "Downtown," and "Peace and Love." The only criticism of the album was Vedder's lack of presence on it (he offered lead vocals on only one tune, "Peace and Love").

However, it turned out that two exceptional tunes with Vedder on lead vocals were indeed recorded during the *Mirror Ball* sessions, but were not included on the album—eventually surfacing on the *Merkin Ball* single ("I God Id" and "Long Road"). Additionally, from August 14 to 27, Pearl Jam sans Vedder backed Young on a tour of Europe (with Brendan O'Brien on keyboards), resulting in set lists that featured new *Mirror Ball* material, as well as classics ("Cortez the Killer," "Powderfinger," "Hey Hey, My My," among others.). The next substantial PJ/NY pairing occurred in 2001, when Vedder and McCready joined Young for a rendition of "Long Road" at the America: A Tribute to Heroes benefit concert, which was also issued on CD and DVD.

Another memorable Pearl Jam / Neil Young moment almost took place on April 7, 2017, when it was PJ's turn to be inducted into the Rock and Roll Hall of Fame. Originally, Young was scheduled to return the favor and introduce his old pals at the Hall, but an illness prevented him from doing so. (David Letterman would serve as Young's replacement.)

18 *MTV Unplugged*

When one thinks of *MTV Unplugged*, several memorable and enduring episodes jump to mind: Eric Clapton's from 1992 (which resulted in the Diamond-certified album, *Unplugged*, the same year), Steve Ray Vaughan's all-too-brief set from 1990 (filmed just a short while before his tragic death in August that year), and, of course, Nirvana's (which also would be issued as a mega-selling hit album in late 1994, just several months after Kurt Cobain's passing). But one episode that is easily on par with these is Pearl Jam's, and perhaps the only reason why it is not as celebrated is because it has never been put up for sale by the band as a stand-alone release (as of this book's writing, its only official release was on DVD as part of the *Ten* expanded reissue in 2009).

Filmed on March 16, 1992, at Kaufman Astoria Studios in Queens, New York (the band was fresh off completing a European tour a few days earlier), Pearl Jam's set leaned heavily on material from *Ten* ("Oceans," "Alive," "Black," "Jeremy," "Porch," and "Even Flow"), as well as a tune from the forthcoming *Singles* motion picture soundtrack ("State of Love and Trust"), and a Neil Young cover ("Rockin' in the Free World"). When the episode first aired on May 13, 1992, the episode was cut to include just "Even Flow," "Jeremy," "Alive," "Black," "State of Love and Trust," and "Porch," and then soon after, subsequent airings included just four tracks—"Jeremy," "Alive," "Black," and "Porch" (I know this, as yours truly unluckily missed my opportunity to recorded the six-song version on a VHS tape—I had to settle for the measly four-song version).

Speaking to *Guitar World* in 1992, Mike McCready gave his thoughts on the episode: "It came out all right, but it could have been a nightmare, because we ordered some specific equipment and they gave us pretty shitty stuff. I wanted to get a Martin, some nice guitars. But when you rent equipment, you don't know what you're getting. Jeff ordered some specific basses and they didn't appear. The acoustic guitar I played had really high action, so it was totally impossible to do leads. But I thought it came out pretty well anyhow."

While researching this book, I realized that I'd never heard a firsthand account from an audience member lucky enough to have attended this taping. Then I recalled, I am in fact good pals with Dan Weiss, a long-time Pearl Jam supporter who was indeed in Kaufman Astoria Studios that evening. Here, Mr. Weiss (whose favorite Pearl Jam song of all time is "Release," with "Given to Fly" and "Corduroy" coming in at a two-way tie for second place), takes an exclusive stroll down memory lane:

I was in high school at the time. We heard that a local radio station, I think it was WDRE, was giving out tickets at a nearby McDonald's, so we headed over there. There were only a handful of people so it seemed our odds were pretty good. At first, two of my friends won tickets by naming the band's name before they were Pearl Jam [Mookie Blaylock]. I think it was getting down to the last pair of tickets or so and I still hadn't won. It wasn't looking good but then the host said my buddy and I could have a pair if we could sing "Alive" to the crowd. I'm not one for public performances, and admittedly have a horrible singing voice, but without giving it much thought, I found my buddy and I belting out the words to "Alive" into the microphone and next thing I knew, I was holding a golden ticket!

It was taped at midnight. I believe the ticket said it was to be held at "a secret location" or something like that. We might've had to call the radio station the day of the show to get the exact address. It was filmed in a TV sound studio and I remember the entire place was draped in black netting, almost like giant fish nets or maybe chains. It was a really cool vibe.

I remember when we got in, the band wasn't onstage yet and I could see these basketball figurines lined up in front of the drum set. I remember thinking, "Oh shit, I'm gonna get me one of those!" After the band was finished playing and people were walking out, you could basically walk right onstage, past their equipment, etc., and as I walked by the drum set I looked down at the figurines... and I couldn't do it. That was the band's property and I felt it wouldn't be right to take their property. I remember I was bummed—that would've been such an awesome souvenir—but I couldn't do it.

At one point during the show, Eddie pulled out a marker and wrote Pro-Choice!!! on his arm. I remember I wasn't so into that at the time [the political aspects of the show], so I didn't understand that side of Pearl Jam. I'm still not a very political person, but I believe in the stances that Pearl Jam has taken and respect their opinions. Eddie used that same marker to hang out either in between takes or after the show—I can't remember which, maybe both—and sign autographs. I remember he was signing a ton of baseball hats. People were tossing them to him, he would sign it and toss it back. I was amazed at how accessible he remained. He didn't run backstage and hide or hit the groupie scene like most bands I was familiar with. Instead, he pretty much just hung out. It was really cool.

Backstage Pass

Curt Kirkwood
Meat Puppets Singer/Guitarist

Isn't it true that when the Meat Puppets appeared as surprise guests on Nirvana's *Unplugged* episode, the higher-ups at MTV were convinced the surprise guest was Eddie Vedder?
That was the rumor! That's what I heard. Definitely, when we showed up there, we did rehearsals and stuff, but everybody was a little indifferent and kind of seemed even a little let down—like they didn't want us there. Like, "What are *these fuckers* doing here?" But I don't think I heard about that until after it actually all went down. It was like, "Oh, okay…*that's* what it was. They thought they were going to get Eddie Vedder, and they wind up with sort of "the prep cooks." But everybody else was really happy with us and the audience was great. Everybody seemed to think it was all cool, and then I realized, "Oh, that's why all the MTV people were hanging back from us." We were dilettantes.

What do you think made Pearl Jam unique at the time?
To me, you had the alternative movement starting in the early '90s, and Pearl Jam had a more sort of loose guitar type thing going on—which I always liked. It just seemed a little more jam-y, a little more folk-y, in the midst of being loud. But still a little bit loose. And I always liked Les Pauls. I liked the rhythm playing of Stone, and I saw him with a Les Paul, and good rhythm players to me are always wonderful, and they kind of get shortchanged with the guitar. John Lennon was like that to me—that's the pulse there, his rhythm playing.

And then the other guitar player just played more jam-y leads, which was supposed to be out with the punk rock, where leads were not that cool. And you were kind of getting them back with a few of those bands—Jerry [Cantrell] from Alice in Chains is a good guitar player, and I thought Mike [McCready] was a really good guitar player. I read that he was into Stevie Ray Vaughan, and I made sense of that. You've got to have some blues in it. It's something that Dean DeLeo told me one time: "Good guitar playing has to have some blues." And I kind of agree with him. If you want to get to the basis of rock music, you've got to bend the strings.

And then Eddie Vedder is just straight-up unique. There's nobody who sounds like him. He had something that I never really felt like achieving or felt like I could, which is a really blatant passion for the voice. I feel like I sing like I talk, so I find it interesting when you've got somebody like David Bowie, Michael Stipe, or Elvis [Presley]—when you have someone who has some sense of emotion. And definitely Eddie had it. Just great players all the way around. Like I said, it's tight, but it feels like it's kind of cool, too. I saw them at Lollapalooza, and they played the Neil Young song "Rockin' in the Free World," really good. And then they played as the backup band on Neil's album *Mirror Ball* around that time, which I thought was a very good album.

I played with Mother Love Bone. They opened for us one time up in Seattle, at the Moore Theatre [on December 13 and 14, 1988]. It was definitely not punk rock—it was different. It was like glam metal, but it was *organic* glam metal—like "forest glam" or something. Not so hair metal, not so "for the ladies." And different than what generally we would play with. I would say during that time—the late '80s—you were getting a lot of stuff that sounded like R.E.M., the [Red Hot] Chili Peppers, or Fairport Convention folk rock. But these guys were definitely coming into their own trip. And Andy [Wood] and I were in the bathroom joking around, and he asked me could he watch me take a piss! I thought that was fucking hilarious.

Ever cross paths with Pearl Jam elsewhere down the line?

Yeah, I played on a song with Eddie—he wasn't in the studio—but on Mike Watt's *Ball-Hog or Tugboat?* album. We played on "Big Train," my brother [Cris Kirkwood] and I—I played slide guitar and Eddie played guitar on that, as well as Dave Grohl. And then right around there, Watt came through town—the first Foo Fighters tour—and I went and hung out there. And Eddie was on there with his wife at the time, with the band Hovercraft, which was pretty bitchin', and they opened the show. And then we all jammed out. So I did jam with Watt, Eddie, and the nascent Foo Fighters.

How do you think Pearl Jam's music holds up?

I think it holds up just fine—like music should. It doesn't seem dated to me, ever. It doesn't have enough ties to everything else that was happening around it at the time. That's the folk music side of it to me—that's something I see in common if you're not talking about classic music that remains timeless, folk music does to me, too. And there's good elements of storytelling in folk music, that seemed to me to keep it ageless—outside of just the uniqueness of the voice, once again. You can't really place that in a time. I think it's still one of the more unique voices. Once again, that was the key, really, across the board with the music from Seattle at the time that was coming out, there were a number of bands that had lots of "big voices"—Chris Cornell, Layne Staley, Kurt Cobain, and Eddie Vedder. I understand that Eddie was not from Seattle, but nonetheless, maybe that's why it doesn't seem quite as...maybe it's a little different. It's a little bit more laid-back in a way. Since he was from San Diego, you've got the surfer element—a more chill element—in the midst of being pretty fucking intense, too. It was fun to watch him early on—climbing around on shit and doing dangerous things, and rolling his eyes back in his head while he was singing.

19 Slamming, Diving, Climbing

According to interviews I've read, seen, or heard over the years with rock musicians, the adrenaline surge they experience while performing in front of large crowds seems to be unparalleled. But for Eddie Vedder throughout the *Ten* tour, performing onstage wasn't enough—during just about every performance of "Porch" (usually as a set-closer), you could find the singer climbing high above the stage in the lighting rigs, or getting up close and personal with the audience via crowd surfing. As a result, PJ became one of the most exciting and unpredictable live rock acts of the era; it didn't hurt that musically, the over-the-top live renditions of the *Ten* material often made the studio renditions seem a bit sleepy.

While slam dancing (also known as moshing, thanks in large part to the Anthrax fellows) had been around since the 1970s—originally in the form of "pogoing"—it became more violent and intense during the '80s. By the early '90s, crowd surfing had also become a semiregular occurrence at hardcore, thrash metal, and alt-rock shows, and was only amplified when the MTV mainstream was turned on to Vedder's antics by footage included in the videos for "Alive" and "Even Flow."

Vedder's daredevil stunts made this era of Pearl Jam live performances feel special, and while they must have become like one big blur after a while to the other band members, several have been well documented either in print or with video footage. For example, Dave Grohl talked to *Spin* magazine in 2001 about the first time he saw PJ live (when Nirvana shared a bill with them and the Red Hot Chili Peppers, on December 28, 1991, at the Pat O'Brien Pavilion in Del Mar, California): "I didn't sit and watch them play until the show in San Diego, where Eddie climbed the fuckin' lighting rig. I swear to God, he was like 250 feet up in the air. It was one of the scariest things I've ever seen live in my entire life. I've seen people cut themselves, I've seen people shit, I've seen people get beat up onstage, and I've seen people break bones, break their backs, and get concussions. Honestly, I was horrified. I was really scared that he was gonna die."

Even Vedder's bandmates expressed fear over his well-being. In the *Pearl Jam Twenty* documentary, Stone Gossard said, "I didn't want him to hurt himself, but at the same time, there was no talking to him. He was going to do what he was going to do. He could have killed himself a couple of times probably, for sure. Which would have been more than I could have taken."

Other memorable excursions included Vedder hitching a ride on a camera crane during a performance at the Pinkpop Festival in the Netherlands on June 8, 1992, before hurling himself into

*Eddie Vedder
ascends the
scaffolding during
Lollapalooza
at Jones Beach
Theater in New
York, 1992.*
(Steven J. Messina)

the massive crowd below, climbing above the stage and then using
his mic cord to slide back down at Magnuson Park on September
20, and even giving a nod to crowd surfers everywhere during the
Unplugged performance, lying down belly-first on a seat with his
hands and legs extended, to replicate the act.

That said, I was lucky to have personally witnessed what in my
humble estimation was one of Vedder's most epic stage climbs, at
a stop on Lollapalooza II at Jones Beach in New York, on August
9, 1992. For those who are not familiar with the venue, it is out-
doors, with water behind and on both sides of the stage (guess it
makes perfect sense, since it's part of a beach that faces the Atlantic
Ocean, eh?). During the jam portion of "Porch," Vedder calmly

walked over to stage right, then climbed atop amps, metal poles, and other scaffolding to stand atop a concrete tower overlooking the ocean water below. By this time, the Chili Peppers' Flea had come out from the side of the stage to watch the entire act unfold. Vedder was possibly even higher than the lofty distance that Grohl had described at the San Diego performance.

Many of us in attendance figured he would do the unthinkable and dive into the water. Thankfully, since it was not entirely clear how deep the water was, cooler heads prevailed, and Vedder scurried back down and returned to the stage to finish the set. Needless to say, no other band topped PJ that day. Years later, I was tickled pink to discover that a fellow attendee that day—sitting not far from where I was situated in the mezzanine section—had snuck in a video camera and documented the whole event. And yes, it can indeed be viewed—as well as many of Vedder's other mid-concert daredevil escapades—via the marvelous YouTube.

Although Vedder's escapades became less frequent after the *Ten* tour wrapped—he no longer does such death-defying stunts in concert nowadays—there was one that occurred at the famous Fox Theatre show on April 3, 1994, about which the Pearl Jam fan site, Five Horizons, offered the following description: "During the long jam during the middle of this incredible version of 'Porch,' Ed throws his mic stand at a huge replica of the 'boy on the cross' figurine (depicted in the *Vs.* book) hanging in the background. Ed dons a Cincinnati Bengals helmet and the gold bat wings and climbs the lighting rig above the stage. Staying there through most of the jam, he throws down a dummy wearing a similar outfit. The crowd screams, thinking that Ed has fallen, but he reappears, and starts singing again. Jeff kicks the dummy into the crowd where it is ripped to pieces. Ed returns to the stage using only his hands on the rope ladder with his feet dangling."

And this, dear friends, is what made Pearl Jam concerts circa 1992/1993 such unforgettable experiences.

20 Watch Pearl Jam's Music Videos

Despite a self-imposed music video ban that stretched over several albums (1993's *Vs.* through 1996's *No Code*), Pearl Jam was still responsible for creating some of the most memorable and enduring music videos of all time. PJ was clearly *the* rock band on MTV circa 1992/1993, as evidenced by all of the shiny Moon Man statues they collected at the 1993 MTV Video Music Awards.

It is the videos from *Ten* in particular that Pearl Jam will forever be best remembered: "Alive," "Even Flow," and "Jeremy." First aired in September 1991, the "Alive" clip marked a departure from the big-budget, storyline-driven videos of other bands. Directed by Josh Taft and shot in black and white, the video is comprised of footage collected at a PJ show on August 3, 1991, at RKCNDY in Seattle, during the tremendously short-lived Matt Chamberlain era. "Alive" served as an introduction to countless soon-to-be PJ fans, who were taken by the images of the sweat-drenched band bashing out the tune, plus images of what seemed like a nonstop display of crowd surfing. The clip began and ended with a shot of a surf-worthy wave on a beach.

Realizing that they were on the right track, PJ reunited with Taft for the "Even Flow" clip. Premiered on MTV in April 1992, the video features more electrifying live footage of the band but this time shot in color, at a headlining performance at the Moore Theatre in Seattle, on January 17, 1992. For fans who had not yet seen the band live—and there were still quite a few who hadn't, as PJ had only just completed their first-ever extended tour, opening throughout the U.S. for the Red Hot Chili Peppers—the video introduced many to the daredevil antics of Eddie Vedder. During the song's breakdown section, he is seen climbing the rafters before winding up on the side of the venue and then leaping quite a distance down into the audience, which caught him with open arms.

But when it came to the audio portion of the "Even Flow" clip, it turns out that it was rerecorded in the studio, and then fit to the live footage. This was confirmed in 2013, when the full show was released as a download, and the version of that song sounded completely different than the version heard in the video. With both the "Alive" and "Even Flow" clips containing such great footage, it remains a head-scratcher as to why PJ doesn't open up their video vaults and issue these complete shows on DVD or for download, as you can only imagine how stellar the other performances from those evenings must have been.

Up to that point, Pearl Jam had not tried their hand at a video that employed a storyline. So it's understandable if they were a bit squeamish when agreeing to do so for their "Jeremy" video. But it turns out they were in very trustworthy hands with director Mark Pellington, who met up with the band in June 1992 at Kings Cross in London, England, to film scenes of Vedder singing along to the lyrics, and the other members either sitting, standing, or flailing around. A wise move was enlisting the aid of a capable young actor to play the role of Jeremy, a boy by the name of Trevor Wilson.

Following the story of a troubled boy who winds up shooting himself in front of his classmates at school (based on the tragic true story of Jeremy Wade Delle, from Richardson, Texas), the scene inside the actual classroom was filmed at Bayonne High School in New Jersey. With the clip completed, MTV's often hard-to-pinpoint "rules" when it came to what could be aired and what couldn't led to the editing out of an admittedly disturbing visual: the Jeremy character putting a pistol in his mouth and pulling the trigger, splattering his blood onto the white shirts of his classmates. To some, the edited scene implied that Jeremy shot his classmates and not himself, which for reasons unknown was perhaps more acceptable viewing in MTV's eyes. Regardless, "Jeremy" was in heavy rotation on the channel.

Interestingly, it turns out that there were alternate videos shot for both "Even Flow" and "Jeremy," directed by Rock Schenck and Chris Cuffaro, respectively. As of this book's release, the Schenck-directed clip has yet to surface, although Stone Gossard did describe it to *Spin* back in 2001: "We made an 'Even Flow' video that never came out that I'm sensitive about, because it was my idea. It ended up being totally rawk: lots of big lights, out on a cliff, definitely comic to look back on now. Hopefully at some point, we'll be able to laugh at ourselves enough to show that one." As for the Cuffaro video, this alternate "Jeremy" clip has surfaced on YouTube—shot in black and white and including scenes of an unknown actor portraying the song's character, but in a much less affecting manner than Trevor Wilson had. (A sad postscript on Wilson: despite receiving widespread accolades for his portrayal of the troubled youth in the video, he rejected Hollywood's overtures to continue acting and returned to leading an ordinary and private life. Tragically, he drowned on August 7, 2016, at the age of 36, while on vacation in Puerto Rico.)

There was a fourth official video, filmed for "Oceans" (directed by Taft), which featured a bold return to black and white. But aside from featuring some great live footage, the clip was ultimately a snoozefest—shots of the band walking around, the beach, airplanes buzzing overhead, etc. Even true PJ fans might be unaware of the "Oceans" music video because it was never submitted to MTV in the U.S., showing that the band was already conscious of overexposure as far back as *Ten*.

So, with MTV spinning the heck out of the officially released videos of "Alive," "Even Flow," and "Jeremy" (the last of which collected four awards at the 1993 VMAs), you would figure that PJ and MTV would have a long and loving relationship, right? Wrong. As a reaction to the media onslaught they were experiencing at the time, the band made the decision to stop making videos. While the move fit the PJ ethos, one can't help but wonder what music videos would have looked like for PJ songs such as "Black," "Daughter," "Elderly Woman," and "Better Man," among others.

By 1998 and the arrival of the *Yield* album, all the hubbub about Pearl Jam had died down considerably, and the band produced their first music video in six years, for "Do the Evolution." Directed by Todd McFarlane and Kevin Altieri, the band members were not featured in a single frame of the animated clip. If you're unfamiliar with the video and are imagining a cartoon fit for all ages, think again: the clip includes scenes of people ripping off their flesh, atomic bombs being dropped, and more. The end result? An extremely well-done and striking video. While the "Do the Evolution" video did enjoy some spins on MTV, it was not given nearly the same attention as more "important" clips such as Backstreet Boys' "I'll Never Break Your Heart," Celine Dion's "My Heart Will Go On," and Limp Bizkit's "Faith."

Think that was a sign that Pearl Jam was prepared to jump headfirst back into making videos? Forget it. Not a single video would be filmed for any of the tracks from 2000's *Binaural*. But they went relatively hog-wild for 2002's *Riot Act*, issuing a total of five (!) videos, all featuring live performances by the band and directed by James Frost—"I Am Mine," "Save You," "Love Boat Captain," "Thumbing My Way," and "½ Full." And while all of the *Riot Act* clips are indeed charming in their own right, the next truly memorable Pearl Jam video arrived in 2006, with "Life Wasted." Directed by Fernando Apodaca, the video features various "heads" with the Pearl Jam members' faces superimposed on them, as wormlike creatures slither around…suffice it to say, it's worth a look. The video, which was nominated for a VMA that year for "Best Special Effects," can be found on Apodaca's website.

PJ has seemed to become quite comfortable with the video-making process once again, recently working with the likes of

Danny Clinch (2006's "World Wide Suicide," plus 2013's "Mind Your Manners" and "Sirens"), Cameron Crowe (2009's "The Fixer"), Gary Menotti (2009's "Just Breathe"), and Ryan Thomas and Brendan Canty (2010's "Amongst the Waves").

21 The MTV Video Music Awards

Although Pearl Jam eschewed making videos for an extended stretch of time, they fully embraced the medium at the beginning of their career, resulting in some of the most played video clips on MTV during the era. And for two back-to-back years—1992 and 1993—PJ was the toast of the MTV Video Music Awards show.

On September 9, 1992, toward the end of their Lollapalooza stint (the VMAs fell between a Lolla stop in Phoenix, Arizona, on the September 8 and a taping for MTV's *Singles* movie premiere party in Los Angeles on September 10), Pearl Jam appeared on the show, held at the Pauley Pavilion in Los Angeles, for a performance of "Jeremy." The band was planning on performing a cover of the Dead Boys' "Sonic Reducer," but supposedly the higher-ups at MTV said, "Thanks but no thanks," and both parties settled on "Jeremy."

The performance was expectedly stellar—PJ had been playing the song night after night on the road for a solid year by that point—with highlights including Eddie (sporting his soon-to-be-trademark corduroy jacket) getting uber intense toward the end of the song and Stone Gossard skipping and stomping around in a perfect circle. Also included was a line from "Sonic Reducer" at the song's conclusion, possibly as a thumb of the nose to the suits at MTV. PJ lost out on their sole nomination that evening ("Best

Pearl Jam accepts an award for "Jeremy" at the MTV Video Music Awards, 1993. (AP Images)

Alternative Video" would go to Nirvana's "Smells Like Teen Spirit" over "Alive"), but Dave Abbruzzese reappeared on stage to beat the drums alongside Chad Smith during the Red Hot Chili Peppers' performance of "Give It Away" (which included a stage full of people going bonkers alongside the band). Furthermore, Eddie and Dave received the interview treatment by MTV VJ John Norris after the show wrapped up (Vedder wore a black helmet with No. 29 emblazoned on it).

At the 1993 VMAs (held at the Gibson Amphitheatre in Los Angeles, California, on September 2), the evening seemed to revolve around Pearl Jam. Their clip for "Jeremy" was up for five awards and would win all but one of them—taking the prize for

"Video of the Year," "Best Group Video," "Best Metal/Hard Rock Video," and "Best Direction" (the "Viewer's Choice Award" went to Aerosmith's "Livin' on the Edge"). The band made the pilgrimage to the stage several times to give acceptance speeches, which were random remarks more than anything lengthy or meaningful (although Vedder did make a good point talking about the power that music can have while accepting "Video of the Year" with the actor who portrayed Jeremy in the video, Trevor Wilson, accompanying the band), and director Mark Pellington solely accepted and offered a speech for the "Best Direction" win.

But the real story and top highlight of the entire VMAs that year was Pearl Jam's performance. To show how immensely popular PJ was at that point, they were given time to play two songs on this night. First up was a performance of the rage-rocker "Animal" off the still-to-be-released *Vs.*, and the second was the big surprise—an unannounced Neil Young joining the band onstage for an intense version of his "Rockin' in the Free World," which ended with Mike McCready smashing his black Les Paul against an amp, plus Vedder bashing his mic stand (and handing it to an audience member) and taking a swig of wine.

And if that wasn't enough Pearl Jam on an awards show for you, the whole band (except for McCready)—along with "Jeremy" Wilson—was interviewed by Kurt Loder after the show, when Eddie turned the tables on Loder when asked how it felt playing with Neil Young ("What do *you* think it would feel like? How do *you* think it felt like?"), and muses that it's "Odd giving out awards for art." Additionally, Jeff selected Beavis and Butthead's appearance as a standout of the evening (the others picked Lenny Kravitz and R.E.M. as additional high points), and they even tried to get young Wilson involved in the chatter at one point.

By not issuing a single music video from 1993 to 1997, Pearl Jam's presence at subsequent VMAs was utterly nonexistent (which turned out to be good for them—the show, like MTV itself, has slowly devolved into an unwatchable mess), but they did receive one more nomination—"Best Special Effects" for "Life Wasted" in 2006—which they failed to secure (Missy Elliott's "We Run This" won the award).

22 **Vitalogy**

Way back when, it was a common occurrence for rock bands to crank out albums each and every year, and in some cases, multiple releases each year (for example, the Beatles in the '60s, Kiss in the '70s, the Minutemen in the '80s, and so on.). But by the '90s, it seemed as though artists were taking their sweet time to craft and sculpt their recordings to perfection, no matter how long it took. But when it came to their third album, *Vitalogy*, Pearl Jam turned back the clock to the good old days of briskly following up a block-buster album with a new offering—in this case, barely a year later.

One of the main reasons for the album's no-nonsense completion was that quite a few songs were written far in advance, with some even premiering on the *Vs.* tour (namely "Satan's Bed," "Tremor Christ," "Not for You," "Whipping," "Immortality," "Last Exit," and "Spin the Black Circle"). The album's best-known track, "Better Man," was one that Eddie Vedder had penned back when he was a teenager, and was demoed and performed live by Vedder's pre-PJ band, Bad Radio (check YouTube for the sonic/visual proof). Another possible reason why the quintet's third album arrived so rapidly? To be blunt, it was padded with several experimental throwaways (namely "Pry, To," "Aye Davanita," and especially, the album-closing soundscape "Hey Foxymophandlemama, That's Me").

Vitalogy, *Pearl Jam,*
1994. (Epic)

Vitalogy saw PJ co-produce once again with Brendan O'Brien, with some recording done during breaks of the *Vs.* tour (Southern Tracks Recording and Doppler Studios, Atlanta, Georgia; and Kingsway Studio, New Orleans, Louisiana). The band also made a conscious decision to record closer to home (Bad Animals Studio in Seattle) as opposed to its predecessor, which was a major gripe of Vedder's. As a result, the album's recording stretched from November 1993 to October 1994. Also, Dave Abbruzzese was "excused" from the band during the making of the album and replaced by Jack Irons. Still, Abbruzzese was credited with playing on 13 of the album's 14 tracks, with "Foxymophandlemama" being Irons' sole contribution.

Always looking to give fans value for their money, the band blessed *Vitalogy* with absolutely gorgeous packaging. The CD version showcased the talents of Jeff Ament's brother, Barry Ament, who was credited with its layout. The disc came in a cardboard case that replicated an obscure medical book of the same name, first published in 1899 and penned by E.H. Ruddock, with the CD booklet including all sorts of images and text that reflected it (hardcore PJ fans have even tracked down authentic yet well-worn editions of the book, thanks to the always accommodating eBay), with a mixture of lyrics, band photos, and doodles drawn by Vedder.

Preceded by the release of a vinyl version on November 22, 1994, the CD and cassette editions of *Vitalogy* were issued on December 6. Again, Pearl Jam scored another bestselling release, nearly matching the first-week sales mark set by its predecessor; *Vitalogy* racked up a whopping 877,000 sales in its first week alone (compared to the 950,378 copies *Vs.* shifted in five days). It topped the charts in five countries (Australia, Ireland, New Zealand, Sweden, and the U.S.), and went 5x platinum in less than a year (on October 13, 1995). Once again, we haven't heard a peep from the RIAA folks ever since regarding how many *Vitalogy* copies have been sold subsequently.

Like *Vs.*, not a single video would be filmed for *Vitalogy*, which makes the colossal sales figures for both albums all the more impressive. It makes you wonder what those numbers would have been had PJ produced a video or two for each release. Still, three singles were offered—"Spin the Black Circle" (whose B-side, "Tremor Christ," received heavy radio airplay, as well), "Not for You," and "Immortality." Surprisingly, the song with the most commercial appeal, "Better Man," was not selected as a single.

As was the case with *Vs.*, *Vitalogy* was reissued and expanded (together with *Vs.*) as a box set on March 29, 2011, which added on three rarities (a "guitar/organ only" version of "Better Man," an "alt take" of "Corduroy," and a demo of "Nothingman"), as well as a third CD, documenting one of PJ's best-ever shows, titled *Live at the Orpheum Theatre: April 12, 1994*, which included early live renditions of several tracks that would eventually be included as studio versions on *Vitalogy* ("Immortality," "Not for You," and "Tremor Christ").

23 Brendan O'Brien

Some rock artists like using a variety of producers throughout their career, whereas others connect closely with a single producer, whom they return to time and time again. In Pearl Jam's case, their "main man" is Brendan O'Brien, the co-producer (along with the band) on such hit albums as 1993's *Vs.*, 1994's *Vitalogy*, and 1998's *Yield*, and sole producer of 2009's *Backspacer* and 2013's *Lightning Bolt*.

Born on June 30, 1960, in Atlanta, Georgia, O'Brien began playing in local bands at an early age, but received his first big break working on the Black Crowes' hit debut album, 1990's *Shake Your Money Maker*, on which he was credited as providing "a potpourri of instruments," in addition to serving as the album's engineer and mixer. That same year, O'Brien worked on the sophomore effort from heavy metallists Danzig, *Danzig II: Lucifuge*.

Speaking with original Danzig guitarist John Christ for one of my earlier books, *Survival of the Fittest: Heavy Metal in the 1990's*, Christ described not only what it was like working with O'Brien, but what he learned from one of the best in the business: "Interestingly enough, Rick Rubin had produced all the records, but our lead engineer was Brendan O'Brien, who went on to huge success and fame working with Pearl Jam, and the list goes on and on. I remember talking to him, because he had just moved to L.A. from Atlanta and he had a couple of kids, and he said, 'I love working with Rick Rubin. I'm going to do whatever that man says, because he's got the Midas touch.' Brendan is also a great guitar player and piano player. He really helped me get my sounds down and helped me get a lot of great little solo ideas recorded. Brendan was a good coach in the studio for timing and overdubs and getting things just right."

After working with Rubin on the Red Hot Chili Peppers' massive commercial breakthrough, 1991's *Blood Sugar Sex Magik* (again credited as engineer and mixer, as well as playing multiple instruments on various tracks), O'Brien branched out on his own and seemingly overnight became one of the most sought-after producers in all of rock music—producing almost all of the studio albums by Stone Temple Pilots (including 1992's multiplatinum debut, *Core*), and enjoying a long and fruitful association with Pearl Jam.

While interviewing Doug Pinnick of King's X in 2013 for the *Songfacts* site, I asked what O'Brien brought to the sessions for *Dogman*, considered one of the heaviest-sounding releases of the band's career (and which the producer worked on directly after the *Vs.* sessions): "With Brendan, what I learned was don't spend a whole lot of time on something. And don't be afraid to turn the knob to the point where it explodes. Everything that I learned with Brendan was, don't be afraid to use compression. But that was back in '94, very few people were doing that, and Brendan had created this whole new sound with compression. So I learned a big deal about compression through him. It gave me comfort to know that after a month of working with the band, he's pretty much lost interest and he's ready to move onto the next one. I'm that way, too. When I'm in the studio after like four and a half weeks, I kind of don't care anymore. And if there are really serious decisions to be made at the end, I let everybody just deal with it, and then I regret it later. But my attention span is about a month making a record and that's it. So when Brendan said that, it made me feel good, because he's made a great living at it."

Subsequently, O'Brien has worked on albums by some of the biggest names in the rock world, including Bob Dylan, Bruce Springsteen, Neil Young, AC/DC, Aerosmith, Soundgarden, and Rage Against the Machine. But it is his work with Pearl Jam that helped cement his stature as "power producer." In an interview with *Paste Magazine* in 2009 (around the release of *Backspacer*), O'Brien discussed the role he plays specifically when working with PJ: "Well, every artist is different. Everybody's different. In this particular situation, they worked a lot on their own with the songs and I helped them with the arrangements. There was another writing session—I didn't write the songs, but I was there—in Montana up at Jeff's place where Eddie wasn't around, it was just the band together, and it was sort of my job to help them pull all the ideas together and get them arranged. I feel like, on this record, they allowed me to be more of a part of it than maybe in the past."

24 Soundgarden

If there is one band most closely associated with Pearl Jam—both in public and behind the scenes—it could quite possibly be Soundgarden, who proved to be one of the most enduring, popular, and influential of all the grunge bands (even serving as an influence on some of their peers, namely Alice in Chains). Originally formed in 1984 in Seattle, the initial SG lineup consisted of Chris Cornell as a "singing drummer," plus guitarist Kim Thayil and bassist Hiro Yamamoto. By 1985, however, Cornell had handed off his drumsticks to Scott Sundquist, and a year later, Matt Cameron was the band's latest—and last—timekeeper.

What made Soundgarden truly unique, especially in their early days, was that they sounded little like much of the mainstream hard rock that was being created at the time. While bands like Black Flag and the Melvins had already begun slowing hardcore-punk's rapid pace down to Black Sabbath-y sublevels, Soundgarden also had the songs to match; all four musicians were strong songwriters who would contribute tunes. Additionally, they were not aligned to a single style; as much as the press wanted to deem them "a heavy metal band," elements of psychedelia, goth, punk rock, and even prog were all present from the start.

On October 1, 1987, the group's first release was issued, the six-track EP, *Screaming Life* (one of the first-ever releases by Sub Pop Records, behind only the *Sub Pop 100* compilation and Green River's *Dry as a Bone* EP), which spawned such early classics as "Hunted Down" and "Nothing to Say." Another Sub Pop EP followed on August 1, 1988, *Fopp.* Their full-length debut on SST Records, *Ultramega OK*, was released on Halloween 1988, and featured the standouts "Flower" and "Beyond the Wheel," the latter of which showcased the enormous vocal talents of Cornell, while the album would eventually earn a Grammy Award nomination for "Best Metal Performance."

With people outside of just Seattle finally taking note of the Pacific Northwest's emerging young rockers, Soundgarden signed with a major label, A&M Records, which led to the release of *Louder Than Love* on September 5, 1989. But the move to a major did not sit well with Yamamoto, who jumped ship, and was first replaced by ex-Nirvana guitarist Jason Everman (who appeared in the album's two music videos, for "Hands All Over" and "Loud Love," and home video, *Louder Than Live*), before Ben Shepherd signed on in 1990, resulting in what many consider the definitive Soundgarden lineup.

It was in the middle of the tour in support of *LTL* that Mother Love Bone's Andy Wood died from a drug overdose, which especially affected Cornell, as he and Wood were friends and onetime housemates. Wood's passing would eventually lead to Cornell penning songs that former MLB members Stone Gossard and Jeff Ament would play on (as well as guitarist Mike McCready and a few vocals from Eddie Vedder). Dubbed Temple of the Dog, their self-titled debut would be issued on April 16, 1991. But a few months before that, Gossard, McCready, and Ament enlisted the aid of Cameron to play drums on a demo of tunes to try out singers for their new band—which eventually found its way into the hands of Vedder and led to the formation of what would become Pearl Jam.

Being successful in the music biz seems to be equal parts talent, luck, and being in the right place at the right time. And Soundgarden scored high in all three sectors when their third full-length was released on October 8, 1991: *Badmotorfinger.* The arrival of Mr. Shepherd into the band signaled the point at which the "Soundgarden sound" truly coalesced, and it certainly didn't hurt matters that the band just happened to offer the public their finest batch of songs yet, including "Rusty Cage," "Slaves and Bulldozers," "Jesus Christ Pose," and "Searching with My Good Eye Closed," among others. But it was "Outshined" (and its accompanying video) that broke Soundgarden commercially, resulting in *Badmotorfinger* going gold, and eventually earning double platinum certification. (It also didn't hurt that the band served as the opening act on Guns N' Roses' U.S. and European tours in support of their *Use Your Illusion* albums.)

It was also this era of the band that spawned an identifiable grunge look: the Dr. Martens boots, cargo shorts, and shirtless torso, with a long hair and goatee (or some other variation of facial hair) combo. It was also during this era that SG and PJ shared concert bills for the first time—October 6, 1991, at the Palladium in Hollywood (as part of *Rip Magazine*'s fifth anniversary party), and then for three Texas-area shows from April 28 to April 30, 1992. It wouldn't be the last time that year that the pair crossed paths—both would be invited to participate in that year's edition of Lollapalooza. A year later, there would be another show featuring both SG and PJ, this time with headliner Neil Young (and a fourth act, Blues Traveler, rounding out the lineup) on August 18, 1993, at the mammoth Canadian National Exhibition (CNE) Stadium, in Toronto, Ontario.

With the release of *Superunknown* on March 8, 1994, Soundgarden had become one of the most popular bands in the world. The album debuted at No. 1 on the Billboard 200, was certified 5x platinum in the U.S. alone, won two Grammy Awards a year later, and spawned the classics "Spoonman," "Black Hole Sun," "Fell on Black Days," "The Day I Tried to Live," "My Wave," and the title track. The resulting tour exposed the first cracks in the band's armor, however, including having to cut the tour short due to Cornell experiencing vocal difficulties.

SG returned with their next studio offering, *Down on the Upside*, on May 21, 1996, which while not as jaw-droppingly brilliant as the two titles that preceded it, still delivered the goods both commercially (peaking at No. 2 on the Billboard 200, selling nearly 2 million copies) and artistically (the standouts "Pretty Noose," "Burden in My Hand," "Blow Up the Outside World," and "Ty Cobb"), and was supported with another appearance as part of Lollapalooza. However, on April 9, 1997, fans were shocked by the announcement that Soundgarden had split. The move ultimately proved to be beneficial for Pearl Jam—with SG now removed from Cameron's daily planner, he was welcomed into PJ during the summer of 1998, their fifth drummer overall (a position he has occupied ever since).

Soundgarden reunited in 2010, and issued their sixth studio album, *King Animal*, on November 13, 2012, which peaked at No. 5 on the Billboard 200 and spawned a pair of standout tracks accompanied by music videos ("Been Away Too Long" and the Dave Grohl–directed "By Crooked Steps"). Various compilations, live recordings, and box sets would also arrive during this reunion era. Pulling double duty between PJ and SG was tricky for Cameron, so he sat out all of SG's touring commitments in 2014. And just who was the fill-in, you ask? None other than Matt Chamberlain, the briefest-tenured drummer in Pearl Jam history!

Cornell and his old PJ pals would reunite for Temple of the Dog shows during 2016. Sadly, this proved to be the last collaboration between them, as Cornell committed suicide while on tour with Soundgarden on May 18, 2017, at the age of 52.

25 Collect the Holiday Singles

Pearl Jam has always been a very giving bunch, showering their fans with free concerts, benefit performances and auctions, and extra-special album packaging. And almost every year since 1991, the band has issued a special "holiday single" on vinyl for members of their fan club, the Ten Club. Each single features exclusive songs not widely available otherwise, except for one (which we will get to when we discuss 1998).

The first holiday single, in 1991, featured "Let Me Sleep," a tender-sounding number with lyrics that seem to alternate between enjoying Christmas as a youngster and being downright miserable in the present. The B-side, "Ramblings," is exactly that: a recording of one of the guys fumbling around on an acoustic guitar, while the others wish everyone happy holidays, curse, and point out that it's being recorded while the Red Hot Chili Peppers are performing in the background (obviously recorded during the PJ / Smashing Pumpkins / Chili Peppers tour in late 1991 and early 1992). One of the few redeeming qualities of the tune is that part of a random statement that Mr. Vedder offers was later recycled for one of the better PJ fansites, twofeetthick.com ("I'm a rhinoceros, and my skin is two feet thick"). Unfortunately, fans would have to endure two more return visits to "Ramblings" land, on the B-sides of the '92 and '93 singles.

A selection of Pearl Jam's holiday singles. (N. Kraetsch)

Subsequently, the holiday single series has produced a number of gems, especially 1993's acoustic sing-along "Angel," 1999's stark and haunting "Strangest Tribe," and 2009's retro-sounding (and from the single's cover, retro-*looking)* "Turning Mist," which features none other than Mike McCready on lead vocals. And while the majority of the tunes included on these special singles are covers, they are by no means mere throwaways. Some of the standouts include 1995's "History Never Repeats," performed by Vedder, Neil Finn, and Tim Finn (originally done by Split Enz); 2000's "Crown of Thorns" (Mother Love Bone); 2001's "Gimme Some Truth" (John Lennon); 2005's "Little Sister" (Elvis Presley) featuring Robert Plant; and 2006's "Love, Reign o'er Me" (the Who). The 2013 single, "99 Problems," featuring Jay-Z, was certainly one of the more surprising selections, while 1998's "Last

Kiss" (written by Wayne Cochran but made popular by J. Frank Wilson and the Cavaliers) though originally the B-side, became a full-fledged hit after receiving a regular single release due to overwhelming demand. And a few tracks off the holiday singles were just too good to not be included on the 2003 double-disc compilation, *Lost Dogs* ("Strangest Tribe," "Drifting," "Let Me Sleep," and "Last Kiss").

If there are some gaps in your collection, copies regularly become available on eBay.

26 Watch *Singles*

Director/screenwriter/journalist/author Cameron Crowe certainly has a way of accurately depicting everyday life and romantic relationships on the big screen—see films such as 1982's *Fast Times at Ridgemont High* or 1989's *Say Anything* for proof. And you have to give Crowe some additional credit for realizing something special was brewing in Seattle at the dawn of the 1990s, as he picked the Emerald City as the backdrop for his 1992 film *Singles*.

The plot follows a group of single twentysomethings doing their darndest to become…un-single. It stars Matt Dillon as Cliff Poncier (the singer in a fictional grunge band named Citizen Dick), Bridget Fonda as his on-again/off-again girlfriend, Campbell Scott as a guy trying to get a speed train proposal off the ground, Kyra Sedgwick as *his* on-again/off-again girlfriend, and Sheila Kelley as a woman who never quite seems to find Mr. Right, plus a handful of cameos from some Hollywood veterans (Tim Burton, Eric Stoltz, Tom Skerritt, and a then-unknown Paul Giamatti).

So how does *Singles* fit significantly into the story of Pearl Jam? Well, to serve as the other members of Citizen Dick alongside Dillon, Crowe cast Eddie Vedder, Stone Gossard, and Jeff Ament. The "band" has some memorable and funny scenes, including one in which the musicians are sitting in a coffee shop reading over an offending review, and another when they are watching a documentary about bees.

While Citizen Dick does not actually perform any songs in the film, Pearl Jam certainly made its presence felt on its soundtrack, thanks to the inclusion of studio versions of two outstanding compositions that had been performed throughout the *Ten* tour, "Breath" and "State of Love and Trust." Additionally, two real-world grunge bands do perform in the film—Alice in Chains ("It Ain't Like That" from *Facelift* and the newly recorded "Would?") and Soundgarden (another exclusive tune for the film, "Birth Ritual"). As a side note, when a Blu-ray version of the film was issued in 2015, viewers were treated to additional scenes, one of which was an absolutely dazzling unedited live version of "Birth Ritual" that has to be seen to be believed.

In addition to his contribution as an actor, Ament inadvertently inspired a few standout tunes that would eventually reside in the Chris Cornell songbook. The PJ bassist worked on the film set as an art director, and for a scene in Poncier's apartment, a stack of cassettes were needed to serve as the singer's demos. Ament went the extra mile and actually came up with fake song titles for the cassettes, despite the fact that they would be indecipherable to moviegoers. Cornell took note of one of the cassettes and penned songs inspired by Ament's song titles, including "Fluttergirl" (which later appeared on Cornell's solo debut, *Euphoria Morning*), and most significantly, the Soundgarden classic "Spoonman" (which turned up on *Superunknown*, while a small snippet of an acoustic take of the tune can be heard in the film).

Released on September 18, 1992, *Singles* was a modest hit upon release (earning $18.5 million at the box office, with a $9 million budget). But over the years, the film has become a cult classic due to its humorous-yet-heartwarming storyline, great music, and the film acting debuts of Vedder-Gossard-Ament. And *Singles* was not the end of Crowe's personal and working relationship with Pearl Jam—he would interview them for a *Rolling Stone* cover story in 1993, direct a music video for the song "The Fixer" in 2009, and, most significantly, direct the exceptional documentary *Pearl Jam Twenty* in 2011.

27 Pearl Jam Clones

Like any musical movement, there are the originators...and then there are the copycats. And the great grunge uprising of the early '90s was no different. Seemingly overnight, bands that just a few months (weeks? days?) earlier were probably sporting spandex and mile-high hair were suddenly wearing Doc Martens and flannels, and trading their Floyd Rose tremolo-equipped pointy guitars for well-weathered instruments. One of the most copied groups of the era was Pearl Jam, and the imitators didn't stop at just their music; they also often attempted to copy Eddie Vedder's unmistakable baritone.

The most obvious copycat of that era was Creed. Although beefcake singer Scott Stapp's Christian-esque lyrics differed greatly from Vedder's, there was no denying that Stapp was well versed in vocal Vedder-isms—the most obvious example found on Creed's popular 1997 tune, "My Own Prison." And while it's hard to single out the most preposterous statement in the history of rock 'n' roll, my vote would confidently go to Creed bassist Brian Marshall, who offered up the following humdinger during a radio interview in 2000 (on KNDD, a Seattle station, no less): "Eddie Vedder wishes he could write like Scott Stapp."

Other bands whose singers felt better with a little bit of Vedder were Seven Mary Three (1995's "Cumbersome"), the Nixons (1996's "Sister"), Tantric (2000's "Breakdown"), Fuel (2000's "Hemorrhage (In My Hands)"), Nickelback (specifically 2002's "Hero," which was credited to Nickelback's Chad Kroeger and Saliva's Josey Scott), and, if you position your ears at a certain angle, bits of Collective Soul (specifically the "Yeah!" right before the chorus of their 1994 hit, "Shine").

One group that for some reason nobody seems to think owes a debt to PJ is Hootie & the Blowfish. Don't believe me? Give another listen (if you're brave enough) to their mega-selling 1994 debut, *Cracked Rear View*, and specifically such light pop rock as "Hold My Hand," "Let Her Cry," and "Only Wanna Be with You," and you will definitely hear some Vedder-esque vocals from Darius Rucker. This point was even referenced in the 2012 comedy film, *Ted*, when the main character (a teddy bear, voiced by Seth MacFarlane) sings "Only Wanna Be with You" karaoke-style at a party and observes, "This is how *everybody* sang in the '90s" and "You can do any '90s song with just vowels."

Not all bands that contained similarities to PJ and Vedder were one-trick ponies, however. Case in point, Stone Temple Pilots. First bursting onto the scene in 1992 with their hit debut album *Core*, the press dismissed the band as a PJ clone early on, not without reason to: not only was singer Scott Weiland's voice on the MTV/radio smash "Plush" very Vedder, but in the song's accompanying video (which was directed by Josh Taft, who also directed the PJ videos "Alive," "Even Flow," and "Oceans"), Weiland even contorts his face and moves a bit like Vedder.

However, much to their credit, STP's PJ approximation was short-lived, as they soon took on a variety of different musical styles and proved to be expert songwriters—just give a listen to any of their other albums for proof, specifically such classics as 1994's *Purple* and 1996's *Tiny Music...Songs from the Vatican Gift Shop*. And one last morsel about "Plush": Weiland and guitarist Dean DeLeo performed an acoustic version of the song on MTV's *Headbangers Ball* back in 1992, on which Weiland sang the tune in a more natural voice. As a result, that rendition is arguably better than the well-known studio version (and can also be heard on STP's 2003 hits compilation, *Thank You*)—which makes you wonder why he didn't sing it that way the first time around.

What was most problematic about the bands that shamelessly stole from Pearl Jam was they were completely missing the point about what made grunge special, important, and enduring in the first place—the originators were putting their own unique spin on rock music, trying different approaches, and injecting their personalities into their work.

When I interviewed Vedder for *Grunge Is Dead*, he discussed this topic, and his oft-copied vocal style: "It took me a while to figure out how to really sing—or not push it. I was a horse being let out of the gate—I was pent up. That first record, it's really 'throaty' [laughs]. It didn't mean to be, but it became a vocal style that became co-opted by certain bands that I feel made really shitty music. And they weren't making those records until we were on like our third record—or even fourth. And what's funny—the bridge would sound like Layne [Staley], the verse would sound like me, and the chorus would sound like Kurt [Cobain]. Or they'd look like me and sound like Kurt, or look like Kurt and sound like me [laughs]. All this weird amalgamation stuff.

"But the bummer was, if you listen to surf music, everybody sounded like the Beach Boys. If you get the Rhino *Cowabunga!* box set, there's all these bands you've never heard of. It all sounded like the Beach Boys, with harmonies, guitars, and "Wipe Out" drum sounds. But it was all kind of good. For me what was weird—I was just like, 'God, I would never listen to this [grunge-copycat] music. This is not good.' And it felt like they were co-opting the angst from whatever I'd been through. I don't know anything about these people, but I didn't feel like they'd lived through it. It wasn't like they were co-opting what we were doing—it was like, the first record. Or those two songs."

28 Drummer No. 1

Although Dave Abbruzzese was Pearl Jam's drummer during their most commercially successful period and Matt Cameron has been their longest-tenured timekeeper, Dave Krusen was certainly one of their most important. The reason? Because he was PJ's first drummer, helping to get the band off the ground, being present for the creation of the band's sound and, most importantly, was a major part of their classic debut, *Ten*.

Born on March 10, 1966, in Tacoma, Washington, Krusen honed his craft playing in a variety of local bands. Eventually he crossed paths with Tal Goettling, who just happened to be friends with none other than Jeff Ament and Stone Gossard. When the two former Mother Love Bone members began looking for a drummer for their newly formed band (Eddie Vedder had just signed on), Goettling recommended Krusen, resulting in Pearl Jam (then known as Mookie Blaylock) playing their first-ever gig a week later, on October 22, 1990, at the Off Ramp Café in Seattle.

Krusen's tenure in PJ would be brief—it lasted only seven months, as his final performance with the band was on May 25, 1991, at RKCNDY in Seattle, at the "wrap party" for the filming of *Singles*. But one of the most important events in the entire history of Pearl Jam occurred during that time span: the recording of *Ten*. In addition to providing the backbeat on some of the group's most instantly recognizable and beloved songs ("Alive," "Even Flow," "Jeremy," "Black," "Porch," and so on), he also earned a songwriting credit—along with all the other—members, on the album's epic closer, "Release." Additionally, Krusen played on quite a few B-sides and rare tracks, including the beloved "Yellow Ledbetter," "Wash," "Alone," "Hold On," and "Brother," among others.

Speaking to *Rolling Stone* in 2016, Krusen was open and honest about his exit from Pearl Jam: "I'm an alcoholic. I had really been just sick of my disease at that point and could just not stop drinking." Subsequently, however, Krusen seemed to get his life back on track and has remained busy as a musician, playing with a variety of artists, including post-grungers Candlebox (1998's *Happy Pills*, plus several other releases), the Blind Melon offshoot Unified Theory (2000's self-titled debut), and the more experimental Hovercraft (1997's *Akathisia*, performing under the alias "Karl 3-30," along with Eddie Vedder's first wife, Beth Liebling). Krusen was also reunited with his former PJ bandmates on April 7, 2017, for a performance of "Alive," when he and the band were inducted into the Rock and Roll Hall of Fame.

29 Madison Square Garden

If there was a single venue that most performers would choose to headline as proof that they'd truly "made it," New York City's Madison Square Garden would certainly be either near or at the very top of the list. Located at 4 Pennsylvania Plaza in Manhattan, the heralded venue has gone through several major renovations—and even relocations—over the years, and is connected to Penn Station, which in turn offers Amtrak, the Long Island Rail Road, New Jersey Transit, and the New York City subway.

MSG is known primarily as the home court for the National Basketball Association's New York Knicks (since 1946), and the home rink for the National Hockey League's New York Rangers (since 1926). It's also hosted myriad other events, including "The Fight of the Century," which saw Joe Frazier defeat Muhammad Ali via unanimous decision in 1971; JFK's 45th birthday celebration in 1962, at which Marilyn Monroe sang her iconic rendition of "Happy Birthday"; the Ringling Brothers Circus; and countless concerts featuring the crème de la crème of performers, such as Frank Sinatra, Elvis Presley, Led Zeppelin, George Harrison's *Concert for Bangladesh*, Bruce Springsteen, Billy Joel, Kiss, Queen, and many more.

The first MSG opened in 1879 and was located at East 26th Street and Madison Avenue in Manhattan. MSG II replaced the old structure in 1890 at the same exact site before MSG III came along in 1925 (at Eighth Avenue between 49th and 50th streets). The fourth MSG opened in 1968, nestled between 31st and 33rd streets from Seventh to Eighth avenues. Additionally, in 1968, a smaller venue also opened within MSG's structure—initially called the Felt Forum, it went through several name changes before settling on the Theater at Madison Square Garden, with a capacity of 5,500, compared to MSG's 20,000.

So, what does all that have to do with Pearl Jam? Well, the band and the venue have forged an extremely strong bond over the years. Eddie Vedder and Mike McCready performed the Bob Dylan song "Masters of War" at the Garden back on October 16, 1992, as part of the star-studded *30th Anniversary Concert Celebration* in honor of Bob Dylan (which also featured performances by the likes of Eric Clapton, Neil Young, Stevie Wonder, Lou Reed, Willie Nelson, John Cougar Mellencamp, Chrissie Hynde, and Tom Petty, among others, as well as Mr. Dylan himself). Also, on April 17, 1994, PJ closed out their tour in support of *Vs.* with an intimate performance at the Theater at Madison Square Garden (then going by the name of the Paramount Theatre).

The next time Pearl Jam played the Garden would be as headliners of "the real deal" MSG—September 10 and 11, 1998, while on tour in support of *Yield.* As a headliner, PJ has always performed two nights back-to-back at MSG: July 8–9, 2003 (touring for *Riot*

The marquee outside Madison Square Garden before a Pearl Jam concert in New York. (Steven J. Messina)

Act, with the first date documented later that year on the *Live at the Garden* DVD), June 24–25, 2008 (not in support of any album), May 20-21, 2010 (*Backspacer*), and May 1–2, 2016 (again, not in support of any album).

There have been quite a few standout guest appearances over the years, such as Ben Harper joining in for both "Daughter" and "With My Own Two Hands" (7/8/03), Ace Frehley guesting on guitar for a cover of Kiss' "Black Diamond" (6/25/08), C.J. Ramone supplying bass for a cover of the Ramones' "I Believe in Miracles" (also on 6/25/08), and Rick Nielsen and Tom Petersson tackling Cheap Trick's "Surrender" (5/2/16).

MSG is also the site of several noteworthy shows in PJ history. In 1998, fans made a coordinated effort to entice the band into playing "Breath," a song that hadn't been played since 1994. The "Breath Campaign" culminated successfully on September 11, 1998. Then, in 2003, the fans became so enthusiastic during "Do the Evolution" that there was a brief moment of panic amongst the band, as the stage beneath their feet began to shake. Vedder later tells the crowd that three other artists shook the stage in MSG history: the Grateful Dead, Iron Maiden, and Bruce Springsteen. The moment is documented on the *Live at the Garden* DVD.

Additionally, Ament, Gossard, McCready, and Cameron would return—along with Chris Cornell—to MSG on November 7, 2016, as members of Temple of the Dog. Sadly, this performance would be Cornell's last-ever true concert in New York (two brief solo performances by Cornell would occur in April 2017 for TV). He would pass away just a few months later, on May 18, 2017.

30 Red Hot Chili Peppers

Although they emerged during the grunge era, Pearl Jam could get downright funky at times—particularly in the groovy rhythm guitar work of Stone Gossard. One of the first bands to successfully merge funk and punk was the Red Hot Chili Peppers, a group that played a prominent part in the PJ story and was an obvious musical influence.

Originally formed in 1983 and hailing from Los Angeles, California, there have been two constant members of the band since its inception—singer Anthony Kiedis and bassist Flea (real name: Michael Balzary)—while several guitarists and drummers have passed through the ranks over the years, the best-known of the bunch Hillel Slovak and John Frusciante on guitar, and Jack Irons and Chad Smith on drums.

Beginning as an explosive and unpredictable live act (their trademark early on was performing in their birthday suits…except for strategically placed tube socks), the group released several original and groundbreaking albums, such as 1984's self-titled debut, 1985's *Freaky Styley*, 1987's *The Uplift Mofo Party Plan* (the last to feature Slovak, who would die from a heroin overdose on June 25, 1988, at the age of 26), and 1989's *Mother's Milk*. After the commercial breakthrough of 1991's *Blood Sugar Sex Magik*, the band got a bit more serious and issued material that leaned more toward the mainstream/pop side of things.

Even before the formation of Pearl Jam, the Chili Peppers had already left their mark on a young Eddie Vedder—so much so that several photos in the *Pearl Jam Twenty* book depict the singer sporting a black leather jacket with RED HOT painted on one sleeve and

Chili Peppers on the other. In another photo, Vedder is wearing the same jacket with the late, great Joe Strummer, the leader of the Clash. By the late '80s, the Clash was no more and Joe had gone solo... and had none other than former Peppers drummer Irons manning the kit. It was during Strummer's tour in support of his *Earthquake Weather* album that Vedder befriended Irons, which led to the duo embarking on a camping trip through Yosemite. And who should also be on that trip but Irons' former Peppers bandmate Flea!

By 1990, Jeff Ament had also befriended Irons, and invited the drummer to join an embryonic version of what would eventually become Pearl Jam. Irons passed on the invite himself, but when Ament asked if he knew of any potential singers for the group, he eventually recommended none other than Vedder, who...well, you know the rest. Additionally, Irons was also supposedly the one who suggested to the Chili Peppers that they take Pearl Jam on tour with them in support of *Blood Sugar* (a trek that also included a pre-fame Smashing Pumpkins) in late 1991 and early 1992. That tour succeeded in introducing the fast-rising band to a large audience and set the stage perfectly for their massive breakthrough success in the summer of '92.

After spending several months on the road with the Peppers (from October 16, 1991, to January 2, 1992, to be exact), their trademark funk had noticeably rubbed off a bit on PJ. This was evident when Pearl Jam recorded the B-side for the "Even Flow" single, a track titled "Dirty Frank." As Stone Gossard told *Guitar World* in the September 1992 issue, "You can't help but be influenced by the Chili Peppers when you watch them night after night. Rather than emulating them, we just wanted to catch their groove and feel it the way they feel it...It's cool to have moments like that."

With *Ten* riding high on the charts by the spring/summer that year and grunge mania peaking, it would make sense that not one but two Seattle bands would be included on that year's Lollapalooza lineup, with Pearl Jam and Soundgarden getting the nod. And who was the tour's headliner? None other than PJ's old touring pals, the Red Hot Chili Peppers. And when both bands were asked to perform at that year's MTV Video Music Awards, a photograph was snapped of Kiedis kissing Vedder full on the lips backstage. (The photo later ran in *Rolling Stone*.)

When Dave Abbruzzese exited Pearl Jam in 1994, he was replaced by former Chili Peppers drummer Jack Irons, who played on the albums *No Code* (1996) and *Yield* (1998), the PJ/Neil Young collaboration *Mirror Ball* (1995), as well as tracks on other assorted releases.

At the 2002 Rock and Roll Hall of Fame induction ceremony, Eddie Vedder inducted the Ramones, and gave a memorable yet lengthy (17 minutes) speech, while sporting a Mohawk. When Anthony Kiedis later took the stage to induct the Talking Heads that same night, he stated, "Eddie Vedder, wherever you are, you are a genius. The Ramones' songs may be two minutes long, but that speech was not!"

One last PJ/RHCP connection: Mike McCready did an in-depth interview with Flea and Smith on SiriusXM Pearl Jam Radio in 2016, right around the time of the Peppers' 11th release overall, *The Getaway*. The conversation included Smith and McCready recalling how PJ landed the Peppers tour way back in '92, and how it proved to be a complete game-changer in their career. And in 2017, McCready thanked the Peppers during his Rock and Roll Hall of Fame induction speech.

31 Best of the B-Sides

Pearl Jam has always focused on doing right by their fans and giving them value for their hard-earned cash. So in addition to offering exclusive holiday singles to members of their fan club, they have often offered non-album tunes on the B-sides of their domestically released singles.

One of their finest non-album B-sides was included on their first single, "Alive," a tune by the name of "Wash." The opening lyric bears a similar sentiment to the thoughts of psychotic cabbie Travis Bickle in the classic 1976 film *Taxi Driver* ("Wash" begins with the lyric, "Oh please, let it rain today / This city is so filthy, like my mind in ways"). The song is one of PJ's best momentum builders in their entire catalog; it starts smoothly before ending with Eddie Vedder hollering, "Wash my love!" The song has gone on to become a concert favorite as well, including an odd, sped-up version that served as a set opener on New Year's Eve 1992, when PJ opened for Keith Richards at the Academy in NYC (Vedder flipped the bird to Marky Mark—aka Mark Wahlberg—at the song's conclusion).

As mentioned in the previous entry, Pearl Jam showcased their funkier side on the B-side to their second single, "Even Flow," via the track "Dirty Frank." While the tune is not played live very often, it was featured on the *Live at the Orpheum Theater, Boston, April 12, 1994* CD, included as part of the *Vs./Vitalogy* box set from 2011. Speaking to *Guitar World* back in 1992, Mike McCready discussed the tune's creation and meaning: "'Dirty Frank' was written while we were touring with the Red Hot Chili Peppers. The song's about our bus driver, Frank—we were convinced he was a serial killer. We would find piles of empty beer cans under his driver's seat after a whole night's drive. It was like, 'Oh man, I'm glad we're still alive!'" Stone Gossard added, "'Dirty Frank' is a pearl jam. The lyrics on that song are amazing, some of the best Eddie's ever written."

For the "Jeremy" single, fans were treated to not one but *two* non-LP tracks—"Footsteps" and "Yellow Ledbetter." The former is one of PJ's most stripped-down tracks (comprised of only a single acoustic guitar, harmonica, and vocals), and lyrically is part of the *Momma-Son* trilogy (sung from the point of view of a killer sitting in his prison cell). The latter track contains sterling guitar work from Mike McCready—straight out of the Jimi Hendrix / Stevie Ray Vaughan songbook—and has become an incredibly popular number amongst fans (and one of its most-often-played in concert). Much has been said about the almost indecipherable lyrics, but in 2015, a writer for Boston's WZLX radio station's website confidently claimed to have cracked the code: "'Ledbetter' reveals its meaning mostly in the refrain commonly perceived as 'I don't know whether I was the boxer or the bag.' This line simply suggests a conflicted man, but it was at a 2003 concert at the Xfinity Center in Mansfield, Massachusetts, (then known as the Tweeter Center) on July 11, 2003, that Vedder sang the lyric as 'I think of him when I go to bed, and he's coming home in a box or a bag.' This strongly implies that the song was about a man receiving a letter about his brother dying in a war. Just three days earlier, at Madison Square Garden, Vedder sang 'I don't know whether my brother will be coming home in a box or a bag.'"

Although no music videos were filmed for any of the tracks on *Vs.*, there were still several singles released, including "Go," that contain a pair of interesting non-album B-sides—"Elderly Woman Behind the Counter in a Small Town" (acoustic) and "Alone." While a full-band version of "Elderly" was included on *Vs.*, the version on the single is a charming one, comprised of just acoustic guitar and vocals. On the other hand, "Alone" had been kicking around even before the recording of *Ten*; a demo of the track had been passed around in bootleg/trading circles for some time prior. McCready's guitar solo on the single version borrows a phrase or two from another PJ tune, "Breath" (which appears on the soundtrack for Cameron Crowe's *Singles*).

When it comes to the *Vitalogy* era, Pearl Jam threw a couple of curveballs. "Out of My Mind" was paired with the A-side, "Not for You." A live recording from the evening of April 2, 1994, at the Fox Theatre in Atlanta, Georgia, "Out of My Mind" is billed as "improv," but since Vedder's lyrics and phrasing fit perfectly, there seems to have been some thought and planning done beforehand. Elsewhere, the flip side of the "Immortality" single is one of the more intriguing B-sides in PJ's entire history—a cover of "Rearviewmirror" by lo-fi alt-rockers the Frogs. Hailing from Milwaukee, Wisconsin, the Frogs are perhaps the cultiest of cult bands, yet their fans included Nirvana, Smashing Pumpkins, and obviously, Pearl Jam. Their original rendition of "Rearviewmirror" is surprisingly great, as their version bears almost no resemblance musically to PJ's rocking version.

Fast-forward to *No Code*, for which non-album compositions included the garage rocker "Black, Red, Yellow" on the "Hail, Hail" single, and the stark and dark "Dead Man" on the "Off He Goes" single. And a healthy amount of leftover tracks from the sessions that yielded *Yield* were plucked off the cutting room floor, including a pair of compositions that backed up the "Given to Fly" single—the mid-paced "Pilate" and the more uptempo "Leatherman"—and "U," a typical-sounding PJ rocker on the "Wishlist" single.

Strangely, aside from an "alternate mix" of the song "Insignificance" on the "Nothing as It Seems" single, there would be no B-side studio originals for any of the *Binaural* singles. But PJ made up for lost time by including three non-LP tracks when it came to singles for *Riot Act*—the slightly country-ish "Down" and the surprisingly strong and melodic "Undone" were tacked onto the "I Am Mine" single," while a Jeff Ament original, "Other Side," was found on the "Save You" single. After *Riot Act*, however, it seems as if the band's main focus was on just the right amount of selections for their respective latest studio album, due to the "digital age" in which artists would issue a digital single with just a lone track rather than two, and perhaps include live tracks or merely another song from the album, as opposed to including studio leftovers.

Luckily for fans who may have learned about these mostly uncommon compositions after the fact—or for those who understandably don't want to dole out the dough for just a few tracks on a CD single—Pearl Jam collected quite a few of the aforementioned B-sides (plus previously unreleased goodies) on the 2003 double-disc compilation *Lost Dogs*.

32 Eddie Vedder's Other Projects

The Pearl Jam member with the most varied appearances outside of the band is Eddie Vedder. While his early band from San Diego, Bad Radio, never got out of the demo stage recording-wise, you can easily find those demos and live footage on YouTube. Once you do, you will find that while the band did contain some Pearl Jam-y tunes ("Believe You Me" and most directly, "Better Man"), some of it is far too derivative to be taken seriously (the obviously Chili Peppers–influenced "What the Funk" is best left in obscurity).

After firmly establishing himself with PJ, other artists began inviting Vedder and his instantly recognizable vocals to their recordings. As a result, you can find Vedder's voice on the Bad Religion tracks "American Jesus" and "Watch It Die" (off 1993's *Recipe for Hate*), Mike Watt's "Against the '70s" and "Big Train" (1995's *Ball-Hog or Tugboat?*), two great collaborations with Nusrat Fateh Ali Khan, "Face of Love" and "Long Road" (1996's *Dead Man Walking* soundtrack), Crowded House's "Everything Is Good for You" (1996's *Recurring Dream*), a cover of the Dave Clark Five's "Any Way You Want It" with the Ramones (1997's *We're Outta Here!*), and a pair of songs with his idol, Pete Townshend, "Magic Bus" and "Heart to Hang Onto" (1999's *Pete Townshend Live: A Benefit for Maryville Academy*). And while Vedder was a member of the spacey/experimental band Hovercraft in the '90s, frustratingly, he only appeared on one studio track: "Hymn" (off the 1997 comp, *Kerouac: Kicks Joy Darkness*).

Vedder's fondness for appearing elsewhere continued into the 21st century; he can be found on Wellwater Conspiracy's "Felicity's Surprise" (2001's *The Scroll and Its Combinations*); a cover of the Beatles' "You've Got to Hide Your Love Away" (2002's *I Am Sam* soundtrack); Cat Power's "Good Woman" and "Evolution" (2003's *You Are Free*); alongside his heroes, the Who, on live renditions of "I'm One," "Gettin' in Tune," "Let's See Action," and "See Me, Feel Me" (2003's *The Who Live at Royal Albert Hall*); a cover of Marvin Gaye's "Mercy Mercy Me" with the Strokes and Josh Homme (the B-side of the Strokes' 2006 A-side, "You Only Live Once"); R.E.M.'s "It Happened Today" (2011's *Collapse into Now*); and Jimmy Fallon's "Balls in Your Mouth" (2012's *Blow Your Pants Off*).

So far, Vedder has issued a pair of solo recordings. Co-produced between the singer and Adam Kasper, *Into the Wild* was issued on September 18, 2007, and contained tracks for the Sean Penn–directed film of the same name. Two singles were selected from the album, "Hard Sun" and "Guaranteed," while the album itself was a hit, peaking at No. 11 on the Billboard 200, and receiving platinum, gold, and silver certifications in Italy, Switzerland, and the UK, respectively. Vedder's second solo offering, *Ukulele Songs*, followed on May 31, 2011, and once more featured the singer and Kasper as the production team. Featuring both original tunes and standards, the album was even more successful in the U.S. for Vedder than its predecessor, peaking at No. 4 on the Billboard 200.

33 Mike Watt

While the rock world was still reeling from the death of Kurt Cobain in 1994, Eddie Vedder began the healing process by recording and touring with one of punk rock's all-time heroes, Minutemen/fIREHOSE bassist Mike Watt.

Born Michael David Watt on December 20, 1957, in Portsmouth, Virginia, it was after his family relocated to San Pedro, California (a town that Watt will forever be closely associated with), that Watt befriended Dennes Dale Boon (best known as D. Boon). Eventually, Watt and Boon took up bass and guitar, respectively, and formed the Minutemen (with drummer Ed Hurley rounding out the trio) in 1980.

Recording for such outlets as Black Flag's SST Records and a label co-founded by Boon and Watt (along with a pal, Martin Tamburovich), New Alliance Records, the Minutemen specialized in a sound that was hard to pin down to a single style, but whose basis was decidedly punk rock. The band seemingly crammed in as much recording and touring as they possibly could, resulting in such classics as 1984's double-album, *Double Nickels on the Dime* (which later became well known for including the tune "Corona," the theme song for the hit TV and movie franchise *Jackass*).

Eddie Vedder, Mike Watt, and Dave Grohl performing at Tramps in New York, 1995. (Steven J. Messina)

Unfortunately, the Minutemen's career was cut short when Boon tragically died in an auto accident on December 27, 1985, at the age of 27. Watt and Hurley would soldier on as fIREHOSE (with newcomer Ed Crawford), issuing solid albums for both SST (1987's *If'n* being a highlight) and Columbia (1991's *Flyin' the Flannel*), before going the way of the dodo in 1994. But instead of resting on his laurels, Watt immediately went to work on his first solo album. Assembling an all-star cast that rotated from track to track (including Krist Novoselic, Henry Rollins, Flea, J. Mascis, and Adam Horovitz, among others), the resulting album, *Ball-Hog or Tugboat?*, was issued on February 28, 1995, via Columbia, and featured input from none other than Dave Grohl (drums on both "Big Train" and "Against the '70s") and Eddie Vedder (guitar and backing vocals on "Big Train" plus lead vocals and guitar on "Against the '70s").

And when it came time to support the album, an idea was hatched to include both Grohl and Vedder on the initial run of dates, which the former Nirvana drummer discussed in 2001 with *Spin* magazine: "For anyone like me or Krist [Novoselic] or Eddie, who may have been somehow disillusioned or jaded or just numb, being around Mike Watt in the studio for just one day renewed that feeling of excitement. He started talking about putting a tour together. He wanted to have Eddie play guitar and me play the drums and he'd play the bass. For three people who were so starved for some sort of thrills, it kind of blew up. Eddie and his wife's band, Hovercraft, had this van they had spray-painted silver—it just looked like a cop magnet; it was such a bad idea. And we had this red Dodge extended van that we called Big Red Delicious. We all had CBs, and through a lot of CB conversations driving through the middle of nowhere, I realized that Eddie is a fuckin' funny motherfucker. I think that for Eddie, at that point, a lot of things had been knocked out of perspective. That tour brought a lot of it back together. We were playing three sets a night for 12 days in a row, with a 10-hour drive every night."

However, beyond that set of dates and a performance on *The Jon Stewart Show*, the Watt-Grohl-Vedder union was short-lived (when Watt toured later in the year, he had a new lineup joining him, dubbed the Crew of the Flying Saucer). Then all three (along with Pat Smear) did a surprise reunion on April 27, 2011, in Seattle at a Mike Watt and the Missingmen show, performing "Big Train" and a cover of the Stooges' "Fun House." Additionally, a killer live recording of the Watt-Grohl-Vedder lineup was issued on November 11, 2016, via Columbia/Legacy: *Ring Spiel Tour '95*. Recorded at the Metro on May 6, 1995, the 16-track set contains renditions of tracks from the Minutemen ("Political Song for Michael Jackson to Sing"), fIREHOSE ("Formal Introduction"), plenty off of *Ball-Hog* ("Big Train," "Against the '70s," "Piss Bottle Man," etc.), and, as a treat to Pearl Jam fans, an embryonic version of the song "Habit" (which would later appear more fleshed out on *No Code*).

Backstage Pass

Mike Watt

Minutemen Bassist/Singer, fIREHOSE Bassist/
Singer, Stooges Bassist, Solo Artist

How did Eddie Vedder wind up appearing on your 1995 album, *Ball-Hog or Tugboat?*

I didn't plan that record to be something with Ed. The whole idea of that album was supposedly a solo record...but there's 48 dudes, it ain't really a solo record! But the idea was I started off with D. Boon and Minutemen and what that all added up to, and then I lost that. And then Edward [Crawford, fIREHOSE singer/guitarist] from Ohio came, and I did seven-and-a-half years of that, which was kind of like the Minutemen. But what I wanted to do was something like a sea change. I thought about the bass—I didn't have to think about it before. "What kind of a bass player are you, Watt?" "Oh, I'm D. Boon's bass player." I remember showing Edward "Piss Bottle Man," and him saying, "Maybe not all your songs are for this band."

It got me thinking, "Maybe I should have different projects." What is a bass player? I got the idea to test this theory I had, which is if the bass player knew the songs, then anybody could come and play drums or guitar or sing. So that's the idea of *Ball-Hog or Tugboat?* It's this Petri dish. I used the metaphor of a wrestling ring, but it's more like a Petri dish, where you try to see the things that are happening. So I picked three towns—West Hollywood, Seattle, and New York City. And I just called people up, and if they were around, they'd come down and get in the ring.

With Ed, there was some kind of charity thing, and we were talking about Captain Beefheart. I think it was at the Palladium. And for some reason, hearing Ed sing at that gig, I thought, "You should try Captain Beefheart." [Laughs] I don't know why. But there's the first song on the other side of *Doc at the Radar Station*, called "Dirty Blue Jean." So when it came time to go up there [to Seattle], Ed wasn't there. Dave Grohl was there, Krist Novoselic, and Mark Lanegan—I did record with some people up there. Ed turned out to be in SoCal, in Cherokee. And we wrote out all the words—we were going to try this tune. I recorded it with Nels Cline on guitar and Michael Preussner on the drums, had the backing track. Ed was in town, and he comes to the studio. And...I don't know, we didn't do it.

So I said, "Y'know what? I've got another song." Because he told me he liked the Who, and D. Boon liked Pete Townshend a lot. Let's see, John Fogerty first, Buck Dharma second, and Pete Townshend third—for D. Boon and guitar influence. We weren't big fans of *Tommy*—we liked *A Quick One* and *Sell Out*—but there's a tune on there called "Christmas." I kind of wrote a tune thinking of Ed. But that lick is kind of in that tune. So I said, "Ed, what about this tune, 'Against the '70s'?" You know how SoCal is, we've got a lot of alleys in our blocks, where people put their garbage. He finds a fucking wetsuit, and he puts it on! Y'know, Ed likes surfing. So this is the only thing in my mind that could make me think, "Why would he put on some wetsuit from the garbage, in the back of the alley, to do this take?" And he sings it, and just tears it up.

What do you recall about the tour with Ed and Dave?
So the record comes out, and then I think Ed is playing with Pearl Jam in Australia, and Dave's down there, too. And Dave had made an album by himself called *Foo Fighters*. Now, he wants to put together a band to tour. So they called me, and said, "Hey Watt, how about a tour?"—where Ed's got a band with this wife at the time, Hovercraft, and Dave has this new project. "We'll open up, and then we'll be your band." And I thought, if I'm really going for the sea change...OK, I'll go for it." So Ed had me come up to their "prac pad" in Seattle, and I spent a couple of days there with him and Dave. I showed some old Minutemen, I showed them some songs from the record. And Ed showed me one of his songs, "Habit," which I really liked.

Ed played guitar, and Dave wanted to mix it up—he was getting the hankering for guitar playing. So he gets [Foo Fighters' original drummer] William Goldsmith, and Pat Smear is there. The guys that were playing with me were so kind, supportive, and really sincere. And it didn't seem jive or hype. I think it was only three-and-a-half, four weeks. But it really helped me. It helped me almost as much as like, D. Boon's mom putting me on bass. Ed was so very cool to me—and Dave, Pat. They were just so beautiful to me, and playing their hearts out...with this weird dude on the bass. [Laughs] They helped me get my nerve up and what I'm doing nowadays—the spring of '95.

And a live album came out in 2016, *Ring Spiel Tour '95*, recorded during that tour.
I know Joe Shanahan [the founder/owner of the venue the show was recorded at, the Metro in Chicago] taped all the shows, and I knew that tape was around. And Tim Smith at Legacy/Sony found it and wanted to put it out. I was scared to even listen to it—because of all the clams. The clams are there, but I was surprised—I didn't do as bad as I thought. And those guys, man, kicked up much dust. But I told Tim, "Look, you've got to ask Ed, you've got to ask Dave." And Pat writes back, "It's about time this is coming out, Watt!" In fact Tim wanted to remix it, and Ed said, "No Watt. *This is it.* This is the thing. This is what happened." And I go, "Ed, you're right."

What are your thoughts today, looking back on the whole experience of playing/touring with Ed and Dave?
Looking back at Watt's music journey, it really was a sea change for me. After that, all of a sudden, I started doing all these projects—I ended up playing in Porno for Pyros, J. Mascis...I ended up playing 125 months with the Stooges! But it really was a sincere sea change for me, and those guys, Ed especially, but Dave, Pat, and William... you think you know it all, and that nobody can teach you anything. Maybe it's just the politics of a bass player. But I just kept the mind open and sure, these guys hadn't been around, but everybody's got something to teach you, Watt. *Just let go.*

One time, when I was doing the first opera [1997's *Contemplating the Engine Room*], I was scared shitless doing that. And Stephen Hodges goes, "Y'know what, Watt? Sometimes being a little bit scared is like being a little bit excited." So that's how I kind of thought about this thing. Because I was shitting a pecan log—to get up there without Georgie [Hurley], without Edward, without D. Boon. Ed's his own man, he's not trying to be a fake D. Boon, but man, looking over at him...it was kind of the same. Because I'm in the middle for the first time [of the stage], but he's the left-hand man—just like D. Boon. And to look back and see Dave, it was really beautiful. Music isn't just notes and technique. A lot of it is rhythm. And a lot of it is people.

34 Rolling Stone and Time Covers

Made famous by Dr. Hook & the Medicine Show, "Cover of the Rolling Stone" focuses—albeit in a humorous manner—on how an entertainer's dream is to one day appear on the cover of the famous music magazine. For many, landing on a RS cover is indeed a sign that an artist has "made it." By this measurement, Pearl Jam has made it four times over.

The band first graced the cover of *Rolling Stone* on the October 28, 1993, issue, with a shot taken the previous June by Mark Seliger in Spokane, Washington, under the headline PEARL JAM: A YEAR IN THE LIFE. The feature was one of the best articles ever penned about the band up to that point, by Cameron Crowe.

For the November 28, 1996, issue, RS opted to recycle a photo of Vedder from the *Ten* era (taken by Ross Halfin in London, sometime in 1992), with the headline INVENTING EDDIE VEDDER: PEARL JAM'S MYSTERY MAN.

Less than three years later, Vedder was once again on the cover of a RS issue—September 30, 1999, this time under the banner THE GREATEST CONCERTS OF THE '90S. The cover featured a photo of the singer in mid–crowd surf, taken by Lance Mercer at the Moore Theater in Seattle on January 17, 1992 (yep, the same night that the footage for the "Even Flow" video was filmed). And while it's not a full-fledged PJ or EV cover, on the October 14, 2004, issue, the singer was included in an all-star group photo (taken by Norman Jean Roy, which also included Bruce Springsteen, John Mellencamp, and Dave Matthews, among others), under the title ROCKIN' REBELS.

The last time Vedder appeared on a RS cover was the June 29, 2006, issue, when a live shot snapped by Nick Stevens was used

Rolling Stone,
October 28, 1993.

with the title The Reluctant Warrior: Eddie Vedder & Pearl Jam Return from Exile. However, Vedder was none too pleased with it; PJ was initially told a photo of the entire band would be featured on the cover before *RS* allegedly took it upon itself to use the solo shot of the singer strumming his Telecaster. (The band photo was used inside the issue instead.)

As a result, at a concert in Cincinnati on June 24, EV got a small bit of revenge by "wiping" his rear end with the issue on stage (while still wearing his trousers, thankfully) and explaining the situation to the audience. Additionally, Pearl Jam and Vedder have appeared on several additional *Rolling Stone* covers outside of the U.S. (the full band on the cover of the April 2009 issue of *Rolling Stone India*, Vedder solo on the July 2006 issue of *Rolling Stone Mexico*, etc.).

As it turns out, the contentious issue with *Rolling Stone* was not the first time Vedder appeared on the cover of a major magazine unhappily or against his will. The October 25, 1993, issue of *Time* featured a photo of the singer in mid-concert scream, alongside the headline ALL THE RAGE: ANGRY YOUNG ROCKERS LIKE PEARL JAM GIVE VOICE TO THE PASSIONS AND FEARS OF A GENERATION. And while appearing on the cover of the heavily circulated and respected publication would be the holy grail for many rock artists, Vedder was allegedly perturbed.

Supposedly, an early plan for the cover was to unite Vedder with Kurt Cobain. In one of his last interviews, Cobain was asked by David Fricke of *RS* about the *Time* cover, to which Cobain replied curtly, "I don't want to get into that." However, in an interview with *NME* in 2016, Cobain's widow, Courtney Love, said, "I remember when Pearl Jam beat Nirvana onto the cover of *Time*, and that pissed Kurt off, let me tell you."

35 Wrigley Field

Although Pearl Jam is most closely associated with Seattle, Eddie Vedder is not originally from the Emerald City; he was born in Evanston, Illinois. So while the majority of his eventual PJ mates and friends from the Pacific Northwest are probably rooting for the Seattle Mariners, he has always been behind one of the unluckiest baseball franchises of the 20th century: the Chicago Cubs. Founded in 1876, the team has won only three World Series titles so far in their history (1907, 1908, and 2016, to be exact), and endured one of the longest-ever droughts between championships: a whopping 108 years. But, despite all of their failures, the Cubs developed one

A view of the crowd at Wrigley Field during Pearl Jam's performance in Chicago, August 20, 2016. (A.Motin)

of the most loyal fan followings in all of professional sports, with their home stadium since 1916, Wrigley Field, considered a home away from home for fans, and is constantly sold out for games.

Located at 1060 W. Addison Street in Chicago, Wrigley is the second-oldest stadium in all of baseball (Fenway Park in Boston is two years older). For years, Vedder has been spotted at Wrigley watching games played by his beloved Cubs, and has sung "Take Me Out to the Ball Game" during the seventh-inning stretch many times. In 2008, Vedder penned and recorded "All the Way," which stands alongside "Go Cubs Go" (by the late Steve Goodman) as one of the most popular tunes about the team. In case anyone ever questioned Vedder's fandom, a charming video surfaced on YouTube in 2013 that was shot back in 1992—March 28, to be exact, on the afternoon that Pearl Jam was headlining the nearby Metro later that night—which sees Vedder taking a friend on a tour of the outside of Wrigley Field. Perhaps the ultimate proof of Vedder's appreciation of Wrigley Field can be seen at the 2:27 mark, when he finds a box of sod supposedly from the field and does the unthinkable: he sniffs it!

Still, the most obvious connection that Wrigley Field has to Pearl Jam are the band's numerous performances there: July 19, 2013, and August 20 and 22, 2016. The 2016 shows became the subject of a 2017 Danny Clinch–directed documentary *Let's Play Two*. And maybe, just maybe, Vedder and the band provided some extra good luck for the Cubs, because later in 2016 the team finally broke their championship drought, defeating the Indians in Cleveland. And who should be spotted on the field, congratulating and whooping it up with the players in celebration afterward (and sporting a Cubs cap)? Mr. Vedder, of course. In 2018, the band announced it would return to Wrigley Field for a pair of shows that summer, on August 18 and 20.

If you are a fan longing to meet the Pearl Jam singer, Wrigley just may be the most ideal surroundings, as he told the *Chicago Tribune* in 2015, "I'm in a pretty good mood at Wrigley. It's a good time to catch me."

36 Drummer No. 2

The shortest-tenured Pearl Jam drummer was a gentleman by the name of Matt Chamberlain. His stay may have been brief, but he has played with a variety of renowned and respected artists over the years, and even drummed in the house band for one of television's all-time most popular shows.

Born on April 17, 1967, in San Pedro, California, Chamberlain began drumming when he was 10, and accepted a scholarship to North Texas State University at the age of 18. His first high-profile drumming gig was on the sophomore effort by Edie Brickell & New Bohemians, 1990's *Ghost of a Dog*, with the drummer earning co-writing credits on two tunes: "Carmelito" and "Forgiven."

Chamberlain's association with the New Bohemians would be short-lived, and by the summer of 1991, he came to the attention of Pearl Jam, who were searching for a replacement for Dave Krusen. Chamberlain was welcomed aboard shortly after the recording of *Ten* was completed—his first show with PJ was at RKCNDY in Seattle, on July 4, 1991. Despite the fact that he exited the band by the end of the following month—accepting a spot in the house band for *Saturday Night Live* for the show's 1991–92 season—it was Mr. Chamberlain who occupies the drum throne in PJ's video for "Alive" (filmed on August 3, 1991, once again at RKCNDY). Also, he was the man who recommended a pal of his from Texas, Dave Abbruzzese, take his spot in PJ.

After his time in Pearl Jam and on *Saturday Night Live*, Chamberlain assembled quite an impressive résumé, including playing on recordings by Fiona Apple, Tori Amos, Lisa Marie Presley, Stevie Nicks, Peter Gabriel, Keith Urban, Kenny Rogers, and Morrissey, among countless others, as well as a release by his old PJ bandmate Stone Gossard (2013's *Moonlander*). And Chamberlain's association with grunge was rekindled in 2014, when he was asked by Soundgarden to sit in for Matt Cameron (who took the year off from Soundgarden to focus entirely on Pearl Jam work) for their tour dates that year—including shows with Nine Inch Nails.

37 Lollapalooza

There is a long tradition of annual outdoor rock festivals in Europe, be they traveling or stationary, including Glastonbury, Monsters of Rock, Reading, Pinkpop, and many others. But in the United States, this phenomenon had never really taken hold. Sure, there had been a few blips on the radar here and there, but none that became a true institution. And certainly none that catered to the alt-rock world.

Lollapalooza changed all of that. Founded by Jane's Addiction frontman Perry Farrell, as well as Ted Gardner, Marc Geiger, and Don Muller, the first Lollapalooza took place in the summer of 1991, and included what was being billed at the time as the last-ever tour by Jane's Addiction (who would split up immediately afterward...until reuniting on a semiregular basis years later). It also featured performances by Siouxsie and the Banshees, Living Colour, a largely unknown Nine Inch Nails, Ice T & Body Count, Butthole Surfers, Rollins Band, and more.

Also included were booths for open-mic debates on political topics, arts, crafts, and info on various philanthropic causes. While obviously modeled after the aforementioned Reading Festival in the UK and the largely forgotten A Gathering of the Tribes Festival in the U.S. (the latter of which proved to be successful in 1990, and probably convinced Perry and pals that such a venture could flourish), Lollapalooza was obviously in the right place at the right time—the precise moment that alt-rock had finally infiltrated mainstream culture.

So when the lineup for the second year of Lollapalooza was announced (with dates running from July 18 to September 13, 1992), it made sense for Pearl Jam to be included. That spring, *Ten* was rocketing up the charts on the strength of the singles/videos

"Alive" and "Even Flow." And the other acts comprised an arguably even stronger lineup than the previous year's—Red Hot Chili Peppers, Ministry, Ice Cube, Soundgarden, the Jesus and Mary Chain, and Lush. With their growing success and popularity, the organizers suggested PJ take one of the spots closer to the headliner. The band declined, instead content to be the second band of the day to hit the stage (after Lush and before the Jesus and Mary Chain). And what made this second year different from the first was the inclusion of a "side stage," which included performances by such soon-to-be household names as Rage Against the Machine, Tool, Cypress Hill, and Stone Temple Pilots, among others, as well as a performance by gross-out kings/queens the Jim Rose Circus.

But it was Pearl Jam that proved to be the big story of Lollapalooza '92. It was the first time that many of their newly acquired mainstream fans had the opportunity to see the band live, and throughout the tour, the band did not disappoint. Despite shows taking place in massive outdoor venues (and PJ's set taking place in broad daylight), Vedder continued his "mountain climbing" routine, often scurrying up lighting trusses during the extended jam section of the set-closing "Porch." Also, lucky fans might catch a Temple of the Dog performance (on August 14 at Lake Fairfax Park in Reston, Virginia, and September 13 at Irvine Meadows Amphitheater in Irvine, California), or pals Vedder and Chris Cornell mingling with the audience and "mud surfing" (photos of which are included in the *PJ 20* and *Grunge Is Dead* books) or spotted enjoying the hijinks of the Jim Rose Circus together.

Lollapalooza would continue as a yearly traveling festival through 1997, going silent until 2003. A proposed Lolla for the following year was canceled. Then, someone came up with the wise idea of relaunching the festival in 2005 as a multi-day event at only one location: Grant Park in Chicago. As a result, Lolla became a giant success again, and has taken place every year since. Pearl Jam returned, this time as a headliner, on the final night of the 2007 edition, on August 5.

38 Listen to Pearl Jam Radio

When it comes to the signs of success, Pearl Jam has ticked many of the traditional boxes: releasing their own albums, headlining Madison Square Garden, etc. Well...what about having your own radio station? On October 22, 2010, Pearl Jam Radio premiered on SiriusXM Radio, the subscription-driven satellite radio service.

Once you are a Sirius subscriber, you can tune into Pearl Jam Radio on either Sirius Channel 22 or XM Channel 22, and you will be treated to an endless stream of studio tracks, B-sides, and concert recordings—all somehow Pearl Jam–related or endorsed by the band (for example, don't be surprised to catch a Brad tune followed by a Who classic). Additionally, guest DJs (such as Kelly Slater and Judd Apatow) are invited to drop by the Sirius Studios in New York City and spin their favorite tunes. You'll also hear interviews (such as Mike McCready chatting with Ace Frehley and the Red Hot Chili Peppers) and exclusive in-studio performances (including Jeff Ament's band, Tres Mts., performing in 2011), among other goodies.

A usual day of programming on Pearl Jam Radio consists of "Pearl Jam Concerts" (which I'm sure you're undoubtedly wise enough to figure out is an airing of a complete PJ concert from any time during their long and lengthy career), "Pearl Jam Radio" (a mixture of studio tracks, B-sides, and concert recordings), and "Pearl Jam Radio's Wishlist" (when one lucky fan gets to act as DJ and choose which tunes get spun). It's fun for the whole PJ-loving family!

39 King's X

Although Pearl Jam is thought of primarily as a grunge or alternative rock band, they have some legitimate ties to heavy metal and hard rock. Some of these connections are obvious (Mother Love Bone), while others are not so clearly apparent—for example, their fondness for rockers King's X.

Originally formed during the early 1980s, King's X is comprised of bassist Doug Pinnick, guitarist Ty Tabor, and drummer Jerry Gaskill. Pinnick is the primary singer, though the other two have sung lead as well, and all chip in to provide stellar three-part vocal harmonies. The trio scored several MTV and radio hits during the late '80s and early '90s ("Over My Head," "It's Love," "Black Flag," and "Dogman"), and produced critically acclaimed albums (1989's *Gretchen Goes to Nebraska*, 1990's *Faith Hope Love*, and 1994's *Dogman*) which remain popular amongst headbangers.

So just how does King's X fit into the Pearl Jam equation? Good question. Here we go. The first sign of Pearl Jam's admiration was including Pinnick's name on the thank you list of *Ten*—quite possibly due to the fact that it was Pinnick's bass sound on such King's X tunes as "Out of the Silent Planet" that inspired Ament to pick up a Hamer 12-string bass, which eventually led to the classic bass riff of PJ's "Jeremy." This was then followed a few months later by Ament sporting a King's X shirt for the whole world to see on PJ's first *Saturday Night Live* appearance (on April 11, 1992). The feelings flowed both ways, as King's X enlisted Brendan O'Brien to produce their fifth album overall, *Dogman* (with O'Brien fresh off producing PJ's *Vs.*).

But the next connection was the most obvious yet: Pearl Jam inviting King's X to open a mini-stretch of gigs from March

24 to April 3, 1994, on the blockbuster *Vs.* tour, including the famous April 3 show at the Fox Theatre in Atlanta, which was broadcast live over the radio. Both Doug and Jerry joined Pearl Jam onstage—supplying vocals and percussion, respectively—for a memorable rendition of "W.M.A." (which would eventually be included as part of the "Dissident" CD single). Additionally, various King's X members would appear with PJ during their set at other stops on this tour, lending a hand when the band covered Neil Young's "Rockin' in the Free World."

In an interview I conducted for the Alternative Nation website in 2015, Gaskill recalled the following about that tour, as well as performing with PJ on the radio broadcast:

I remember every night feeling like I was watching history being made. It was a true honor to be a part of something as special as what Pearl Jam had become. We had known those guys before they were Pearl Jam and to be a part of this historic event was something I'll always be thankful for.

I remember one night, Doug was to sing "W.M.A." with them, and David Abbruzzese asked me to play octobans. He told me they never did this song because there was nobody to play those extra percussion parts. So he kind of told me how it went and I got up there and played alongside him. It felt great! We did the encore with them and I remember walking on the stage and the ovation from the crowd was overwhelming. After the song, Eddie introduced Doug to the crowd, but never mentioned me. David stood and started shouting, "And goddamn Jerry Gaskill!" Of course no one heard him, and that's okay with me. It was just an honor to be a part of it.

I also had my oldest son, Jerrimy, out with me, who was 15 at the time. He hung with the guys quite a bit. I believe Eddie would come to the bus and get Jerrimy to shoot hoops together. At the end of the tour Eddie said to me, "Tell Jerrimy wherever we are, he's always welcome." When we got home I remember one day taking Jerrimy to school and he said, "You know, Dad, almost everybody at my school would give their right arm to do what we just did, and that's just what we do." I thought that was really special as well…

After Pearl Jam wrapped up their set that evening in Atlanta, Vedder quickly played DJ for radio stations that kept the signal going, and the very first tune he spun was…"Cigarettes" by King's X.

It would be 10 years for another public Pearl Jam / King's X reunion—this time occurring on the first official live release by King's X, 2004's *Live All Over the Place*, on which Ament guested and supplied bass on a cover of the Jimi Hendrix Experience's "Manic Depression."

But perhaps the most complete Pearl Jam / King's X collaboration was the band Tres Mts., which will be discussed in greater detail shortly.

Backstage Pass

Doug Pinnick
King's X Singer/Bassist, Tres Mts. Singer/Guitarist

You go way back with the members of Pearl Jam.
I knew Jeff when he was in Mother Love Bone, and he used to come to New York and to King's X shows, and hang out with the guys at Megaforce Records. He would just come out and hang out, and we were his favorite band. He was very quiet and didn't say much. He'd reach out to me every now and then and we'd chat. And we stayed in touch. Then, after Andrew [Wood] died, he sent me a cassette, and said, "Hey man, check out my new band and tell me what you think."
Side one was Mookie Blaylock—which was Pearl Jam. It was a demo. And side two was Temple of the Dog, which nobody knew about. When that record came out, it was like, "Where did it come

from?" and "Oh my god, what a great record." So I remember playing it, and I remember playing side one, and thinking, "It's okay." I didn't quite get it at first. I played side two, and I'm going, "Oh my god, who is this singer? I'm intimidated. Oh no, they kind of sound like King's X...what am I doing to do?" [Laughs] And I didn't know it was them and Chris Cornell. I had no idea. I didn't even think Chris could sing like that.

But to go back to Pearl Jam, King's X was playing in Tacoma, Washington, and Alice in Chains were playing at a club in town, after we had played—we were opening for AC/DC. And Pearl Jam and Alice in Chains came to see us open for AC/DC, and they came backstage and said, "Come to our show!" So we all went—the whole road crew and everybody. It was a little club—probably about a hundred people there. Alice in Chains' first record had just barely been out, and there was no Pearl Jam at the time—they were still Mookie Blaylock.

And I remember watching them, and I went, "Wow...this band is good!" And Mike McCready was a little Jimi Hendrix—I just loved the way he played—and they were so young. They were so green and wide-eyed. And they were giving it all. It was like, 120 percent—just the vibe, the attitude, the honesty. And I'm going, "Oh my god. This is so cool." And then Alice in Chains came on and just rocked the house. And we've been friends ever since. Jeff told me that he saw us when we played Seattle before I met him. We all go way back.

And then we toured with Pearl Jam [in 1994], and we watched every show. It just reinforced how incredible that band was. I remember one night, me and [King's X guitarist] Ty [Tabor] were sitting on the side of the stage, watching the show, and *Dogman* was out at that time. And King's X...nothing was really happening. We were putting these records out, we were doing videos, but nothing was going on. We were getting these breaks—here we are, opening for Pearl Jam, when Jeff and those guys used to say they can't wait to open for us, and now, we're opening for them. I remember Ty and I sat on the side of the stage watching them, and he looked at me, and said, "Y'know Doug, these youngins are kicking our ass. Man, we ought to just give this shit up." And I went, "Yeah." It was like, "Wow.

These Seattle bands have come along and are just ruling. It's not a fad. It's the real deal."

Seattle brought back real music. People were just like, "Let's not do our hair. Let's not put tight jeans on and prance around. Let's fucking make real music." King's X wanted to be that—and we were that—but we were at the end of an era where maybe if we had lived in Seattle, things would have been different. But where we came from, we came out and we had hair and we had hairspray, but we hated that kind of music, and we didn't want to be a part of it. But just a part of the appeal was to have hair sticking up and be a little glammy looking. We were rock stars.

In the '70s, you had that little glam look—you had to look like you played in a band. So we had that look. But I didn't feel our *music* had that look. If I had any insight, I would have dreaded my hair and grown it out long, and we would have changed the way we looked a little bit, because after a while, we did—Jerry [Gaskill, King's X drummer] grew his hair out really long and Ty had long hair. We were all trying to be real. But we had already been established as a "hair metal band," even though we weren't. So we knew we would never be accepted in the '90s as part of that.

Besides you and Jerry joining Pearl Jam on stage for a rendition of "W.M.A." at the Fox Theatre, were there any other standout memories of when King's X opened for Pearl Jam in '94?
One night I said to Eddie, "How are you doing?" And he seemed really troubled. He said he felt like he just wasn't giving enough to the audience. He felt like he needed to give more. And it was really bothering him. I told him, "Dude, you put all of yourself in that record. We all love what you've done and we come to hear you sing those songs. You don't have to run around. You don't have to jump off the rafters. You don't have to be in everybody's face. You've already proved yourself and your integrity. We love your songs. *Sing to us.*" And that night, he walked up to the mic and never left it. He stood right in front of the mic and sang the whole night. And I cried, because he did some of the most incredible things—emotionally and

physically—I've ever seen a person do in one spot in my life. I truly at that point realized he was a great performer.

And what are your thoughts now on Tres Mts., looking back?
That record was just a lot of fun to make and was easy to make. The first time we went together, the three of us—me, Jeff, and Richard [Stuverud, Tres Mts. drummer]—wrote eight songs, and then a month later, Jeff flew us all back out there and brought Mike McCready in, and we did eight more songs. And Jeff paid for everything. He just flew us all out. He was sort of like the record company, which was pretty cool. I think we all pretty much own that record. We had lots of fun. I learned a lot just hanging around and sitting around the table, talking to the guys. Y'know, behind the scenes stories, Pearl Jam stories, just between me and them. Getting to know them as people. Because I'd known those guys for a long time, but to be in a house with Jeff and Mike for two weeks or so and living with them and waking up and going to sleep, was pretty cool to get to know them. They're really cool people.

40 Mookie Blaylock

When the Vedder-Ament-Gossard-McCready-Krusen lineup first came together, finding a suitable band name proved to be a bit of a challenge. Eventually, a rather curious name, Mookie Blaylock, was used when the quintet began playing out live and for early recordings. Just where did this name come from, you ask? Don't fret—I have the answer for you.

Born Daron Oshay Blaylock on born March 20, 1967, in Garland, Texas, the man better known as Mookie played point guard in the NBA for three different teams during a career that spanned from 1989 to 2002—the New Jersey Nets (1989–92), the Atlanta Hawks (1992–99), and the Golden State Warriors (1999–2002). He had a respectable career (an NBA All-Star in 1994, twice named to the NBA's All-Defensive First Team, and had his No. 10 jersey honored by the University of Oklahoma, from which Pearl Jam supposedly got the idea of titling their debut *Ten*), but when the band chose his name for its own, it was not exactly for complimentary reasons. Case in point, this exchange between Vedder and Gossard for a *Rip Magazine* article from December 1991:

"Mookie's kinda out there. He's kinda this cult player," Eddie says.

"Kinda mediocre," Stone cuts in, laughing.

Pearl Jam, including Eddie Vedder in a Mookie Blaylock New Jersey Nets jersey, performing at the Roseland Ballroom in New York, 1991. (Steven J. Messina)

"He's really got to bust his balls out there every night," Eddie continues.

"He's not really good looking; he's just tough," Stone adds.

Might there be a parallel somewhere here?

"There's something about the mediocre sports hero that this band can relate to," Stone says, referring to the volleyball game he and Eddie had earlier in [the *Rip* writer's] visit—a definite lesson in male bonding and competition. "Just knowing that someday even a regular guy off the street can win the championship, if the team has the right chemistry."

41 Jeff Ament's Other Projects

Along with his pal Stone Gossard, Jeff Ament had already constructed quite an admirable discography prior to the arrival of *Ten*. Since both were previously members of Green River and Mother Love Bone, they had their music etched in vinyl several times already. But even prior to those two bands, Ament was a member of hardcore-punkers Deranged Diction, who issued an 18-song demo cassette, *No Art, No Cowboys, No Rules*, in 1983; musically it had much in common with the work of Black Flag, the Dead Kennedys, and the Ramones, among others. The album would be reissued in 2009, along with songs that were never properly recorded by the band, titled *Life Support / No Art, No Cowboys, No Rules*.

We've already covered Temple of the Dog earlier in this book, as well as the Neil Young *Mirror Ball* project. Ament took part in a near-TOTD reunion track, "Hey Baby (Land of the New Rising Sun"), credited to "M.A.C.C." on 1993's *Stone Free: A Tribute to Jimi Hendrix*, before, making special guest appearances on songs by onetime PJ bandmate Jack Irons, "Dunes" (2004's *Attention Dimension*), and a live cover of the Jimi Hendrix Experience's "Manic Depression" with King's X (2004's *Live All Over the Place*).

There have been several instances when Ament was part of a side project that lasted beyond just a single album, including the alt-rock / world music–sounding Three Fish, who issued a pair of recordings, 1996's self-titled debut and 1999's *The Quiet Table*, as well as two albums with the hard-to-pin-down RNDM, 2012's *Acts* and 2016's *Ghost Riding*. Also, we mustn't forget Tres Mts., which saw Ament team up once again with drummer Richard Stuverud (who also kept the beat in Three Fish and RNDM), as well as Doug Pinnick from King's X, for 2011's *Three Mountains*. And wouldn't you know it, Mr. Ament has also found the time to issue a pair of solo efforts: 2008's *Tone* (which saw guest input by his pals in Tres Mts.) and 2012's *While My Heart Beats* (which saw Stuverud, Mike McCready, and Matt Cameron lend a hand).

42 Studio Litho

Back in the day, it was just about every musician's dream to have his own recording studio. The reason I write "back in the day" is because nowadays, almost every musician has his own studio with the advent of computer programs such as Garage Band. But I'm talking about *before* home recording was convenient and potentially professional-sounding. And in 1995, Stone Gossard realized that dream as the owner of Studio Litho, located at 417 N. 36th Street in Seattle.

According to the studio's Facebook page, Litho is all about accommodating a wide variety of artists at various levels of professionalism—"From small budget, self-financed records to platinum selling, major label masterpieces, we do it all. Litho mixes the best in vintage analog and cutting edge digital equipment with a comfortable atmosphere where you can relax and make your music. Part of our mission is to support the development of new talent in the Northwest music community."

And when the studio opened, Gossard surrounded himself with gentlemen who certainly knew their way around recording studios—studio manager Ed Brooks previously worked with a variety of artists, including production work (the Walkabouts) and engineering (the B-52's *Cosmic Thing* and R.E.M.'s *Automatic for the People*), plus later mastering Pearl Jam's *Live on Two Legs* and *PJ 20 Motion Picture Soundtrack*, as well as various other live PJ releases, while "founder and chief strategist" Jim Haviland was involved in designing and/or working at studios since 1987 (including Bad Animals in Seattle and Universal Recording in Chicago).

Gear-wise, Studio Litho has everything a musician looking to create a worthwhile recording could ever want: vintage recording gear (API mid-1970s custom 44-input console with 550A, 550B, and 560 EQs...got that?), modern-day technology (Pro Tools), and some nifty-sounding instruments at your fingertips (Hammond C-3 with Leslie cabinet, Hohner Clavinet D6, Ludwig Tack Piano, Wurlitzer, Fender Rhodes, Vox Jaguar, Prophet 5, and more).

The overall vibe both inside the studio and its surrounding area sounds appealing, via further info on the Litho Facebook page: "Our clients enjoy access to the entire building, which includes a fully functioning kitchen, one full and two half baths, two lounges, a territorial-view sun deck, the ping-pong death-match dungeon of doom, PlayStation, wireless Internet access, and an extraordinary array of reading material. The grounds include a play court for basketball, volleyball, or pickle ball, a meditation garden, and off-street parking. The studio is within walking distance to many great bars, restaurants, coffee-houses, and funky shops."

And while these descriptions are fine and dandy, it's really the impressive array of artists who have recorded at Studio Litho that serve as a testament to its success and staying power—Soundgarden (1996's *Down on the Upside*), Screaming Trees (2011's *Last Words: The Final Recordings*), Dave Matthews Band (2012's *Away from the World*), Deftones (1997's *Around the Fur*), Mastodon (2006's *Blood Mountain*), Brad (all of their albums, except for their debut), and, of course, Pearl Jam (1996's *No Code*, 1998's *Yield*, 2000's *Binaural*, 2002's *Riot Act*, and 2013's *Lightning Bolt*).

43 Key Arena

Pearl Jam has played at a variety of venues in Seattle over the years—Moore Theater (1990, 1992, and 1995), Off Ramp Café (1990, 1991, and 1993), the Vogue (1991), RCKNDY (1991 and 1992), Mural Amphitheater (1991), Magnuson Park (1992), Mercer Arena (1993), the Showbox (1996 and 2002), Crocodile Café (1998), Memorial Stadium (1998), Benaroya Hall (2003), Westin Hotel (2004), Easy Street Records (2005), and the Paramount Theater (2005). But the one they've been most closely associated with is KeyArena.

The arena first opened its doors in 1962 (April 21, to be precise), initially as the Washington State Pavilion before changing its name to Washington State Coliseum later that year, then changing to Seattle Center Coliseum (1964–94), before being renovated in 1994–95 and being reopened/renamed KeyArena (full name: KeyArena at Seattle Center). For quite a few years, the now-extinct NBA team the Seattle SuperSonics called the arena their home, and it even hosted the NBA All-Star Game in 1974. But it was probably best known as a venue for major touring musical acts, including Elvis Presley, the Beatles, the Rolling Stones, the Who, the Beach Boys, the Police, Nirvana, and many more.

Between 1996 and 2013, Pearl Jam performed a total of nine shows there, which is almost as many as they've played at Madison Square Garden (10, as of this moment). And if you were in attendance at any of these performances, you very well could have witnessed such memorable moments as Mudhoney's Mark Arm and Steve Turner and Soundgarden's Kim Thayil ripping it up on a cover of the MC5's "Kick Out the Jams" (on December 6, 2013), the live debut of "Just Breathe" (September 21, 2009), a rarely performed cover of the Sonics' "Don't Believe in Christmas" (December 9, 2002), and Supergrass joining PJ for a cover of "Timeless Melody" by the La's (November 5, 2000).

In April 2017, an intriguing article in the *Seattle Times* stated that a renovation proposal for KeyArena was in the discussion stage, and one of the ideas was to enlist Pearl Jam to play an "extended residency" at the arena, similar to what Billy Joel has been doing since 2014 at Madison Square Garden in NYC (playing the venue once a month indefinitely). The chances of this idea coming to fruition seem promising, especially since longtime PJ manager Kelly Curtis is part of the advisory board of the company seeking to do the renovation (Oak View Group).

44 The Ukulele

"Ukulele" and "rock 'n' roll" do not usually go hand in hand. But you have to give credit to Eddie Vedder—although he's best known as a rock singer, on his second-ever full-length solo release, 2011's appropriately titled *Ukulele Songs*, he made an entire album comprised of just his ukulele and his voice. Ever wonder just how this miniature-guitar-looking instrument with usually only four strings came into creation and gained popularity? Well, you're in luck—you're about to receive a history lesson.

The birth of the instrument can be traced to Portuguese immigrants who settled in Hawaii in the late 1800s, and was a combination of two different instruments—the machete (not to be confused with the broad blade that goes by the same name) and a five-string rajão (pronounced "rah-zhow"). The first ukuleles made in Hawaii were supposedly done so by four Portuguese gentlemen—Manuel Nunes, Joao Fernandes, Augusto Dias, and Jose do Espirito Santo—who first found work as sugar cane field workers.

By the early 21st century, the Martin instrument company began manufacturing its own ukuleles worldwide (made out of Hawaiian koa wood), and shortly thereafter, Sears Roebuck purchased the Harmony guitar company, which led to the mass production of ukuleles. Part of the ukulele's attraction was its relative ease to play. With a miniature neck and few strings, all you need is a very basic knowledge of playing a stringed instrument and, voilà, you could quickly fumble your way through a song that summoned up the sounds of Hawaii! Subsequently, several different styles of ukuleles have been manufactured—pocket, soprano, concert, tenor, baritone, bass, and contrabass.

Over the years, several notable ukulele players have gained recognition, among them entertainer Don Ho, novelty artists such as Tiny Tim (who scored a surprise hit in the '60s with "Tiptoe Through the Tulips," one of the few pop hits to ever prominently feature the instrument), comedians Martin Mull and Steve Martin (the latter even performed a vocal-ukulele duet, "Tonight You Belong to Me," with actress Bernadette Peters in the 1979 hit comedy film *The Jerk*...which Vedder would later also perform with Cat Power on *Ukulele Songs*), the Cars' Greg Hawkes (who issued an album comprised of Beatles songs played on the instrument, *The Beatles Uke*), and of course, Vedder's aforementioned solo album.

In an interview with NPR to promote *Ukulele Songs*, Vedder explained his attraction to the uke: "It is a happy sound, and by using it to process some emotions that were less than joyful, it somehow balanced it out to where it didn't sound like suicide music."

Vedder has also used the uke to great effect during PJ shows, particularly during encores. He told NPR it's ideal for encouraging audience participation: "It's such a small instrument. People are like, 'Let's help it out!'"

45 The Who

Since the beginning of Pearl Jam, Eddie Vedder has been vocal about how big of an influence the music of the Who has been on him. And while the majority of music fans never get the chance to perform with their heroes, Vedder has been lucky enough to perform alongside the Who onstage on several different occasions over the years, in addition to PJ covering Who songs themselves.

Originally going by such names as the Detours and the High Numbers, the classic Who lineup was solidified in 1964: singer Roger Daltrey, guitarist/singer Pete Townshend (who was also the band's chief songwriter), bassist John Entwistle, and drummer Keith Moon. And during the band's "glory period," between 1964 and 1978, the Who went through several different musical phases, which proved to be incredibly influential—mod-pop ("I Can't Explain," "Substitute"), proto-punk ("My Generation," bits of

Eddie Vedder and Pete Townshend performing at the Rosemont Theatre outside Chicago, 2015. (AP Images)

"Happy Jack"), conceptual/prog (*Tommy, Quadrophenia*), merging synthesizer and rock ("Baba O'Riley," "Who Are You"), and arena rock ("Squeeze Box," "Won't Get Fooled Again").

As a result, the Who quickly became one of the world's most popular bands and most explosive live acts—highlights including Daltrey twirling his mic high in the air; Townshend doing the "windmill" on his guitar, leaping in the air, and smashing his instruments; Moon's manic drumming style (which served as the inspiration for Animal on *The Muppets*), and Entwistle…standing still as a statue.

After Moon's drug-related death in 1978, the Who soldiered on for a few more years with Kenney Jones behind the kit before embarking on a so-called farewell tour in 1982. The Who would then reunite countless times in future years, and have been a full-time proposition since 1996, although Daltrey and Townshend are the sole original members left in attendance (Entwistle died in 2002, also drug-related).

And while many grunge bands' chief influences could be directly linked back to two particular "Black" bands (Black Sabbath and Black Flag), Vedder's love for the Who would wind up seeping into Pearl Jam, most obviously when they broke out a high-energy cover of "Baba O'Riley" circa 1992 (a wildly drunken version that was played at the *Singles* movie premiere party can be found on YouTube), and "The Kids Are Alright" the following year.

From there, the next Who/Vedder union would take place on February 23 and 24, 1994, at Carnegie Hall in New York City, at concerts dubbed *Daltrey Sings Townshend*, when an unannounced Vedder performed solo mini-sets both nights. Night one included renditions of "The Kids are Alright," "Sheraton Gibson," and "My Generation," while night two featured airings of "Let My Love Open the Door," "Squeeze Box," "Naked Eye," and "My Generation." It also turns out that Vedder got a bit nutty the second evening—trashing his dressing room Keith Moon–style, and attempting to scrawl an infamous lyric from "My Generation" ("Hope I die before I get old") on the wall...in his own blood. A photo of part of the carnage is included in the *Pearl Jam Twenty* book.

Subsequent Who covers have been recorded/released by Pearl Jam, including "Leaving Here" (on the 1996 compilation *Home Alive: The Art of Self Defense*), "The Kids Are Alright" (on the 2001 tribute album, *Substitute: The Songs of the Who*), and "Love, Reign o'er Me" (on their 2006 holiday single). PJ also preformed at the *VH1 Rock Honors* ceremony for the Who in 2008, where they performed "Love, Reign o'er Me" and "The Real Me." And on September 19, 2006, Vedder joined My Morning Jacket onstage at the Palaisozaki in Turin, Italy, for a rendition of the early Who classic "A Quick One, While He's Away" (one of the Who's first extended compositions, a clear stepping stone toward *Tommy*).

Vedder forged friendships with the members of the Who, particularly Townshend, who in 2008 told *Rolling Stone* that he once gave important career advice for his then-new friend: "To think he nearly quit in 1993 and went back to some surfing beach. Lucky he came to speak to Uncle Pete. I told him—submit."

Vedder has performed onstage with both Townshend and the Who over the years, with these performances documented on the Pete Townshend release, *Pete Townshend Live: A Benefit for Maryville Academy*, in 1999 (the songs "Magic Bus" and "Heart to Hang Onto") and the Who's *The Who Live at Royal Albert Hall* in 2003 ("I'm One," "Gettin' in Tune," "Let's See Action," and "See Me, Feel Me").

In 2016, Vedder penned an article for *Rolling Stone* titled "Eddie Vedder on How the Who Blew His Mind as a Kid, Changed His Life," in which he explained how the Who's music continues to inspire him and future generations: "The songwriter-listener relationship grows deeper after all the years. Pete saw that a celebrity in rock is charged by the audience with a function, like, 'You stand there and we will know ourselves.' Not 'You stand there and we will pay you loads of money to keep us entertained as we eat our oysters.' He saw the connection could be profound. He also realized the audience may say, 'When we're finished with you, we'll replace you with somebody else.' For myself and so many others (including shopkeepers, foremen, professionals, bellboys, gravediggers, directors, musicians), they won't be replaced. Yes, Pete, it's true, music can change you."

46 *Saturday Night Live*

Although there is some question about just how "live" its musical guests' performances are (Ashlee Simpson, we mean you), the enduring television program *Saturday Night Live* is one of the few shows on TV you can count on to provide a wide variety of music performances throughout any given season. As of this moment, Pearl Jam has had the honor of performing a total of four times on the program over an 18-year span.

Premiering on October 11, 1975, *Saturday Night Live* is comprised of a set cast of comedic actors and actresses and has served as the career launching pad for numerous notable names, including Chevy Chase, Gilda Radner, John Belushi, Dan Aykroyd, Bill Murray, Eddie Murphy, Adam Sandler, Chris Farley, Will Ferrell, Jimmy Fallon, and Tina Fey, among others. *SNL* features a special guest host each week (the most popular recurring hosts being Christopher Walken, Tom Hanks, Alec Baldwin, and Steve Martin), as well as comedy sketches, including such classics as the Coneheads, Samurai Futaba, the Blues Brothers, Mr. Bill, Mister Robinson's Neighborhood, Wayne's World, and More Cowbell, among countless memorable bits.

Now that we've gotten a bit of background out of the way, let's focus on how Pearl Jam fits into the *SNL* universe. Their first appearance on the show occurred on April 11, 1992, just as *Ten* was breaking through commercially, on an evening when actress Sharon Stone was the host (and, interestingly, with former PJ drummer Matt Chamberlain playing in the *SNL* house band). Pearl Jam appeared in a seconds-long mini-bit at the beginning during Stone's monologue (just a shot of the band looking startled after supposedly catching a glimpse of Stone based on a famous scene from her hit film *Basic Instinct*).

Two tunes were eventually performed, "Alive" and "Porch," with Eddie Vedder wearing a backward baseball cap, a blue jacket similar to Mickey Rourke's Henry Chinaski in *Barfly* over a Sub Pop/LOSER shirt for the first song, then taking off the jacket and wearing a green shirt with a homemade coat hanger design on the front, and the message NO BUSH '92 on the back. I recall watching the initial broadcast and discussing with friends afterward how good PJ sounded (something that is not always the case on *SNL*). When the entire cast bids the viewing audience adieu at the show's end, Vedder is spotted having changed his shirt yet again, this time to one with the Rock for Choice logo on it.

The band's next *SNL* appearance would take place almost exactly two years later, on April 16, 1994 (right as the *Vs.* tour was winding down), when actor Emilio Estevez was the host. To gauge just how popular and how much demand there was for Pearl Jam at the time, *SNL* did the unthinkable, awarding the band the time to perform *three* songs, one of the few times in show history they've allowed that to happen. As a result, PJ fans were treated to renditions of "Not for You," "Rearviewmirror," and "Daughter." The first selection was a pretty daring one, as artists usually stick with well-known tunes on *SNL* (usually their latest singles). Instead, PJ opted to get things rolling with a tune that had yet to be issued on any album (*Vitalogy* was still several months away).

"Rearviewmirror" succeeded in kicking things up a notch—so much so that Jeff Ament's hat flies off toward the end to expose his shaggy bleach-blond hairdo. "Daughter" comes off as soft and sweet as ever, with Stone Gossard playing a sunburst Hamer Duo-Tone model (a break from his usual Gibson Les Pauls), Ament seated while playing an upright bass, and McCready fiddling around on his Strat. Years later, McCready disclosed that his alcoholism had gotten so bad that he completely blacked out for the evening's performance of "Daughter" and did not even recall that the band had played it that night.

With Kurt Cobain's death still looming large (his body had been discovered just eight days earlier), Vedder made two references to the late Nirvana singer/guitarist that evening. The first was reciting some lyrics from Neil Young's "Hey Hey, My My" toward the end of "Daughter" (Cobain had borrowed a line from the song, "It's better to burn out than to fade away," in his suicide note) and the second was during the end credits, when Vedder opened his jacket to expose the letter *K* written on his shirt.

Given that they made two *SNL* appearances in two years, it seemed safe to assume that fans wouldn't have to wait long for Pearl Jam's next visit to the show. They were mistaken. It would be almost exactly 12 years before the group would reappear—April 15, 2006, while the band was out promoting their soon-to-be-released self-titled album, with Matt Cameron now behind the drum kit (Dave Abbruzzese was the drummer for their first two *SNL* appearances). During the episode hosted by Lindsay Lohan, PJ played "World Wide Suicide" and "Severed Hand" in an inspired yet professional manner.

Four years later, PJ was prepared for their fourth *SNL* performance overall, on March 13, 2010, in support of the *Backspacer* album (which had been released several months before). The night's host was actor Jude Law, and keyboardist Boom Gaspar joined PJ on *SNL* for the first time, performing "Just Breathe" and "Unknown Thought." While video of the latter tune is easily accessible online and is another inspired performance, the former is quite difficult to locate on free online streaming services, but is available for purchase via iTunes. Audio of the song's *SNL* performance was included on the *Pearl Jam Twenty Soundtrack*, which confirms that the rendition was indeed a winner.

Shall we touch upon the times when Adam Sandler and Bill Hader impersonated Eddie Vedder on *SNL* sketches? I agree with you...the less said about that, the better.

47 Drummer No. 3

Dave Abbruzzese may not have played on *Ten*, but he did tour in support of it, and he did play on Pearl Jam's next two blockbuster albums, which makes him the drummer of the definitive PJ lineup to many of the band's fans.

Born on May 17, 1968, in Stamford, Connecticut, Abbruzzese first began drumming at the ripe old age of four, and continued to bash away after he and his family relocated to Mesquite, Texas, in 1976 (with the music of AC/DC, Pink Floyd, Led Zeppelin, and Peter Gabriel serving as inspiration), before dropping out of high school without even completing his freshman year.

Subsequently, Abbruzzese would drum in such local acts as Dr. Tongue, Segueway, the Flaming Hemorrhoids, and Course of Empire. It was through his affiliation with Texas bands that he befriended fellow percussionist Matt Chamberlain, who in turn suggested Abbruzzese as his replacement in PJ. Trying out for the fledgling band was an easy decision for Abbruzzese—his profession at the time was selling bongs and grow lights—and he arrived in Seattle on August 4, 1991 (23 days before the release of *Ten*). He promptly landed the gig, with his first performance with the band taking place on August 23 at the Mural Amphitheater in Seattle.

As previously stated, Abbruzzese would be present for all of the touring in support of *Ten* (including many dates opening for the Red Hot Chili Peppers, plus Lollapalooza '92), as well as appearing in the popular videos for the songs "Even Flow" and "Jeremy," plus PJ's performances on *MTV Unplugged* and both the 1992 and 1993 MTV Video Music Awards. Abbruzzese's first studio recordings with the band would include such B-sides as "Dirty Frank," two outstanding tracks that PJ contributed to the *Singles* motion picture soundtrack—"Breath" and "State of Love and Trust"—plus a re-recording of "Even Flow," which would be utilized as the audio for the song's music video.

Abbruzzese also quickly proved that he could contribute in the songwriting department, as evidenced by his penning of the music for the song "Angel" (included on PJ's 1993 holiday single), as well as writing all of the music to "Go," the album-opening track of their sophomore album, 1993's *Vs.*, co-writing "W.M.A." with Jeff Ament, and co-authoring "Last Exit" with Stone Gossard (another album-opener, this time on 1994's *Vitalogy*), plus earning further songwriting credits alongside all of the band on "Pry, To" and "Aye Davanita."

But as the years went by, a gap was widening between the band and Abbruzzese. Eddie Vedder was inspired to pen the lyrics to "Glorified G" after hearing the drummer talking about purchasing a gun, as well as this memorable example of the drummer not being on the same page as his bandmates in the group's *Rolling Stone* cover story from 1993: "'So are we talking about "Daughter" as the first single?' drummer Dave Abbruzzese asks casually. Suddenly, all air leaves the room. The other four members dog pile on Abbruzzese. 'What single? One meeting at a time! What do you mean, single?' Abbruzzese shrugs."

As a result, the "Five against one" catchphrase used by the band at the time was not as pure as fans thought, and the drummer got the heave-ho by the band in August 1994 (his final performance with the band was April 17, 1994, at the Paramount at Madison Square Garden in New York City). He was replaced by the man Pearl Jam supposedly wanted all along: Jack Irons. In a 2001 *Spin*

Magazine article, Ament discussed what led to Abbruzzese being excused from the band: "Dave was a different egg, for sure. There were a lot of things, personality-wise, where I didn't see eye to eye with him. He was more comfortable being a rock star than the rest of us. Partying, girls, cars. I don't know if anyone was in the same space. Also, with Dave, musically, when you'd say, 'I want this to sound more like the Buzzcocks,' I don't think he related to that at all. He was a technical guy, and we all played by feeling, or by seeing bands."

In the wake of his exit, Abbruzzese would record as part of the band Green Romance Orchestra (1997's *Plays Parts I & V*), appear on two selections on the 1995 Jimi Hendrix tribute album, *In from the Storm*, plus several albums by six-string shredder Stevie Salas (the first being 1997's *Alter Native Gold*). However, Abbruzzese has also received the type of publicity that nobody wants: trouble with the law. First, in 2010, he was arrested on several charges in Denton, Texas (including possession of a controlled substance and speeding), and in 2015, two warrants were issued for his arrest in the same town (for possession of a controlled substance and failure to appear on a manufacture or delivery of substance charge). When I placed a call to the Denton County Police Department in August 2017 to find out the status of these two warrants, I was informed that they were both still active.

With the announcement that Pearl Jam was being inducted into the Rock and Roll Hall of Fame in 2017, fans began to wonder if Abbruzzese would be welcomed back into the fold. Despite abundant rumors on the Internet, Abbruzzese was ultimately not in attendance the night of the induction on April 7. Mike McCready did state on SiriusXM shortly afterward that he thought Abbruzzese "should've been in the Rock and Roll Hall of Fame," and continued by saying, "Dave was integral at the part when we were starting to take off, and we were playing at Lollapalooza and we were opening for the Chili Peppers and Soundgarden and all that stuff. And we had to have a drummer because things were blowing up really quickly and he was there right when that was happening."

Abbruzzese weighed in via a Facebook post, later reposted by *Rolling Stone*: "For the band to put me in the same light as Matt Chamberlain & Dave K really was a slap in the face. Nothing to do with those guys as people or players. Respect...but as a contributor? A band member? A definitive contributor to the energy and power of where the band went?...The sacrifices, the work, the physical and emotional contributions...not to mention the personal weight of carrying on through and after unceremonious and disrespectful way I was fired. I gave this band all I had to give every single moment I was in it."

48 Magnuson Park

If you were to pick a single Seattle-area performance that signaled Pearl Jam had truly arrived, you'd have to look no further than their headlining performance at Magnuson Park on September 20, 1992, when they played to 29,000 attendees on a bill that also included Pete Droge, Lazy Susan, Cypress Hill, Shawn Smith, Seaweed, and Jim Rose.

The idea for the free concert in Seattle first came about during the spring of '92, when it was announced that on May 20, Pearl Jam would be performing a free concert at Gas Works Park, where voter registration booths would be set up in advance of that year's U.S. presidential election. But with PJ's popularity surging, concern was raised by officials regarding safety and crowd control. Apparently they were not convinced by a news report on K5 News, in which Eddie Vedder and Stone Gossard explained that the band

Drop in the Park, *Pearl Jam, 2009.* (Sony Legacy)

and management actually had all the bases properly covered, even showing a map of how the stage and the grounds were to be set up in the segment.

With PJ booked solid for the remainder of the spring and summer (with a European tour and Lollapalooza), they had to return to the drawing board and come up with another plan. Ever a man of the people, Vedder actually showed up at Gas Works Park the day of the aborted show to mingle with fans and explain the band's side of the story. And that plan eventually led to a redo at the much more spacious Magnuson Park (which stretches across 350 acres, making Gas Works' 19.1 acres seem rather puny), with the performance now going by the name of "Drop in the Park."

Located in the Sand Point neighborhood, Magnuson Park was the first public park within Seattle (which was "a gift" to the city in 1884 by David Denny, a member of a group of pioneers known as the Denny Party, who are credited with founding Seattle). By 1887, the Board of Park Commissioners was put into place, which supervised the growth of the park. The name of the park has been changed several times—first Carkeek Park, before being used by the military (from 1922–75) and renamed Naval Station Puget Sound, followed by Naval Air Station Sand Point. By 1975, a large chunk of the land previously used by the Navy was donated to Seattle and the National Oceanic and Atmospheric Administration, which led to the park being named Sand Point Park, before finally settling on Magnuson Park in 1975 (named after former U.S. senator Warren Magnuson, who was also a former naval officer from Seattle).

By September of '92, Pearl Jam as a live act was a well-oiled machine, possessing enough firepower to blow more established/ veteran acts off the stage. Their performance at Magnuson was no different, as they provided a firm set that included all the expected standouts from *Ten*, as well as airings of "State of Love and Trust," "Sonic Reducer," and "Rockin' in the Free World."

Vedder went through several costume changes throughout the course of the performance. He hit the stage for "Even Flow" wearing a black helmet (which he was also spotted sporting backstage at the VMAs earlier that month), a strange wig, and what looks like a yellow-ish pullover shirt. He then transitioned to a gray sweatshirt for "Deep," modeled an unbuttoned shirt over a green olive-colored T-shirt for "Jeremy," and by the time "Garden" was performed, boldly went with just the now–sweat drenched green T-shirt, which he stuck with for the remainder of the performance. (Dark-colored cargo shorts and black Dr. Martens boots remained in place throughout the show.)

Judging by the crowd-shot footage, the expected highlight of the performance was when Vedder decided to climb the lighting rig on stage right during "Porch." He then climbed hand-over-hand to the middle the rig, alternating between dangling high above between his feet and hands with his mic and mic cord hanging by his mouth, and at other times wedging it in the rig. Shortly after pointing out that he now possessed the best seat in the house, he announced "I can see you all from here!" to the crowd, then used the mic cord as a means of scooting back down to the stage before swinging back and forth on it Tarzan-style, then hurling himself into the crowd. (All of this footage can be found on YouTube.)

Pearl Jam's Magnuson Park performance has gone on to become somewhat legendary amongst fans, and collectors must have thanked their lucky stars when it was announced that a pre-recorded version of the performance would be included (albeit in truncated tracklist form) on vinyl as part of the "super deluxe" edition when *Ten* was reissued on March 24, 2009.

49 The Photographers

It seems like you can count on one—or maybe two—hands the amount of people who have been admitted entrance into Pearl Jam's inner circle over the years. In terms of photographers, there are three of them who PJ has worked with on a consistent basis and granted full access: Charles Peterson, Lance Mercer, and Danny Clinch.

Of the group, the photographer probably most associated with grunge is Peterson, a native of Longview, Washington, whose black-and-white photographs that showcase his trademark "flash and drag shutter effect" were utilized in photographs for many Sub Pop recording artists in the early days of the label, including classic images of Soundgarden, Green River, Nirvana, and Mudhoney, among others. And he has taken quite a few subsequent classic PJ photos, especially at the Drop in the Park performance at Magnuson Park in 1992.

Another photographer who has worked closely with PJ throughout the years is Seattle native Lance Mercer, who took the now-iconic "all for one" photo of the band that adorns the cover of *Ten*, the early photograph of the band that is featured on the cover of the *Rearviewmirror (Greatest Hits 1991–2003)* comp, plus images associated with the *Vs.*, *Vitalogy*, *No Code*, and *Live on Two Legs* releases. Both Peterson and Mercer pooled their resources in 1998 for the hardcover book, *Pearl Jam: Place/Date (The Official Photographic Record)*, while Mercer dug deep into his stash of PJ pics for the 2006 book, *5x1: Pearl Jam Through the Eye of Lance Mercer*.

Finally, there's Danny Clinch. Although the only photographer in this entry not originally from the state of Washington (he's from New Jersey), Clinch has forged a special relationship with PJ over the years, including capturing an iconic image of the band when they played at Wrigley Field in 2013 that features the backs of both Eddie Vedder and Jeff Ament as they leapt into the air at exactly the same moment. Clinch also directed the 2007 PJ concert film, *Immagine in Cornice*, the music video for "Sirens" off 2013's *Lightning Bolt*, plus short films with the band, in addition to taking great photos of Vedder holding his beloved ukulele for the booklet of the *Ukulele Songs* release. (A Vedder/uke shot was also used for the cover of Clinch's 2014 photo book *Still Moving*). Lastly, Clinch directed the 2017 documentary *Let's Play Two*, which focuses on PJ's pair of historic shows at Wrigley Field a year earlier.

Still not convinced that Peterson, Mercer, and Clinch are PJ's "go-to guys" when it comes to photography? Then perhaps the most convincing proof is all three have images prominently featured throughout the exhaustive coffee table photo book from 2011, *Pearl Jam Twenty*.

50 "Last Kiss"

There are many songs throughout music history that, because of their melody or hooks, become popular despite their dark or disconcerting lyrics—for example, "Suicide Is Painless," "Tom Dooley," "Hey Joe," "Ode to Billie Joe," "Down by the River," and even specific children's nursery rhymes such as "Humpty Dumpty." And you can certainly include the song "Last Kiss" (which Pearl Jam would score a massive hit with) to this list, as it tells the gloomy tale of the aftermath of a car wreck that involves two lovers, which leaves one dead and one alive.

The song was originally written by Wayne Cochran (known as "the White Knight of Soul" and for sporting a humorous-looking pompadour), Joe Carpenter, Randall Hoyal, and Bobby McGlon, resulting in Cochran recording the song four times over the years (the original was issued in 1961 via the Gala label). But it was not until 1964, when J. Frank Wilson and the Cavaliers covered the tune (on the Josie label), that "Last Kiss" finally became a hit—peaking at No. 2 on the Billboard Hot 100 and possessing impressive staying power (coming in at No. 9 on the year-end Billboard charts).

In 1974, the Canadian pop group Wednesday covered the song and scored a modest hit with it (peaking at No. 34 on the Billboard Hot 100); as a result, interest in J. Frank Wilson and the Cavaliers' version was renewed, triggering their version's return to the lower reaches of the charts for a spell. In an interesting quirk, for three weeks on the Cashbox Top 100 Singles Chart, Wednesday's version and J. Frank Wilson and the Cavaliers' version were listed back to back.

Subsequently, however, the song seemed to get lost in time, perhaps due to the overabundance of rock 'n' roll classics from the golden era of the late 1950s and early '60s, or because youngsters of the '80s and '90s seemed to lose interest in the style and period. But that's where Pearl Jam swooped in.

For their 1998 holiday single, PJ opted to revisit this bygone era, covering "Last Kiss" as well as "Soldier of Love" (the latter a song penned by Buzz Cason and Tony Moon and subsequently recorded by Arthur Alexander, the Beatles, and Marshall Crenshaw, among others). Both songs were recorded at a sound check in Maryland. To show that PJ had no expectations for people to go ape over "Last Kiss" outside of hardcore fans, the tune was allotted to the single's B-side.

In a true case of a happy accident, PJ's version of "Last Kiss" caught the attention of rock radio, which resulted in the song being placed in heavy rotation, and the band being forced to issue the song as an honest-to-goodness A-side in 1999, which nearly topped the charts (peaking at No. 2—behind only Jennifer Lopez's "If You Had My Love") and earned gold certification. And to show once more what sets the band apart from the majority of other music artists, instead of pocketing the proceeds from the single themselves, they donated all the earnings to the aid of refugees of the Kosovo War. The song would also be included as the first track on the benefit album *No Boundaries: A Benefit for the Kosovar Refugees*, the same year. Later, "Last Kiss" would also find a spot on two different PJ comps—2003's *Lost Dogs* and 2004's *Rearviewmirror (Greatest Hits 1991–2003)*.

51

Eddie Vedder...the Song!

You know you're quite an icon when you have a song titled after you. And that is precisely what happened in 1996, when Chicago-based alt-rock duo Local H issued their album *As Good as Dead* and included a song titled simply, "Eddie Vedder." While it was not the most successful tune off the album (the Nirvana-esque "Bound for the Floor" was, peaking at No. 5 on the Billboard Modern Rock Tracks chart), it did earn some radio attention and even MTV spins, once a video was filmed for it. And here, exclusively for this book, Local H singer/guitarist Scott Lucas opens up and discusses just how and why he penned the tune.

The story concerning the inspiration behind the song is a noteworthy one. "It was originally a song called 'The King,' and it was kind of directed at a girl that didn't really give a shit about the music you were writing. I think the original lyric was, 'Would you like me any better if I was Eddie Vedder? Fuck you to the both of you, and Prince can kiss my ass.' So there was a Prince thing in there, as well. And that was probably why the song was called 'The King.' But that wasn't very good.

"At the time, there were so many times on the radio that the singers sounded like Eddie Vedder. And it was everywhere. It was really annoying. You'd have strangers—and even friends—tell me, 'You should sing lower and you should change your singing style.' So I think that there was sort of an oblique comment on that, and sort of a joke, like, 'If this is the only way to get on the radio, why don't we just name a song...'Eddie Vedder'?' So that's a smart-ass type of thing. But the original idea just came down to somebody who liked Eddie Vedder's songs more than mine. It's kind of a

'Why don't you like me?' type of song. There are a ton of them and they're boring, and this was just a way to spice up that formula."

Local H would also film a video for the song, as well. "That was a cool video," Lucas says. "I really liked the way that Phil Harder's head worked—the director. We didn't really get along with many video directors. I think that was the first video we did with him, and then we went on to do three or four more with him. His ideas were always pretty simple and interesting. He always let me throw my two cents in—in a nice way. So I was like, 'Let's do a *Vertigo*-type thing.' And he figured out a way to put some *Vertigo* lines in one of the scenes of the video. So, he tolerated me that way—that was cool."

As a result of penning a song titled "Eddie Vedder," some have wondered if Lucas was indeed a fan of Pearl Jam or not. It turns out…he is. "Oh yeah!" Lucas says. "There was a point where people had told me that they had asked Eddie about the song, and he was like, 'It's a good song. I just don't understand why they had to put my name in it.' And there was a point when we were recording our next record, *Pack Up the Cats*, and we were working with Nick DiDia, who had worked with Pearl Jam on quite a few records, with Brendan O'Brien. So he was talking to Stone Gossard, and telling him that he was doing our next record, and Stone said, 'Well, tell those guys to name a song after *me* this time!' So there is a song on *Pack Up the Cats* called 'Stoney,' and that is a nod to that conversation."

I know what you're wondering: did Lucas ever actually meet Vedder, and if so, was the song discussed? "It took me a long time to actually cross paths with Eddie Vedder," Lucas says. "Finally, there was a night he was doing his thing in Chicago [Lucas estimates that it would have been circa 2015]. And I was like, 'Fuck this…I'm going to go meet him.' I just wanted to say 'Hey' or apologize or whatever. I was like, 'I'm *finally* doing to meet this guy.' So I made a concerted effort to do that. I finally did meet him, and I was like, 'Hey, I heard this song might have bummed you out slightly. I just wanted to apologize.' He was like, 'Well, I don't really remember saying that. It probably bummed me out a lot less than you think.' So I'm not even sure if it was ever even actually on his radar—somebody might have been telling me bullshit. But the night ended up okay—we ended up at a bar and sang along to Who songs on the jukebox. So, it was a pretty good night."

52 "My Baby's in Love with Eddie Vedder"

Interestingly, Local H's song was not the only composition of the '90s to include Eddie Vedder's name in its title. Case in point— "Weird Al" Yankovic's "My Baby's in Love with Eddie Vedder," off his 1999 album *Running with Scissors*. But while Local H is looked upon as a serious rock band, Yankovic has made a career out of poking fun at pop stars with often witty parodies: "Another One Rides the Bus" was a parody of Queen's "Another One Bites the Dust," "Eat It" was a goof on Michael Jackson's "Beat It," "Amish Paradise" was a spoof on Coolio's "Gangsta's Paradise," and so on.

So with Pearl Jam being one of the leading rock bands for nearly a full decade by 1999, it only made sense for Al to take the PJ plunge. Admittedly, "My Baby's in Love with Eddie Vedder" is not the cleverest of parodies Yankovic ever committed to tape, but it should still tickle the fancy of most fans of the band. Instead of parodying a specific Pearl Jam tune, the only thing that "My Baby's in Love with Eddie Vedder" has in common with the band is its inclusion of Vedder's name in the title and its lyrics, which interestingly is somewhat similar in approach to the

Local H tune. Musically, the tune does not contain one speck of grunge—instead, it draws upon zydeco music, and showcases Al's accordion skills.

During an "Ask Al" segment on his website back in September 1999, Yankovic was asked, "Why do you think Eddie Vedder is pretty cool? It says so at the end of the 'special thanks' section." Yankovic replied, "I met Eddie after a Pearl Jam show in Akron, Ohio, a couple years ago. I talked to him backstage for a few minutes, and he seemed like a decent, down-to-earth kinda guy. I don't know what he thinks of my song, but I really hope he's not offended by it. Of course, it was written from the perspective of a guy who's bitter and jealous because his girlfriend's got a crush on him, so it may seem a little harsh…but hopefully Eddie understands that it's a JOKE."

And it turns out that Yankovic just may be a closet grunge fan, as "My Baby's in Love with Eddie Vedder" was not the first time he took note of the genre—"Smells Like Nirvana" preceded it, in 1992 (and its video that expertly recreated the look and vibe of the original "Smells Like Teen Spirit").

Rick Parashar

When discussing the greatest rock 'n' roll producers of all time, several names quickly come to mind: George Martin, Rick Rubin, Mutt Lange, Butch Vig, and many others. But one man who never seems to get the credit he deserves is the late Rick Parashar.

Born Rakesh Parashar on December 13, 1963, in Seattle, Parashar and his brother Raj founded London Bridge Studios in their hometown in 1985. By the early-to-mid-'90s, both Rick and his studio were in high demand. The results speak for them-selves: he co-produced three classic grunge releases—Pearl Jam's *Ten*, Temple of the Dog's self-titled album, and Alice in Chains' acoustic EP *Sap*—and also co-produced Pearl Jam's "Breath" and "State of Love and Trust" plus Alice in Chains' "Would?" on the *Singles* motion picture soundtrack. He also co-produced various PJ B-sides, including fan favorite "Yellow Ledbetter."

Blind Melon chose Parashar to produce the band's self-titled debut in 1992, which included such classics as "No Rain," "Change," and "Tones of Home," among others.

Sadly, Parashar passed away on August 14, 2014, at the age of 50. Blind Melon guitarist Christopher Thorn was willing to chat exclusively for this book about what it was like working with Parashar and helped shed some light on what made him special as a producer and as a person.

"I believe the first thing we got from the record company [before choosing a producer] was probably *Ten*, and it just blew our minds away. It just felt like guys that were making music for *us*. And then shortly after that, we heard Temple of the Dog, which at the time for some reason hit me harder. And the *Sap* record. That's what we heard, and we said, 'Oh, hell yeah. Rick is positively the guy for us.'

"He was kind of this Buddha. He had this calming quality, which for us at that time was really important, because we were out of our minds—we were super young and just got a record deal.

"When you think about the history of rock 'n' roll, this is a guy who made some of the most important records—and I'm not even including my own record. And whether you like it or not, he made a record with Nickelback [2001's *Silver Side Up*] that sold like a zillion [copies]! The guy didn't get lucky once; the guy had a track record. Once is good enough, but if you do it more than once, you're in a whole different category. And Rick was there."

Thorn also recalls running into Pearl Jam while Blind Melon was recording. "Back in the '90s in Seattle, it was really small," he says. "There were a few places you were all going to go to. Those guys were always super cool. I probably knew Stone [Gossard] and Mike [McCready] the most, and still to this day when I see them, we're all friendly and it's great to see them. What a great role model; a band that was like, 'We're not doing that bullshit fame thing. We're just going to make great records.' They had a great moral compass, more so than us. They inspired us, for sure. We just had the most amazing time playing with Pearl Jam and Neil Young in 1993. And those guys were on top of the world. I'll tell you, Pearl Jam...man, they were ferocious at that point. It felt like they had so much to prove. They came out with such a force, that honestly, it felt like the ground shook every time."

54 Mike McCready's Other Projects

Mike McCready has guested on quite a few recordings by other artists over the years. And much like his bandmate Eddie Vedder, a good amount were with renowned artists.

Let's start with the aforementioned Temple of the Dog (1991's self-titled release), the near-TOTD reunion track, "Hey Baby (Land of the New Rising Sun") (credited to "M.A.C.C." on 1993's *Stone Free: A Tribute to Jimi Hendrix*), plus Neil Young's *Mirror Ball*, Screaming Trees' "Dying Days" (1996's *Dust*), Brad's "The Day Brings" (1997's *Interiors*), several tracks with the Wallflowers (on 2002's *Red Letter Days*), Heart's "I'm Fine" (2004's *Jupiter's Darling*), Peter Frampton's "Blowin'

Smoke" and a cover of Soundgarden's "Black Hole Sun" (2006's *Fingerprints*), and Soundgarden themselves, on the track "Eyelid's Mouth" (2012's *King Animal*). McCready has contributed to a few motion picture soundtracks, as well, including *The Cable Guy* ("Oh! Sweet Nuthin'," credited to $10,000 Gold Chain) and *Almost Famous* ("Fever Dog," credited to the movie's fake band Stillwater).

Outside of Pearl Jam, McCready has been a part of several true side bands. The one largely considered to be the best—or at least most renowned—of all the grunge offshoots is Mad Season, which saw McCready team up with the late Layne Staley, as well as bassist John Baker Saunders, and drummer Barrett Martin (with additional vocals provided by guest Mark Lanegan), which resulted in one classic full-length, *Above*, released on March 14, 1995, peaking at No. 24 on the Billboard 200. The albums spawned three singles: "River of Deceit," "I Don't Know Anything," and "Long Gone Day." Although both Staley's death (on April 5, 2002) and Saunders' death (on January 15, 1999) would prevent an authentic Mad Season reunion from ever taking place, the band has experienced a few partial reunions with others filling in for Staley and Saunders, including a performance in 2015 that saw Chris Cornell providing lead vocals and Duff McKagan handling bass duties.

Other side bands McCready has been a part of include Flight to Mars and the Rockfords. Flight to Mars is comprised of McCready, Paul Passereli (vocals), Tim DiJulio (guitar), Gary Westlake (bass), Ryan Burns (keyboards), and Mike Musburger (drums), and serve primarily as a tribute band, focusing on material by '70s hard rockers UFO. Since they specialize in covers, no recordings have been issued by the band, but they are quite generous in other ways—for example, they perform an annual benefit each year at the Showbox in Seattle for Crohn's disease and Colitis research.

On the other hand, the Rockfords—which also features input from Carrie Akre (vocals), Danny Newcomb (guitar), Rick Friel (bass), and Chris Friel (drums)—do offer up original tunes, with a sound leaning more toward pop. Thus far, the band has issued one self-titled studio album (issued on February 1, 2000, and featuring Heart's Nancy Wilson supplying vocals on the tune "Riverwide"), the live album *Live Seattle, WA 12/13/03* (released just two weeks after being recorded, on December 28, 2003), and the 2004 EP *Waiting...* However, not a peep has been heard from the Rockfords since.

And in case you were wondering, as of this book's release, McCready has yet to issue a solo album.

Backstage Pass

Richard Christy
Charred Walls of the Damned Drummer,
***The Howard Stern Show* Writer**

How did you first get into Pearl Jam?
My first exposure to Pearl Jam was when the video for "Alive" came on MTV. I saw "Alive" and thought it was a really cool song and really liked it. So, I had to drive like 40 miles away from where I lived to find a record store that had their cassette, because it was right when it came out. None of my friends had really heard of them, so it was fun to expose them to all of my friends in high school, and then to see later on, everybody knew who they were. But I'm proud to say I was one of the early Pearl Jam listeners, because I also was familiar with Mother Love Bone—just from reading music magazines. When their singer unfortunately passed away, that was big news, and I sought out the band after hearing about that. So I was familiar with who was in Pearl Jam—that it was some of the Mother Love Bone guys. And when I heard "Alive," I just became a big fan right away.

When Pearl Jam first came out, they were kind of marketed as a heavy metal band. Their videos were shown on *Headbangers Ball*, and Eddie Vedder and Mike McCready even had a sit-down interview with the show's host, Riki Rachtman.

Totally. I just kind of looked at them as a hard rock, almost heavy metal type band. I actually identified a little bit with their look, too, because growing up on a farm in Kansas, I used to wear flannel shirts all the time when I would haul hay because it would keep my arms from getting cut up by the alfalfa hay bales. So I was like, "Oh, those guys look like they haul hay too, because they're wearing flannel like me." To me, they were just a cool rock band. I had no idea that they would go on to create a whole new genre of rock called grunge.

Is it true you attended a Pearl Jam show at the University of Kansas?

Yeah. I saw an ad for a free Pearl Jam show and I couldn't believe it. I was like, "Wow. That's pretty frickin' awesome!" And it was in Lawrence, Kansas, on the KU campus [on May 2, 1992], on this big hill. And I lived maybe a little over an hour south, and me and a bunch of my buddies who were about to graduate went up there.

I remember Pearl Jam's drummer, Dave Abbruzzese, hanging out in this area near the stage and just kind of hanging with all the fans. I remember going up and talking to him, and he was real nice. The bass player was hanging out, too. If I remember right, they were both throwing a football to the fans before they played. It was just really low-key. And then when they played, people just went *insane.* It was like a dust storm in the mosh pit, because it was just so dry and hot there that day.

So I got right into the mosh pit, and to this day, it's probably [one of] the funniest and coolest things that's ever happened to me at a concert. I had been moshing for a long time and crowd surfing in all this dust. And Mike McCready spots me from the stage and points at me—while they're playing. I'm like, "Holy shit…is Mike McCready pointing at *me*?" I pointed at myself, and he nodded, like, "Yes. I'm talking to you." And then he takes his finger and acts like he's brushing his teeth, and then points back at me!

So I took my fingernails and scraped my teeth, and a ton of dirt came off onto my fingernail. Then I realized, "Oh, he's saying my teeth are covered with dirt." So I looked back at Mike McCready and he started laughing and giggling, and gave me the thumbs-up. This was all while he was playing a song. I could not stop laughing. And none of my friends even believed me that that happened. But I swear, one day I'm going to meet Mike McCready and tell him about this. I'm sure he won't remember, but I just want to let him know that he made one of the most memorable concert moments ever for me by doing that—just by him taking the time out of playing a song, to show me that my teeth were covered in dirt.

You can actually go on YouTube and search for "Pearl Jam, Day on the Hill, 1992," and watch the video. If you look closely, you see a long-red-haired guy crowd surfing—you can see me in the video! And then Eddie Vedder was amazing, too. He climbed the scaffolding just like a spider—climbed to the top, while it was shaking. I was like, "Man, that guy's got some balls." It was a lot of fun to watch.

Any last thoughts?

Another thing I want to throw in—I thought it was really awesome that Mike McCready went on *That Metal Show* and talked about his love of metal. Because there was a time where grunge bands...it wasn't cool for them to say that they were into metal. And I loved that Mike McCready is a confessed metalhead, and he's not ashamed to say it. I love that. And that's another reason for me to be a big Mike McCready fan.

55 Crohn's Disease

As discussed more thoroughly elsewhere in this book, Pearl Jam does an extraordinary amount of philanthropic work. One illness that Mike McCready has been very outspoken about is Crohn's disease. The reason? He was diagnosed with this condition back in 1986, and has been living with it ever since.

Crohn's disease (which is named after gastroenterologist Burrill Bernard Crohn) is considered a chronic inflammatory bowel disease, which is linked to an inflammation of the digestive or gastrointestinal tract. There is no part of gastrointestinal tract that is safe from possibly being affected (it can be found anywhere from the mouth to the anus), but it's most commonly located at the end of the small intestine.

Symptoms of those affected by Crohn's disease can include any of the following: diarrhea, fever, fatigue, abdominal pain and cramping, blood in the stool, oral sores, reduced appetite, weight loss, or pain or drainage near or around the anus due to inflammation from a tunnel into the skin (also known as a fistula). Additionally, inflammation of skin, eyes, and joints; inflammation of the liver or bile ducts; and delayed growth or sexual development in children can also serve as symptoms. What exactly causes Crohn's disease has yet to be pinpointed, but if untreated, it can lead to obstruction, fistulae, abscesses, and possibly colon cancer.

McCready was first diagnosed several years before the formation of Pearl Jam, after he had relocated for a spell to Los Angeles and was still a member of the heavy metal band Shadow. After experiencing stomach troubles for two weeks, he visited a doctor who identified it as ulcerative colitis, which has led to the guitarist treating the condition with a drug called prednisone (often used to treat inflammatory diseases) on and off over the years.

Speaking to EverydayHealth.com in 2007, McCready recalled one particular episode of a Crohn's disease attack he experienced on the same day a career highlight was scheduled to take place: "The one kind of classic one that I tell that sticks out in my mind was when we were opening for the Rolling Stones. I think it was in 1997 in Oakland. And they are my favorite band of all time, so this was a huge honor for us to be even part of it. So I was kind of sick at that time. We were about to go on. It was within a minute of us going on stage, and I had what I call a Crohn's attack, and so I'm about to just lose it right there, right before we go on, and I run up to Eddie [Vedder], and I say, 'Hey, Ed, can you start with this song called "Sometimes" because I'm not really on that song. I just do some little atmospheric things,' and he said sure. And those guys go out. I ditch and go find a bathroom. And I got to look into us open up for the Rolling Stones in the bathroom onstage, in a Port-A-Potty. And then I went out and did the show, but that's happened a few times. I mean, we were in, I think it was Rotterdam one time, and I was running around, and I was playing the lead, and all of a sudden it hit me again, and I couldn't go anywhere, but there, and I was in extreme pain, didn't want to hunch over or anything because we were playing in front of like 10,000 people. So I'm trying to hold it together and play, and I had to go, and I went right there while I was playing. And it stopped, and I had to change, and, you know, it was a nightmare."

Over the years, McCready has performed benefit concerts to help raise awareness about Crohn's disease, including one particular concert in May 2016 at the Showbox in Seattle, in which he was joined by Guns N' Roses bassist Duff McKagan and his bandmate in Mad Season, Barrett Martin. The following year, the guitarist and his wife, Ashley, helped raise more than $350,000 for the Crohn's & Colitis Foundation and the Jennifer Jaff CareLine for People with IBD [inflammatory bowel disease], through two benefit events—the Annual Crohn's and Colitis Luncheon and two shows by McCready's UFO tribute band, Flight to Mars.

56 Top 10 Pearl Jam Songs (Actually, Let's Make That 11)

A shelfful of books could be written about Pearl Jam's top songs, all fans have their own personal favorites. But since I am the author of this book, I am the lucky duck who has the opportunity to select what I believe are the best Pearl Jam songs of all time.

"Alive" (1991)

Probably Pearl Jam's best-known track, and for many of us fans, the song that served as our initial introduction to the group. Combine one of Stone Gossard's best chord progressions with one of Mike McCready's best solos along with some of Eddie Vedder's best lyrics, and you have what just may be the top PJ tune of them all.

"Even Flow" (1991)

The topic of homelessness had been touched upon by other artists over the years (Jethro Tull's "Aqualung," Phil Collins' "Another Day in Paradise," Anthrax's "Who Cares Wins," among others), and "Even Flow" was Pearl Jam's contribution to this troubling topic; the opening line, "Freezin', rests his head on a pillow made of concrete, again," is about as potent as it gets. Musically, PJ impressively proved they could walk the line between rockin' and groovin' even at this early stage of their career.

"Jeremy" (1991)

Bullying and school shootings have been intractable problems across the U.S. for decades, and Pearl Jam used the sad and disturbing tale of Jeremy Wade Delle as lyrical inspiration for the song and video that truly catapulted *Ten* from a platinum success to mega-platinum behemoth.

"Black" (1991)

The song that could have been a mega-hit for Pearl Jam. Lyrically, it remains one of Vedder's crowning achievements, as it deals with someone who is torn up inside about a breakup. All you have to do is hear the "Doo doo doo doo doo doo doo" part once, and it will stick in your noggin until the cows come home. And really, how can you go wrong with one of David Letterman's all-time favorite songs?

"Yellow Ledbetter" (1992)

Mike McCready has never been bashful about his love of James Marshall Hendrix. And he shows off his superb Hendrix-like guitar chops throughout this B-side, which has become a highlight of most every PJ concert.

"Breath" (1992)

If you forced me to pick a single favorite PJ track, I may very well select this tune off the *Singles* soundtrack, as its highly melodic yet rubbery-sounding riff (thanks to the presence of Jeff Ament's fretless bass) merged with a great Vedder-sung chorus created a simply sublime song. How this tune didn't make the cut for *Ten* remains a mystery; it's mind-boggling to consider how an already perfect album could have become more perfect if rejects such as "Breath" and "Yellow Ledbetter" had appeared on PJ's debut.

"Elderly Woman Behind the Counter in a Small Town" (1993)

I think we can all agree that Eddie Vedder is one of the best rock lyricists of all time, can't we? This tune tucked away toward the back of *Vs.* is one of the many times when he creates wonderful images with his choice and careful placement of words.

"Better Man" (1994)

Did Eddie Vedder just wake up one day and become a gifted singer/songwriter/lyricist? *Nyet.* "Better Man" had been kicking around since Vedder's high school days (and was even tackled by his pre-PJ band, Bad Radio, in the late '80s), before finding its way onto *Vitalogy*. It's proof positive that Vedder's talent was always there.

"Do the Evolution" (1998)

Who says punk rock can't have a groove to it? Pearl Jam proves 'em wrong again with this snappy little rocker, which contains a brief-yet-awesome "choir" bit that seemingly appears out of nowhere.

"Life Wasted" (2006)

Eddie Vedder was deeply affected by the passing of one of his best friends, rock legend Johnny Ramone. So much so that it allegedly inspired him to pen the raggedly rockin' "Life Wasted," one of the best tunes off the band's self-titled offering.

"Just Breathe" (2009)

Until "Just Breathe," many Pearl Jam fans may have figured that Vedder would not be able to top the poetic lyrics of such tunes as "Black," "Elderly Woman," and "Better Man." But the crowning lyrical achievement of his entire career may just be "Just Breathe."

57 "Sonic Reducer"

Think "first-wave punk rockers," and bands such as the Ramones, the Sex Pistols, and the Clash come to mind, right? Well, there was also a horde of other acts who don't get nearly as much time in the limelight. For example, the Dead Boys, who penned a ditty that most Pearl Jam fans will be familiar with: "Sonic Reducer."

The D. Boys' roots lay in Cleveland, Ohio, and a precursor band called Rocket from the Tombs, which featured guitarist Cheetah Chrome and drummer Johnny Blitz. After eventually morphing into the Dead Boys with singer Stiv Bators, guitarist Jimmy Zero, and bassist Jeff Magnum, the group's full-length debut, *Young Loud and Snotty*, was released in October 1977 and established the band as a true punk rock force. That force was particularly notable on the album's opening track, "Sonic Reducer." When I interviewed Chrome (real name: Eugene Richard O'Connor) in 2014 for *Alternative Nation*, I asked him what he recalled about the writing and recording of "SR" (as well as another DB classic that would appear on their second/final album, 1978's *We Have Come for Your Children*, "Ain't It Fun?"), to which he replied, "Both just remind me of the old Rocket from the Tombs' loft in Cleveland, where we were when we wrote those, and of the intense rehearsals…"

According to the official Pearl Jam website, the first time "Sonic Reducer" was covered by PJ was September 8, 1992, at the Desert Sky Pavilion in Phoenix, Arizona, on one of the last stops of the Lollapalooza tour. The second performance of the song was September 11 at Irvine Meadows, but if the band had its way, it would have also been performed on September 9 at the Pauley Pavilion in Los Angeles. The occasion? The MTV Video Music Awards. But when Pearl Jam ran the idea past MTV, they were convinced to perform their current single, "Jeremy," instead. But Eddie Vedder was able to insert a lyrical snippet of "Sonic Reducer" at the very end of the tune, singing, "I don't need no mom and dad."

The song was included on that year's Christmas single for members of the Ten Club (the B-side being "Ramblings II"), and has gone on to become one of PJ's most often performed cover tunes over the years (as of the writing of this book, it has been played a total of 77 times). When I asked Chrome if he'd made a respectable amount of dough via publishing rights, he said, "Yeah, but assholes like Seymour Stein and Warner Brothers got a chunk too, so not as good as it should have been. Careful what you sign, kiddies."

58 Drummer No. 4

Not many people can say they drummed in two of the most popular and important rock bands of all time. Jack Irons is one of the few gentlemen that can stake that claim, as he served in both the Red Hot Chili Peppers *and* Pearl Jam.

Born on July 18, 1962, in Los Angeles, California, Irons would meet his future Chili Peppers bandmates Hillel Slovak, Anthony Kiedis, and Flea via school, and eventually, provided drums while attending high school for the band Anthym (which also featured Slovak on guitar, and another renowned musician, singer/guitarist Alain Johannes).

Irons, Slovak, Flea, and Kiedis would go on to form the Red Hot Chili Peppers in 1983, but when it came time to sign on the dotted line with a record company, Irons and Slovak got cold feet, and opted to go with Johannes in another band they had formed, What Is This? Irons would go on to play on a total of three releases by the band in 1984–85 (a self-titled full-length, plus a pair of EPs—*Squeezed* and *3 Out of 5 Live*). And while he would not appear on the first two Chili Peppers albums (their 1984 self-titled debut and 1985's *Freaky Styley*), he would indeed be listed as a co-writer on several tracks. Eventually, Irons must have recognized the error of his ways, because he returned to Pepper-land in time for the band's third release, 1987's *The Uplift Mofo Party Plan*.

Despite worldwide commercial success just around the corner, tragedy struck when Slovak died from a heroin overdose in 1988, resulting in Irons quitting the Peppers again (this time for good), and reuniting once more with Johannes to form the alt-rock group Eleven. And it was right around this time that the drummer befriended a certain surfer/singer by the name of Eddie Vedder and puts him in touch with a new band looking for a singer. (Irons was also invited to join the band, but turned it down because of his happiness with Eleven.)

Three Eleven albums with Irons would be released (1991's *Awake in a Dream*, 1993's self-titled, and 1995's *Thunk*) before he was invited by his old PJ pals to replace Dave Abbruzzese. He wisely accepted the second invitation, resulting in playing on one tune on Pearl Jam's third release, 1994's *Vitalogy* ("Hey Foxymophandlemama, That's Me"), as well as two full-lengths, 1996's *No Code* and 1998's *Yield*, the 1995 two-song EP *Merkin Ball*, and the band's collaboration with Neil Young, 1995's *Mirror Ball*. Irons was also credited as a co-writer of several PJ tunes— "Who You Are," "Red Mosquito," and "I'm Open" (as well as being the sole author of an untitled tune on *Yield* that is often referred to as "Red Dot").

But despite being a member of one of the world's most successful bands, Irons opted to exit the band in 1998. Talking to *Drum Magazine* in 2011, the drummer explained his decision: "When I left Pearl Jam in '98, I wasn't in a good place. Honestly, the way I felt, the last thing on my mind was music. Music is, I believe, something you do when you're feeling strong. I pretty much had to kind of give up my career to get my life together."

Subsequently, Irons regained his vigor and returned to music, issuing several solo albums (2004's *Attention Dimension*, 2010's *No Heads Are Better Than One*, and 2011's *Blue Manatee*), another album with Eleven (2003's *Howling Book*), and co-forming the band Spinnerette along with Johannes and singer/guitarist Brody Dalle (2008's *Ghetto Love* EP and 2009's self-titled release). Additionally, Irons has appeared on recordings by various other renowned artists, including Joe Strummer, Keith Levene, Hole, Mark Lanegan, and the Wallflowers, among others. Irons served as an opening act on the Red Hot Chili Peppers' 2017 U.S. tour...and who should appear on stage with Irons as a surprise guest on a cover of Pink Floyd's "Shine On You Crazy Diamond" when the tour visited Seattle's KeyArena on March 17, 2017? Eddie Vedder!

No Code

Whenever Pearl Jam and Brendan O'Brien had joined forces in a recording studio, the results were either raw and rocking (*Vs.*) or raw and experimental (*Vitalogy*). So, it would be understandable to assume that for their third collaboration, 1996's *No Code*, we would be receiving more of the same. It turns out the answer was "yes and no." The first PJ album to fully feature new drummer Jack Irons showed that his exotic percussion skills added an interesting ingredient to an even richer Pearl Jam recipe.

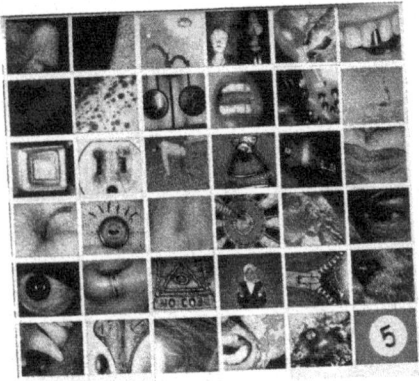

No Code, *Pearl Jam,*
1996. (Epic)

Recorded between July 1995 and May 1996 (at Chicago Recording Company in Chicago; Kingsway Studio in New Orleans, Louisiana; and Stone Gossard's Studio Litho in Seattle, Washington), *No Code* was released on August 27, 1996. Whereas each previous Pearl Jam album had a clear song or two that possessed crossover appeal (*Ten's* "Black," *Vs.'* "Daughter," *Vitalogy's* "Better Man"), *No Code* was the first to *not* do so—although the lead-off single, "Who You Are," came closest. And once more, the band should be applauded for not taking the easy way out; you can just picture an exec somewhere at the record label, chomping on his cigar, wondering why he wasn't getting *Ten Part II.*

The arrival of his old pal Irons seemed to have worked wonders for Eddie Vedder, who was caught in a calm—even meditative—state of mind at various points (especially the sleepy opening track, "Sometimes," and the gentle, lullaby-ish album closer, "Around the Bend"). But lest you think PJ had gone soft, *No Code* also offered a number of sonic karate chops to the solar plexus, such as the blink-and-it's-already-over "Lukin."

The tunes that most feature Irons adding a new and interesting percussive component were stacked side-by-side on the album— "Who You Are" and "In My Tree." Elsewhere, you'll find a tune that sounds like *Harvest*-era Neil Young alongside "You Don't Know How It Feels"-era Tom Petty ("Smile"), a tune that sounds like Mike McCready is doing his best to summon his inner Leslie West of Mountain ("Red Mosquito"), and the aforementioned "Lukin" (which lyrically captures the manic state of mind Vedder must have been in at the time, still grappling with fame).

Videos? Forget it. PJ was still not going to allow themselves to be bitten by the video bug, but were still A-OK with issuing singles. *No Code* would spawn three: "Who You Are," "Hail, Hail," and "Off He Goes." The album cover of *No Code* was comprised of random Polaroid photo images contributed by various "photographers," including Vedder, Jeff Ament, and Mike McCready, including a closeup of former NBA player Dennis Rodman's eyeball. But on the CD version, when you completely unfolded the little booklet, it would unveil what is now commonly referred to by fans as the "*No Code* logo"—a single eyeball staring at you from within a triangle. As far as the meaning behind the album's title, while chatting with *Rolling Stone Australia* in their August 2000 issue, Vedder simply stated, "For me, *No Code* meant 'Do Not Resuscitate.'"

As expected, *No Code* once again found its way to No. 1 on the Billboard 200, the third PJ release in a row to accomplish this impressive feat, while also topping the Australian, Canadian, Danish, New Zealand, Portuguese, and Swedish album charts. However, *No Code* took a noticeable dip in sales compared to its predecessors—certified both gold and platinum on January 8, 1997, but not receiving any further certifications since then.

Travis Stever
Coheed and Cambria Guitarist

What do you recall about getting into Pearl Jam's music initially?
I think everybody name-checks Nirvana's "Smells Like Teen Spirit" and *Nevermind* being the changing of the tide in rock. And there's no doubt that that's the truth. But I remember the first time I saw the "Alive" video—with the wave coming—and I feel like that was a change, also. Pearl Jam was more of the authentic back-to-the-roots rock thing.

A lot of our friends—young bands that Claudio [Sanchez, Coheed and Cambria singer/guitarist] and I were in—the whole Seattle grunge scene was something that we were all admiring from New York and wishing to be a part of, as kids. I remember covering a couple of Pearl Jam songs in one of our bands, called Toxic Parents, and I remember even later, creating a band specifically in the more B-side/rarity thing—that's how deep it went—to play at a high school thing, and playing "State of Love and Trust" from *Singles*. And all the bands we were in, I'd say probably half of *Ten* was covered!

Which other Pearl Jam albums besides *Ten* did you get into?
You move on to *Vs.*, *Vitalogy*, every record was incredible. But I want to fast-forward to 1996. Now, I have a lot of full-on love for hip-hop, don't get me wrong, but I hung out with people that would go to a lot of raves. And here I am, this "rock guy." And even the way the radio was at that point, it's funny, I feel like it's similar to now—the Spice Girls were just coming around, and it just felt like rock had dried up, and it wasn't happening. And then two records really got me excited that things would be moving forward—Pearl Jam's *No Code* and Porno for Pyros' *Good God's Urge*. Both of those albums coincided with each other, but *No Code* is still one of my favorite Pearl Jam records—"Red Mosquito," "Who You Are."

Ten is incredible and it's a genius record. For the most part, they all are. I kind of fell off after *No Code* until years later, but I remember being with Claudio, and he bought *Yield* at Tower Records. He grabbed that album and put it in, and I was like, "Holy shit! It's still going!" But by that time, what we were both listening to was back to more aggressive kind of music. It's interesting how we all flow back and forth with the music that we want to listen to. But *Yield*, as far as I remember, was a little slower, atmospheric. It wasn't as heavy as most of them. And I remember hearing *Binaural*, and it just wasn't the "mode" I was in. Now, I've listened to all that stuff later, and I'm just blown away. So it's a band that ages so well consistently.

If I take some time from *Ten*, I still go back and hear things I've never heard before, and find new love for that record, because it has so many aspects and so many different sounds. But at the same time, it was this raw, familiar sound that they brought back—I think that's why it went so well, because it was *real* rock. It's kind of like a very different sound and vibe, but that's what Guns N' Roses did with *Appetite for Destruction*—it gave rock, and even aspects of punk, a little shot of new life. And that's what *Ten* was. And then I feel like *No Code* did the same thing, but it just wasn't...it's kind of like how you and I have discussed Blind Melon's *Soup*. I feel like *No Code* was kind of their *Soup*—it should be known as an incredible record. And those of us that know the band know it is, but some other people are like, "Well, it only had the one hit." It's like, "Yeah, well...*fuck you.*"

Any memories of seeing Pearl Jam live over the years?
I had the luxury of playing a festival with Coheed, and Claudio and I—and our wives—were able to get side-stage for a Pearl Jam show in Spain. And I've never seen anything like it, man. I've been on stage for a lot of bands...just this sea of people all over the place, and they just hung on every note and every word. It's inspiring, man. Really inspiring.

60 Mudhoney

In Green River, it became clear that Mark Arm was on a different musical path than Jeff Ament, Stone Gossard, and Bruce Fairweather, with Arm seemingly more into the vintage garage rock side of things. So after the band split in 1988, Arm reunited with original GR guitarist Steve Turner, and that same year, Mudhoney was born. Rounding out the lineup were previous members of other Washington State bands—bassist Matt Lukin of the Melvins and drummer Dan Peters of Bundle of Hiss—and Mudhoney quickly developed a local following.

Part of what made the band unique was that while most rock bands at the time seemed to think that their guitarists could only fulfill their potential by shredding away on high-end instruments, Arm and Turner made it a point to play only second-hand guitars, with Arm favoring a Hagstrom II and Turner a Fender Mustang. Fast-forward a few years later in the '90s, and thanks to Mudhoney and such bands as Sonic Youth, seemingly every band had been bitten by the vintage guitar bug—and the more obscure and battered, the better. Another ingredient of the Mudhoney sound was the guitarists' use of a then somewhat forgotten piece of gear, the Big Muff Pi (usually just called "Big Muff") from the Electro-Harmonix company, which when combined with their odd guitars created a gloriously fuzzy tone that recalled the sounds of the Stooges and Blue Cheer.

Immediately signed to Green River's label, Sub Pop, Mudhoney issued a single ("Touch Me I'm Sick") and a six-track EP, *Superfuzz Bigmuff*, both of which are considered to be two of grunge's all-time classic recordings (*Superfuzz Bigmuff* would be reissued in 1990 with its tracklist doubled in length, under the title *Superfuzz*

Bigmuff Plus Early Singles). From there, Mudhoney would issue albums and tour on a regular basis (including making the jump to a major label—Reprise Records—in the wake of grunge's commercial advancement) until 1998, before Lukin exited the band and was replaced by Guy Maddison.

At this point, you may be wondering—is there any connection between Mudhoney and Pearl Jam besides the Green River one? You betcha! It turns out that Eddie Vedder is quite fond of Mudhoney's music, and as a result, PJ has taken Mudhoney out on tour numerous times over the years. In fact, they were on tour together when the news of Kurt Cobain's death broke, and right afterward, both bands embarked on a trip to visit the White House. It was also during that 1994 tour that Arm joined PJ on stage for a rollicking rendition of "Sonic Reducer" at a performance on April 12 at the Orpheum Theater in Boston, which would later be officially released as part of the deluxe edition of their *Vs./Vitalogy* reissue in 2011.

Over the years, Vedder developed a friendship with the guys in Mudhoney, resulting in a song simply titled "Lukin" from the 1996 PJ album, *No Code* (according to the lyrics, Vedder could seemingly experience some normalcy visiting the home of his bass-playing pal from Mudhoney). And Vedder also explained to me in *Grunge Is Dead* that to a certain degree, the members of Mudhoney also helped keep him in check: "And at the same time, not take yourself so fucking seriously. You do things and in the back of your head you could just hear Danny Peters and Matt Lukin laughing at you. [Laughs] As they watch some MTV awards or whatever the fuck it is. Or seeing them in a pool hall and them going, 'Dude, what was that about?' Thinking you did something intense and cool, and they're like, 'Yeah, whatever, guy.' I owe them a lot."

61 Fox Theatre Broadcast

While it's almost impossible to pick a single Pearl Jam performance as their best, certainly one of their most widely heard took place toward the end of the *Vs.* tour—April 3, 1994, at the Fox Theatre in Atlanta, Georgia, to be exact. The reason it's known by so many fans is because it was broadcast for free to any interested radio station in the U.S. As a result, supposedly 300 stations did so, helping the show become one of the most bootlegged PJ concerts of all time (with yours truly even joining in on the fun, taping it on cassette via a boom box in my dorm room during its original airing).

It certainly didn't hurt that Pearl Jam was on fire and intensely focused that night at the Fabulous Fox (a venue that saw Lynyrd Skynyrd record their classic 1976 concert album, *One More from the Road*), dishing up a seemingly never-ending set (26 tracks total!) that opened with "Release" and closed with "Indifference," and included all the classics up to that point ("Rearviewmirror," "Jeremy," "Animal," and "Alive," among others.). Also, listeners got a taste of what was to come on the band's third album, *Vitalogy*, with airings of the yet-to-be-released "Whipping," "Better Man," and "Satan's Bed."

But what made this performance stand out from the rest were a few interesting little quirks, such as the line "I love God" being replaced by "I love Frogs" (in reference to the rock band) in "Glorified G," lyrics from Pink Floyd's "Another Brick in the Wall (Part 2)" inserted at the end of "Daughter," Vedder dedicating "Go" to Kurt Cobain (as Cobain's whereabouts were unknown at the time, and he would be found dead only five days later), Doug Pinnick and Jerry Gaskill of King's X guesting on "W.M.A.," and a snatch of the guitar riff to Kiss' "Detroit Rock City" played just before "Porch," among other treats. And if all the live rock 'n' roll wasn't enough, Vedder played DJ for a period of time immediately after the show's conclusion (playing tunes by King's X, the Frogs, Sonic Youth, Mudhoney, Shudder to Think, and Rollins Band, among others.

Always looking to give their fans the most bang for their buck, when a single was released on May 16, 1994, for "Dissident" in the U.S., it was issued over three separate CDs, and included almost the entire Fox Theatre performance as a B-side (only *Vitalogy* material and a cover of "Sonic Reducer" were left on the cutting-room floor). One final significant fact concerning the Fox performance: it was one of the last PJ shows with Dave Abbruzzese on drums (he would play only seven more shows with the band before being excused that summer). The success and popularity of the broadcast soon led to further radio explorations for the band, which just so happens, we will discuss next.

62 Self Pollution Radio / Monkeywrench Radio

Having obviously enjoyed his first on-air DJ gig after the Fox Theatre performance and with *Vitalogy* having just been released almost exactly a month earlier, what better way to promote the album than by having Eddie Vedder spin some more of his favorite tunes, in addition to live performances by Pearl Jam and other notable Seattle bands?

Taking place on January 8, 1995, *Self Pollution Radio* was offered via satellite for free to radio stations across the United States. The four-and-a-half-hour show originated from a rehearsal space in downtown Seattle, and once again showed how much Pearl Jam embraced unconventionality.

What fans heard that night were live performances by the Fastbacks (the songs "On Your Hands," "Run No More," "Old Address of the Unknown"), Mudhoney ("Judgement, Rage, Retribution and Thyme," "Generation Spokesmodel," "What Moves the Heart"), Mad Season ("Lifeless Dead," "I Don't Know Anything"), and Soundgarden ("Blind Dogs," "Fell on Black Days," "Kyle Petty, Son of Richard," "No Attention"). And of course, a whole lotta PJ ("Spin the Black Circle," "Satan's Bed," "Corduroy," "Not for You," "Immortality," "Last Exit," "Blood," "Tremor Christ," "Porch," "Indifference"). Also, special guest Krist Novoselic dropped by to chat (and read from a book), phone calls were placed (to the Frogs' Dennis Flemion, Mike Watt, and L7's Dee Plakas), and many other tunes were spun (Sonic Youth's "Teenage Riot," Wesley Willis' "They Threw Me Out of Church," the Who's "Tattoo"). Luckily, someone on site was equipped with a video camera, so all it takes is a virtual trip to YouTube to view some of the shenanigans from that day.

Three years later, the time was right for another PJ satellite broadcast offered free to radio stations that expressed interest—this time from a warehouse in Seattle on January 31, 1998 (the *PJ 20* book lists the actual address as 225 Terry Avenue North), and going by the name of *Monkeywrench Radio*. One hour shorter than its predecessor, the program again featured live performances, including a return appearance by Mudhoney, plus Brad, Tuatara, and Zeke, along with a healthy helping of Pearl Jam ("Do the Evolution," "Given to Fly," "Pilate," "Wishlist," "Brain of J," "In Hiding," "Spin the Black Circle," "Nothingman").

Additionally, listeners were again treated to phone conversations (Gloria Steinem and Mike Watt), and a wide variety of other songs (The Ramones' "Rock and Roll Radio," Sleater-Kinney's "Dig Me Out," Hot Chocolate's "You Sexy Thing") throughout the broadcast. Unfortunately, unlike its predecessor, not a lot of video has surfaced from *Monkeywrench Radio*; the only footage readily available is PJ's rendition of "Do the Evolution," which combines *Monkeywrench* footage with animation from the song's music video.

Despite both programs being successful, Pearl Jam has yet to assemble another radio offering. But according to a quote from Jeff Ament in the *PJ 20* book, that all may change someday: "We need to do that again!" he said.

Read, Watch, and Listen to *Pearl Jam Twenty*

There have been quite a few Pearl Jam books issued over the years, but never a fully authorized one. Nor has there ever been an authorized career-spanning documentary about the band. But that all changed in 2011, with the arrival of a coffee table book and documentary of the same title—*Pearl Jam Twenty*. As its title alludes to, 2011 marked the 20th anniversary of the release of PJ's classic debut album, *Ten*, so what better way to mark this important career milestone than with a no-stone-unturned-styled look back?

The book portion of the two-part equation was issued on September 13 and published by Simon & Schuster. Its hefty 384 pages were authored by Jonathan Cohen and Mark Wilkerson, while the book's foreword was provided by old PJ pal Cameron Crowe. Set up chronologically and comprised of 37 interviews set largely in the oral history format, with contributions from all band members past and present, plus manager Kelly Curtis, Neil Young, Bruce Springsteen, Pete Townshend, Dave Grohl, Chris Cornell, and many more, the book is also crammed with oodles of previously unseen photographs. The last entry is marked December 1, 2010, so when the sad day comes when Pearl Jam is no more, an updated version will be in order.

Premiering in the U.S. on September 20, the documentary impressively matched the promise of the book. Directed by Crowe, the two-hour doc does a superb job of telling the band's story both visually and sonically, featuring vintage concert clips, behind-the-scenes footage (much of which is seen for the first time here, as PJ has always been quite a secretive bunch post-'93), and all-new interviews with all of the current band members and Chris Cornell (plus archival quotes from Kurt Cobain and Neil Young). Standout scenes include Vedder being presented with the actual *Momma-Son* cassette that got the PJ story rolling in the first place, footage of one of the band's first shows (December 22, 1990), and exploring the tough subjects of Cobain's suicide and the Roskilde tragedy, among others.

A two-disc soundtrack for the film was also issued on September 19, covering the band's first two decades and comprised of both live renditions of classics and obscurities, as well as rare demos. When issued on DVD and Blu-ray on October 24 (after it was premiered on PBS' *American Masters* three days earlier), *Pearl Jam Twenty* proved to be a solid seller, earning platinum certification in the United States. And for the hardcore fanatic, there was an extra digital-only release, *The Kids Are Twenty*, comprised of more than two hours of interviews and full-length live performances that didn't make the *PJ 20* cut, or had not been shown in their entirety.

Visit Easy Street Records

In the early 21ˢᵗ century, record store chains had become virtually extinct in the United States, the most obvious example being the complete collapse of the once-mighty Tower Records. But while the chains were going under, independent record shops soldiered on, and some even thrived. In Seattle, one such establishment is certainly Easy Street Records.

Founded in 1988 by Matt Vaughan, the store is located at 4559 California Avenue SW. The store has expanded its space over the years and now even reaches beyond just selling music—in 2001, they opened a café, so customers could also sip and nosh. There was also a somewhat short-lived second location in Queen Anne (which was also much larger than the original, albeit being café-less), which opened in 2002 and remained in business until shutting its doors for good in 2013.

So what does Easy Street Records have to do with Pearl Jam? It turns out that the members of the band are major fans (and customers) of the store, so much so that on April 25, 2005, PJ packed the California Ave. location for a performance. The occasion was to celebrate the fact that Easy Street was picked to host a national, 10-year anniversary conference for the Coalition of Independent Music Stores, which is an independent record retailers convention. An invite-only Pearl Jam performance was then arranged, which resulted in a memorable performance in front of 200 lucky individuals, captured for posterity in the release of a special EP, *Live at Easy Street*, which contained seven highlights from the band's set ("Half Full," "Lukin," a cover of the Avengers' "American in Me," "Save You," a cover of the Dead Kennedys' "Bleed for Me," a cover of X's "New World" featuring X's singer/bassist John Doe,

and "Porch." According to the store, two pressings of the CD have
sold out, and it is their best-selling title ever.

Pearl Jam has not been the only renowned artist to appear at
the store. Over the years, both locations of Easy Street have played
host for signings or performances from the likes of Lou Reed, Elvis
Costello, Patti Smith, Mudhoney, Tom Morello, the Black Keys,
Meat Puppets, the Sonics, Ben Harper, Cage the Elephant, and
Macklemore/Ryan Lewis, among many others. But undoubtedly,
the top highlight of the store's entire history was when yours truly
did a reading and signing for my *Grunge Is Dead* book on April
25, 2009!

It also became known in 2017 that none other than Eddie
Vedder once worked a spur-of-the-moment shift at Easy Street.
Speaking to Seattle radio station 107.7/The End, Vedder told a
remarkable story about how one day back in 1995, he was shop-
ping at the store, left to go to a bar, then came back to see a line
going up the street—with only a single worker, Clarke Canfield,
inside the store. Why the crowd? The Seattle Mariners would be
playing a one-game playoff against the California Angels at the
Kingdome, and it just so happened that Easy Street was the only
Ticketmaster-selling agent in West Seattle. Vedder automatically
leapt into action, returning to the store, offering his services to an
overwhelmed Canfield, and lending a hand behind the counter,
until a sense of calm could be reestablished and order restored.

Another ESR/PJ connection was made on April 29, 2017,
when the first "Pearl Jam Pop-Up Store" was announced at Easy
Street to celebrate that HBO was premiering footage of the band's
induction into the Rock and Roll Hall of Fame from earlier that
month. Available for purchase were all sorts of cool PJ-related
doodads—music, shirts, caps, books, mugs, and more.

 **Yield**

On Pearl Jam's first full-length album with drummer Jack Irons, 1996's *No Code*, the band took a stirring shift toward letting the percussion assume control on several tracks. But rather than following that path and/or exploring it further on the follow-up, *Yield*, it sounded as though Pearl Jam made a conscious decision to get back to their earlier sound.

The band united once again with Brendan O'Brien to help co-produce the album with them, the fourth PJ album in a row that saw O'Brien's name listed in the credits (and interestingly, his last with the band for quite some time). The material on *Yield* would be recorded between February and September 1997 at several different studios, including Studio Litho and Studio X in Seattle and Southern Tracks Recording and Doppler Studios, in Atlanta.

Straight away, you're walloped with a raging rocker, "Brain of J." (the "J." in question short for JFK), but instead of offering a relentless one-two punch as they did with *Vs.* (which saw "Go" followed by "Animal"), the intensity is turned down a notch for one of the album's best tunes, "Faithful." It seemed like Pearl Jam was out to flaunt their mellower mood by the two tunes they selected for singles—"Given to Fly" and "Wishlist." Then, just when you start feeling drowsy, you are offered one of the top rockers of the entire disc, "Do the Evolution."

Released on February 3, 1998, the album cover for *Yield* consisted of a color photograph featuring a stretch of a desolate landscape and a highway that stretches on indefinitely. To the right of the cover image, you will spot a YIELD street sign, providing the album's title. And if you're ever interested in taking a road trip and trying to locate the exact spot where this photo was taken,

Yield, *Pearl Jam,*
1998. (Epic)

according to a fan going by the username "maverick" on the discussion boards of the official Pearl Jam site, the coordinates are "Rt 200 29 miles east of Lincoln [Nebraska] just past mile marker 100." Just don't look for a YIELD sign to mark the spot—it was likely edited into the photograph.

Yield marked the first Pearl Jam album since *Ten* to spawn a music video—and in this case, they picked a song that was not even a single, "Do the Evolution." The video was an entirely animated clip, co-directed by Todd McFarlane and Kevin Altieri. Also, the album would prove to be the last PJ studio offering to feature Irons on drums—who would abruptly quit the band mid-tour and be replaced by their old pal Matt Cameron (still fresh off Soundgarden's breakup). Lastly, *Yield* was the first PJ album since *Ten* to not top the Billboard 200 (albeit peaking at an oh-so-close No. 2), but did manage to go the distance on the Australian, Mexican, New Zealand, and Norwegian album charts—and successfully matched the platinum certification of its predecessor stateside.

66 Drummer No. 5

When Matt Cameron accepted an invitation to join Pearl Jam in 1998, he brought some much-needed steadiness to the lineup, as the group's rotating cast of drummers up to that point was second only to Spinal Tap. And if you were to pick *the* drummer of grunge, it would undoubtedly be Cameron, as he has provided the backbeat for numerous notable bands from Seattle—Pearl Jam, Soundgarden, Temple of the Dog, Wellwater Conspiracy, Hater, and Skin Yard.

Born on November 28, 1962, in San Diego, California, Cameron began playing drums professionally at the age of 14. He was influenced by the usual suspects of the day, including Queen and Kiss; concerning the latter, he played in a local tribute band saluting the self-proclaimed "hottest band in the land," complete with makeup and costumes. He relocated to Seattle in 1983, and by 1985, Cameron was a member of Skin Yard, a group often credited as being one of the earliest grunge bands and featuring none other than Jack Endino on guitar—the man who would become best known as a producer for Soundgarden and Nirvana.

But it was when Cameron joined Soundgarden in 1986, replacing early drummer Scott Sundquist, that he had truly met his musical match. Until the band's split in 1997, Cameron would play on a pair of EPs (1987's *Screaming Life* and 1988's *Fopp*), as well as five full-lengths (1988's *Ultramega OK*, 1989's *Louder Than Love*, 1991's *Badmotorfinger*, 1994's *Superunkown*, and 1996's *Down on the Upside*), and after their reunion in 2010, one more album (2012's *King Animal*). It was during this time that Soundgarden became one of the top dogs of hard rock, with Cameron lending a major hand in the songwriting department, including co-authoring such classics as "Jesus Christ Pose," "Room a Thousand Years Wide," "Birth Ritual," and "By Crooked Steps," among others.

And despite being quite busy with Soundgarden, Cameron found time for several extracurricular projects, including Temple of the Dog, Hater, and Wellwater Conspiracy. However, with Soundgarden's split in '97, Cameron found himself a free agent... but not for long, as he recounted to *Spin* magazine in 2001: "I got a phone call out of the blue, from Mr. Ed Ved, Stoney, and Kelly. I was ambushed. It was really short notice. He called and said, 'Hey what are you doing this summer?'"

As a replacement for Jack Irons in Pearl Jam, Cameron has played on a total of five studio albums (2000's *Binaural*, 2002's *Riot Act*, 2006's self-titled, 2009's *Backspacer*, and 2013's *Lightning Bolt*), and just as he had with Soundgarden, has made his presence felt in the songwriting department, co-writing such standouts as "Save You," "You Are," and "The Fixer," among others. And while he's best known for his work with Soundgarden, Pearl Jam, and Temple of the Dog, he has also appeared on recordings by a variety of other renowned artists, including Smashing Pumpkins (1998's *Adore* and 2001's *Judas O*), The Prodigy (1997's *The Fat of the Land*), Tony Iommi (2000's *Iommi*), and Geddy Lee (2000's *My Favourite Headache*).

67 Collect the Official Bootlegs

In the pre-Internet era, bootleg recordings of live concerts could be big business for those crafty individuals who managed to sneak a recording device into a concert. But with music listeners now able to download files over the Internet or stream concerts, having to pay overblown prices for a bootleg record, tape, or CD is not as appealing as it once was.

Pearl Jam has always been open to allowing fans to tape their shows, and upon the dawn of the 21ˢᵗ century, the band decided—to borrow a quote from the late, great Frank Zappa—to "beat the boots," by exercising some quality control and getting into the bootleg biz themselves. As a result, since 2000 (circa the tour in support of *Binaural*), Pearl Jam has issued countless recordings as part of their "official bootleg" series, and have reaped the financial rewards—a *Billboard* article way back in 2008 quoted the number of live albums that PJ had sold at 3.5 million.

As of this book's publication, countless shows are available for purchase on iTunes from the following tours: Europe 2000, North America 2000, North America 2003, Japan and Australia 2003, North America 2006, North America 2008, South America 2013, and North America 2013. And if you're in the mood for some vintage PJ, there is a "From the Vault" series that specializes in such blasts from the past as *Seattle, WA 17-January-1992*, *New York, NY 31-December-1992*, and *Washington, DC 19-September-1998*. And for even more shows and tours to choose from, there is a "bootlegs" page on Pearl Jam's official site, where you can purchase as many CDs or digital downloads of concerts that your senses can handle.

And if you just don't have the time nor patience to sift through the seemingly endless amount of bootleg recordings being offered, another option is to stick with such official live releases as 1998's *Live on Two Legs* (which includes standout performances from the band's summer tour that year in support of *Yield*) or 2011's more expansive *Live on Ten Legs* (which is comprised of standout performances spanning 2003 to 2011).

68 Gold and Platinum

Prior to the advent of downloading and streaming, the commercial success of a given album was measured by record sales. Seemingly every month, a rock band was storming the charts with a new multi-platinum album; as of the early 21st century, an album merely reaching gold status is reason to pop the champagne corks.

For those unfamiliar with this "platinum speak," the Recording Industry Association of America (RIAA) certifies an album gold for half a million sales, platinum for 1 million, double platinum for 2 million, and so on. During the 1990s, sales were so booming that a new certification was created—the Diamond Award—which marked 10 million copies sold of an album or single. And as most people reading this book are aware, Pearl Jam—especially early in their career—sold a gargantuan amount of albums throughout the world, and especially within the United States of America.

The best-selling album of Pearl Jam's career is, unsurprisingly, the band's landmark debut, 1991's *Ten*, which peaked at No. 2 on the Billboard 200, and at last count (March 31, 2009) has sold 13 million copies, making it the only PJ album to obtain the cherished Diamond Award. According to businessinsider.com, as of 2016, *Ten* is the 36th best-selling album of all time (sandwiched between the Boss' *Bruce Springsteen & The E Street Band Live 1975–85* and Prince's *Purple Rain*).

The next-best-selling PJ album was 1993's *Vs.*, which topped the Billboard 200 for an impressive five straight weeks, and at last count (May 24, 2000) is sitting pretty at 7 million copies sold. Next on the list is 1994's *Vitalogy*, another chart-topper that racked up 5 million albums sold (as of October 13, 1995).

From that point forward, sales of Pearl Jam albums dipped considerably, with not a single album earning multi-platinum status. Of course, this was somewhat self-inflicted, as the band refused to film any music videos from 1993 to 1997, and failed to launch a major tour during their battle with Ticketmaster. That said, 1996's *No Code* (which also hit No. 1 on the Billboard 200), 1998's *Yield* (No. 2), and 1998's *Live on Two Legs* (No. 15) each received platinum certification, while 2000's *Binaural* (No. 2), 2002's *Riot Act* (No. 5), 2006's *Pearl Jam* (No. 2), and 2009's *Backspacer* (No. 1) all peaked at the gold certification mark. The band's 2013 release, *Lightning Bolt* (No. 1), is the first PJ album to not receive a single certification—a baffling fact considering its chart-topping status.

When it comes to long-form video certifications, 1998's *Single Video Theory* (No. 2), 2001's *Touring Band 2000* (No. 1), and 2011's *Pearl Jam Twenty* (No. 1) have all gone platinum, while 2003's triple-platinum *Live at the Garden* (No. 2) is the best-selling of the bunch; 2007's *Immagine in Cornice* (No. 1) went gold. Singles certifications? "Jeremy" (No. 79, 1992), "Merkin Ball" (No. 7, 1995), and "Last Kiss" (No. 2, 1999) struck gold, while "Just Breathe" (No. 78, 2009) hit platinum.

And what about compilations, you ask? The 2003 double-disc rarities comp *Lost Dogs* (No. 15) went gold, while 2004's double-disc *Rearviewmirror (Greatest Hits 1991–2003)* (No. 16), peaked at platinum. So, the facts certainly speak for themselves—over the years, Pearl Jam has earned plenty of metal.

Backstage Pass

Chuck Mosley
Faith No More, Singer

I recall you telling me that Eddie Vedder was one of your favorite singers. What makes him so special?

His voice, because it's a baritone. That's what I like. I don't really like any tenors—I like more alto-sopranos. But some of them I like—Stevie Wonder is a tenor. And I like a lot of Eddie Vedder's lyrics. I'd be like, "Why didn't I think of that?" or "That's something I would say."

Would you say he's one of your all-time favorite singers?

I'm old, man, so I've got a lot of people that I like. He's definitely in the top 30, probably. But I like a lot of people from way back—Billie Holiday, Patsy Cline, Michael Jackson, Stevie Wonder, Robert Plant, Ozzy Osbourne, Isaac Hayes, Melvin Franklin from the Temptations. David Bowie is my all-time favorite. There's a lot, but he's definitely up there.

What is it about Eddie's voice that makes it unique?

You can hear his soul. And he's honest. And it makes me laugh when he does that [imitates a Vedder croon]. I just like the tonality of it. And I totally look up to anybody that can stay in tune 100 percent of the time. I know I struggle with it. And I know I've been called out on that a million times—it's no secret that everybody says I'm not the perfect singer. But that's my charm. I don't sing out of tune on purpose, but I always admire and look up to anybody who can pull it off. Because I was never a singer before I started singing. [Mosley was a keyboardist before joining Faith No More.]

Why do you think Eddie was one of the most copied singers in the 1990s?

Every time one band comes out and makes a huge splash—like Nirvana or Pearl Jam, or Faith No More back in the '80s—there are a thousand bands that come out just like them. Because that's a formula thing that's half the fault of the record companies, and half the bands that are just so fanatic about them, they just want to be just like them, and they don't even realize they're being just like them. It happens all the time. And then out of that thousand, there's like, maybe 10 of them that break out that you know about. For that one in particular, it would be like, "Okay, now we've got to get a band, but we've got to get a singer that's a baritone, so he sounds like Eddie Vedder." *What?* That's too much thought put into it. [Laughs] Do you know any bands that had singers that were "tenor" that copied them?

Darius Rucker from Hootie and the Blowfish comes to mind.
He did! You're absolutely right. Eddie Vedder sounds...well, he kind of tries to sound soulful. But you're totally right, he did it in that one song [sings a bit of Hootie's "Only Wanna Be with You"]. I actually sound like a baritone Ethel Merman. [Laughs] Having said that, Eddie reminds me of that too, a little bit, now that I say that—but in a totally respectful way. I love him to death. I love his voice. You know who *really* sounds like Ethel Merman? Axl Rose!

Loosegroove Records

In the wake of Pearl Jam's massive success with *Ten*, Stone Gossard found himself with a bit of discretionary income. And what better way to celebrate and enjoy the fruits of his labor than to form his own record label with old pal Regan Hagar (ex-drummer of Malfunkshun)? In addition to serving as the heads of Loosegroove Records, Gossard and Hagar were bandmates in the band Brad— in fact, the first time the "Loosegroove" name ever appeared on a recording was the debut release from Brad, *Shame*, in 1993 (as a doodle on the inlay where the CD fits).

After Brad's debut, the label seemed to focus mostly on artists specializing in funky sounds, as well as good old-fashioned rock 'n' roll—including releases by Devilhead (which featured both of Andrew Wood's brothers, Brian and Kevin), Critters Buggin (which included onetime Pearl Jam drummer Matt Chamberlain), Weapon of Choice (featuring singer/bassist Lonnie Marshall, brother of onetime Red Hot Chili Peppers guitarist Arik Marshall), a compilation of vintage recordings from Malfunkshun (1995's *Return to Olympus*), and the solo debut by Urge Overkill's Nash Kato (2000's *Debutante*), among others.

But the best-known Loosegroove release is undoubtedly the self-titled debut by Queens of the Stone Age, issued in 1998. Fresh out of the band Kyuss, this was guitarist Josh Homme's first foray into being the undisputed leader of a band and handling lead vocals. The results were extraordinary, as evidenced by such tunes as "Regular John," "Avon," "If Only," and "You Would Know," which are now considered QOTSA standards. And while the album did not exactly set the charts alight upon its initial release, today it is looked upon as a classic release (especially within the "stoner rock" genre) and set the stage for 2000's *Rated R* and 2002's commercial breakthrough, *Songs for the Deaf.*

And while the label should be commended for going after artists who were off the beaten path (especially during an era when most bands on rock radio were mind-numbingly similar in sound), shortly after the dawn of the 21st century, Loosegroove Records would unfortunately go kaput.

70 Soundtracks

Pearl Jam has appeared on quite a few motion picture soundtracks over the years, mostly offering tunes that were exclusive to the specific project. Here, I will try my darndest to neatly categorize and make sense of them all, in chronological order.

PJ started off their soundtrack career with an absolute bang in 1992, when they pitched in a pair of tunes penned back during the *Ten* era, "Breath" and "State of Love and Trust," for Cameron Crowe's film *Singles*. Besides both songs being winners, the songs are significant in the band's history, as it was the last time Rick Parashar worked with PJ in a production capacity.

Up next was a rap-rock tune for the 1993 film *Judgment Night*, "Real Thing." Now, before you start fretting about the proposition of Eddie Vedder attempting to spit out some rhymes, the song was a collaboration between Pearl Jam and Cypress Hill, who handled the vocals. Two years later, PJ joined singer/writer Jim Carroll on a song he penned, "Catholic Boy," for a film based on Carroll's troubled life: *The Basketball Diaries*, starring Leonardo DiCaprio. Pearl Jam had offered a preview of the tune—albeit Carroll-less—on their *Self Pollution Radio* broadcast earlier the same year.

Hype!, the critically acclaimed grunge documentary, was released in 1996, and Pearl Jam offered their rendition of "Not for You" from their aforementioned *Self Pollution Radio* broadcast for the soundtrack. (Video of the performance is also included in the film.) Notably, it was one of the only times in Pearl Jam's entire career that they would work with the label most closely associated with grunge, Sub Pop. (The band also contributed a live rendition of "Even Flow" for the label's 2000 comp, *Wild and Wooly: The Northwest Rock Collection.*)

PJ's next soundtrack appearance would take place in 1998, when a Vedder/Gossard original, the slow-burning "Hard to Imagine," appeared in the film *Chicago Cab.* Interestingly, the version of the tune for the film was an outtake from the *Vitalogy* sessions, but the song was originally recorded for *Vs.* (the earlier version would turn up on the 2003 odds-and-ends collection *Lost Dogs*). Come 2003, Pearl Jam was ready to take the soundtrack plunge once more, this time for Tim Burton's *Big Fish*, to which they contributed "Man of the Hour." It became such a fan favorite that it would eventually find its way onto the *Rearviewmirror (Greatest Hits 1991–2003)* collection. Stacy Peralta's 2004 documentary about surfing, *Riding Giants*, saw the opener of *Vs.*, "Go," get dusted off and included on the soundtrack, while another surf-related film, the computer-animated mockumentary comedy *Surf's Up*, recycled a standout track from Pearl Jam's 2006 self-titled album, "Big Wave," a year later.

While that's it for Pearl Jam's soundtrack work up to this point, Eddie Vedder has contributed to quite a few more as a solo artist over the years. And just as Pearl Jam hit a home run in their first soundtrack appearance, Vedder did the same with his first solo contribution to a film. Of course, I'm talking about the classic *Dead Man Walking*, which featured outstanding acting performances by both Sean Penn and Susan Sarandon, and included two exceptional Middle Eastern–tinged Vedder tunes, "Face of Love" and "The Long Road," which saw him teamed with legendary Pakistani vocalist Nusrat Fateh Ali Khan (a singer who the late Jeff Buckley once praised as being his "Elvis").

Vedder's next soundtrack appearance would be another pairing, this time with Sarandon as his duet partner, on the old timey "Croon Spoon" from the *Cradle Will Rock* soundtrack in 1999.

Although best known as an actress, Sarandon proves to have a good singing voice, though that shouldn't come as a surprise to longtime fans of the cult-classic, *The Rocky Horror Picture Show*.

For his next solo soundtrack appearance, Vedder covered the Beatles' "You've Got to Hide Your Love Away" for the film *I Am Sam* (which starred his old Penn pal), which was comprised entirely of artists covering Fab Four classics. That was followed by a curious "credit" on the song "Lucky Country" for the 2004 surf documentary *The 5th Document*. Although the tune is credited to Red Whyte, Kelly Slater, and Eddie Vedder, in reality, Vedder's contribution is just casually chatting with some folks at the beginning of the song.

Come 2006, Vedder inadvertently gave a sneak preview of the direction he would pursue on his sophomore solo album, by offering the song "Goodbye"—comprised of only voice and ukulele—for the soundtrack to another documentary surf film, *A Brokedown Melody*. Next, Vedder (credited as "Eddie Vedder & The Million Dollar Bashers") covered a tune originally penned by Bob Dylan but made famous by Jimi Hendrix, "All Along the Watchtower," for the 2007 Dylan-inspired film *I'm Not There*.

The same year, Vedder offered his first full-length solo album that also doubled as the soundtrack for the film *Into the Wild*.

71 Watch *Hype!*

Grunge music was one of the most talked about topics in pop culture during the 1990s. However, there was no documentary that told the complete story. That all changed in 1996 with the arrival of *Hype!* Directed by Doug Pray (a UCLA film student who had directed music videos for such obscure Seattle groups as Flop and the Young Fresh Fellows), the nearly 90-minute documentary was shot between 1993 and 1994, and features vintage footage as well as interviews with some of the major contributors to the movement, including Soundgarden, Mudhoney, Screaming Trees, Seven Year Bitch, Jack Endino, and Charles Peterson, among others.

In an interview with the *Lip TV* in 2013, Pray recalled what made him want to do the documentary in the first place:

I had some really good friends who lived in Seattle during its '80s heyday, before I started filming, who were in bands who are well known in Seattle, and I visited there a few times and it was always just—I lived in San Francisco at the time, which is of course a great music city—and I just was totally blown away by the intensity of Seattle's music community. It was way richer. It was just phenomenal to me. And I remember saying that and thinking that.

And then later, it got famous, and then I was approached by a producer saying, "Hey, let's do a movie about the Seattle music scene," and I thought there would be 20 of them being done. And the more we got into it, the more I talked to my friends and they talked to their friends, and the more I just kept talking to everybody in that community, the more I started realizing, "You know what? Nobody is really doing this film." Everybody is covering the scene like it's Liverpool, but nobody is really doing this film, which would be more honest, like, "What is it like when a scene gets discovered? What is it like on the inside? What does it mean?" That's why it's named *Hype!* and that's what it became.

In addition to the interviews, you will find some great concert footage, including Nirvana's first-ever live performance of "Smells Like Teen Spirit," Mudhoney's "Touch Me I'm Sick," and Soundgarden's "Searching with My Good Eye Closed." But one of the main standouts for Pearl Jam fans is snippets of an interview with Eddie Vedder (sitting next to his first wife, Beth Liebling) throughout the film, as well as a morsel of a Hovercraft rehearsal. The chat was conducted when Vedder was still coming to terms with being in one of the world's most successful rock bands; he talks about what made him feel guilty about the success of his band, the humor of the grunge bands, and how many of the local bands of Seattle were not in it for the money, among other topics. And toward the end, a live rendition of "Not for You" (recorded at the *Self Pollution Radio* live broadcast in 1995) is thrown in for good measure.

When *Hype!* was first released, Siskel and Ebert gave it two thumbs up, and it caught the attention of both the Sundance Film Festival and South by Southwest. It won Best Documentary at the Seattle International Film Festival, which resulted in a home video release a year later. Additionally, *Rolling Stone* placed the film at No. 10 on a Top 25 Music DVDs of All Time list. *Hype!* was first issued on home video in 1996 (along with a 23-song soundtrack) before being reissued as a collector's edition by Shout! Factory in 2017, on DVD and Blu-ray.

72 *Binaural*

With Pearl Jam's albums selling fewer and fewer copies post-*Ten*, something unexpected transpired in 1999: they had a bonafide hit single, "Last Kiss" (which was first issued as a B-side to their 1998 Ten Club Christmas single, then included on the *No Boundaries: A Benefit for the Kosovar Refugees* compilation). For many artists, this would quite possibly result in their next album embracing a more "pop-friendly" sound, in hopes of keeping this winning streak going. Not Pearl Jam. Their next studio full-length, *Binaural*, recorded entirely at Studio Litho in Seattle from September 1999 to January 2000, was released on May 16, 2000, and it made clear that the band was uninterested in chasing commercial success.

The cover image of *Binaural* is a telescopic photo of the Engraved Hourglass Nebula, which is located in the southern constellation Musca, in case you ever feel like dropping by for a visit. It was the first Pearl Jam album since *Ten* that Brendan O'Brien was not listed as co-producer; Tchad Blake would get the nod, along with the band. It was the recording technique that has become a trademark for Blake—binaural recording—that inspired the album's title.

According to the DPA Microphones website, the principles of the binaural stereo technique are as follows: "Binaural recordings are often used as ambience sound or in virtual reality applications. This two-channel system emulates the human perception of sound, and will provide the recording with important aural information about the distance and the direction of the sound sources. Required to be played back on headphones, binaural stereo offers the listener the experience of a spherical sound image, where all the sound sources are reproduced with correct spherical direction." If all this

Binaural, *Pearl Jam,*
2000. (Epic)

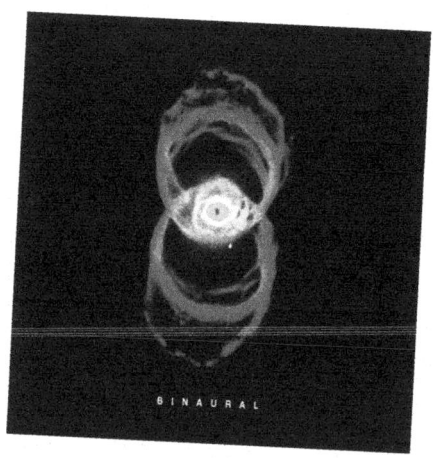

technical mumbo jumbo has left you puzzled, don't worry—you don't have to invest in a special sound system to enjoy Pearl Jam's sixth studio album. It sounds just dandy on traditional speakers or earphones.

Binaural is also the first Pearl Jam studio album to feature the drumming talents of Matt Cameron. And as he did with Soundgarden, Cameron also proved to be a valuable asset in the songwriting department, penning all the music to a rocker known as "Evacuation."

Elsewhere, you'll find that PJ kept their string for exceptional album-openers intact, this time with "Breakerfall" (which contains a pleasantly surprising Roger McGuinn–like 12-string guitar motif). What follows runs the gamut from brash rockers ("God's Dice," "Grievance") to brooding tunes ("Sleight of Hand," "Parting Ways") to songs that lie somewhere between the two ("Insignificance," "Rival"). As for which tracks were lucky enough to be released as singles, two mid-paced selections—"Nothing as It Seems" (which contains some great slow-burn solos from Mike McCready) and "Light Years"—proved to be ripe for the picking.

After dipping their toes back in the treacherous waters of video-making for "Do the Evolution" on their previous album, it's understandable if fans assumed the band would release more videos for this record. But no such luck. The band was not oblivious to the fact that making videos might result in more album sales, as McCready recalled in the *Pearl Jam Twenty* documentary: "Around this time, I think we were less popular. I don't think we were doing any press. We had meetings about those things, like, 'How far are we going to do press on this tour? Are we going to do this? Are we going to do that? Or are we not going to do any of it?' And when you don't do any of it and the changing times fluctuate, people get over you. That's probably around that time—*Binaural*. People are like, 'Okay, I'm kind of over these guys. What's next?'"

To the casual Pearl Jam fan, *Binaural* may be the album that elicits the most perplexed looks when mentioned in conversation. And while the album didn't do the type of business that many of the bands making a career out of regurgitating the *Ten* sound were, it still made its presence felt on the charts—peaking at No. 2 on the Billboard 200 just as its predecessor had (while hitting the top of the Australian, New Zealand, and Portuguese album charts), and managing gold certification stateside.

And the Winner Is...

When a musical artist enjoys a long and successful career, awards from the industry have a tendency to follow. That is indeed the case with Pearl Jam, as they have either been nominated or have won numerous awards over the years.

The American Music Awards, originally created by Dick Clark back in 1973, have been the most kind to Pearl Jam: they have taken home a total of five awards, twice winning two awards on the same night (1993 for both Favorite Pop/Rock New Artist and Favorite New Heavy Metal/Hard Rock Artist, and again in 1996 for both Favorite Alternative Artist and Favorite Heavy Metal/Hard Rock Artist), as well as an award in 1999 for Favorite Alternative Artist.

The most distinguished award an artist can win is the Grammy, presented annually by the National Academy of Recording Arts and Sciences. But despite receiving a whopping 15 nominations since 1993, Pearl Jam has only taken home two trophies: 1996 for Best Hard Rock Performance for "Spin the Black Circle," and again in 2015 for Best Recording Package for *Lightning Bolt*.

Why hasn't PJ taken home more Grammys over the years? Maybe, just maybe, it has something to do Eddie Vedder's acceptance speech when the band won in '96. Whereas most winners are happy to fete the Academy and the music industry at large, Vedder spoke honestly about an "institution" that has fumbled the ball time and time again over the years: "I don't know what this means. I don't think it means anything. That's just how I feel. There's too many bands, and you've heard it all before…but my dad would have liked it. My dad died before I got to know him and he would have liked it, so that's why I'm here. Thanks…*I guess.*"

That wasn't the only award show Vedder has been lukewarm about over the years. Take, for example, MTV, and their sacred Video Music Awards. In 1993 alone, PJ earned four wins out of a possible five, when the "Jeremy" video was awarded Video of the Year, Best Group Video, Best Metal/Hard Rock Video, and Best Direction. But when accepting the award for Best Group Video, Vedder put it all perfectly into perspective: "I don't know how you could say it was 'the best.' It's just a little piece of art. You can't really put art into a competition, y'know?"

Pearl Jam has won lesser-known awards and earned placements on a magazine's best-of list so many times you could probably write a mini-book about just those. But just as a taste, some of the more intriguing ones include winning an Esky Award (awarded annually by *Esquire* magazine) for Best Live Act, "Jeremy" coming in at No. 48 on *Rolling Stone*'s "The 100 Greatest Pop Songs Since the Beatles" list, "Alive" being placed at No. 26 on *Total Guitar*'s "100 Hottest Guitar Solos," "Rearviewmirror" being one of many tunes earning a spot on *Q*'s "The Ultimate Music Collection," "World Wide Suicide" arriving at No. 54 on *New York Post*'s "206 Best Songs to Download of 2006," and the entire band being named Planet Defenders by *Rock the Earth*, among countless other honors.

74 The Corduroy Jacket

Whenever a rock movement first becomes popular, you can expect many fans of the style will soon adopt a similar fashion to the musicians from the bands—gentlemen growing their hair long like the Beatles, punk rockers adopting leather jackets and ripped jeans à la the Ramones, or hair metallists squeezing into spandex trousers and sculpting heavily hairsprayed, mile-high hair. When the grunge movement hit, things were no different. Seemingly overnight, countless fans of Pearl Jam, Soundgarden, Nirvana, and Alice in Chains began wearing Doc Marten boots (à la Chris Cornell) and flannel shirts (à la Kurt Cobain).

One look that became specifically ascribed to Pearl Jam was a corduroy jacket that Eddie Vedder bought at a thrift store and wore for most of 1992 (as seen in the *Unplugged* performance, the "Jeremy" video, the MTV Video Music Awards performance that year, and various performances at Lollapalooza that summer). In fact, it was such a hot item at one point that a few fellow rockers were spotted wearing a similar jacket (including the Lemonheads' Evan

Dando), and clothing companies began selling a replica for prices far higher than what Vedder paid for it originally (in the *PJ 20* book, a photo of the jacket's price tag is included, with a style description of simply "'70s Jacket," size medium, and a price tag of $24).

By 1993, Eddie had retired his infamous jacket, but it would serve as the inspiration for one of the standout tracks on 1994's *Vitalogy*, "Corduroy." Speaking to the AV Club website in 2002, he explained, "That song was based on a remake of the brown corduroy jacket that I wore. I think I got mine for 12 bucks, and it was being sold for like $650. [Laughs] The ultimate one as far as being co-opted was that there was a guy on TV, predictably patterned, I guess, after the way I was looking those days, with long hair and an Army T-shirt. They put this new character on a soap opera, so there was a guy, more handsome than I, parading around on *General Hospital*. And the funny thing is, that guy was Ricky Martin."

In the *PJ 20* book, Jeff Ament recalled an amusing story about confronting two designers—Marc Jacobs and Anna Sui—who had released a "grunge line" that included a $300 replica corduroy jacket, in NYC on New Year's Eve 1992: "I went down, did a fake fashion twirl, and went, 'Hey, Marc, what do you think of this for the next line?' I was probably wearing red velvet shorts and tights. We were young and full of shit and energy."

75 Victoria Williams

By now, you know well that the guys in Pearl Jam are good people, as evidenced by their philanthropic work and their standing up for causes they believe strongly in. One of the earliest signs that the band was all for helping others in need occurred in 1993, when they covered a song penned by singer/songwriter Victoria Williams for a tribute album designed to help offset her medical costs as she battled multiple sclerosis.

Born on December 23, 1958, in Shreveport, Louisiana, Williams issued a pair of obscure solo albums (1987's *Happy Come Home* and 1990's *Swing the Statue!*) that showcased a style best categorized as either alt-country or folk. In 1993, Williams was diagnosed with multiple sclerosis, and did not have any health coverage. As a result, several prominent artists united to cover songs penned by Williams for a tribute album, *Sweet Relief: A Benefit for Victoria Williams*, including Soul Asylum ("Summer of Drugs"), Lucinda Williams ("Main Road"), Lou Reed ("Tarbelly and Featherfoot"), and, of course, Pearl Jam ("Crazy Mary," which included Williams herself pitching in on backing vocals).

Almost instantly, "Crazy Mary" became a live favorite for Pearl Jam and their fans; they have performed the song more than 150 times in concert as of 2016. Two particular standout renditions include Williams joining PJ on stage on September 6, 1993, at the Portland Meadows Race Track in Portland, Oregon, and when PJ solely performed it on July 8, 2003, at Madison Square Garden in NYC, which was included on a DVD issued later the same year, *Live at the Garden*.

Speaking to the Songfacts site in 2016, Williams was asked who the real "Crazy Mary" was, to which she responded, "She is a fantasy I suppose I made up out of some facts…a very old black lady, she used to walk into Shreveport but would never get inside a moving automobile. One day, she met her demise when a car went out of control and slammed into her shack. That which you fear most can meet you halfway."

The song and tribute album succeeded in raising awareness about MS, and also led to Williams creating the Sweet Relief Musicians Fund to aid other musicians in need. Atlantic Records issued her third full-length, *Loose*, in 1994, which also included a version of

"Crazy Mary" (Williams had yet to record the track herself), as well as contributions by R.E.M.'s Mike Mills and Soul Asylum's Dave Pirner. Williams continued to issue solo albums on a semiregular basis until the early 21st century, while also recording and touring as part of the Original Harmony Ridge Creekdippers with her husband, singer/guitarist/songwriter Mark Olson. Pearl Jam's studio version of "Crazy Mary" would also be included as a bonus track on an expanded reissue of *Vs.* in 2011.

In 2015, Williams suffered a seizure, injuring her back and fracturing her shoulder, and a donation option was set up on the Sweet Relief website as once again, as her health insurance did not completely cover her recovery—a problem far too many Americans are dealing with in the 21st century.

76 Surfing, Basketball, and Skateboarding

Judging from the physicality on display during their concerts, it would appear that the members of Pearl Jam are quite an athletic bunch. In addition to all the running around, leaping through the air, and sweating it all out on stage, two members in particular are major fans and participants of surfing and basketball. Of course, I'm talking about Eddie Vedder and Jeff Ament, respectively. In fact, surfing played a major part in Vedder joining Pearl Jam in the first place, as it was during a morning surf in San Diego that the lyrics and storyline to what became the songs on the *Momma-Son* cassette ("Alive," "Once," and "Footsteps") came to him. Over the years, either video or photographic proof of Vedder surfing with pro surfers (such as Kelly Slater) and fellow musicians (such as

Jeff Ament skates at the new skate park he funded in his hometown of Big Sandy, Montana, 2010. (AP Images)

Stewart Copeland) has surfaced, but perhaps the biggest proof of all that Vedder enjoys surfing is that he owns a house in Hawaii!

However, the sport has also proven to be a bit hazardous for the singer. In March 1995, while out surfing with Tim Finn of Split Enz / Crowded House in New Zealand, Vedder was carried about 250 feet off coast and had to be guided back to shore by lifeguards. Ten years later, Vedder was almost lost at sea while trying to paddle from Molokai to Oahu, when the six-man canoe he was on overturned. Luckily, a father and daughter, Keith and Ashley Baxter, were boating nearby and rescued Vedder and his friends (inspiring Vedder to eventually pen the song "Future Days"). Another 10 years later, Vedder was able to repay Keith Baxter when it was brought to his attention that Baxter had been involved in a boating accident that nearly cost him his leg. A GoFundMe page was set up to cover treatments not covered by insurance and reached $70,000;

and Vedder and his PJ bandmates matched the amount, bringing the total to $140,000.

Basketball has proven to be a much safer hobby. The most obvious hint that the band fancied the sport was their choosing of Mookie Blaylock as their first name. Another early hint that Ament was a particularly passionate basketball fan was his wearing of Nike shirts, shorts, and high-top sneakers onstage, as well as playing a bass adorned with the names of NBA players he admired (and figurines of basketball players would be set atop his amplifier). Ament is a solid player himself; he was a standout on his high school team (the Big Sandy Pioneers), and also participated in two *Rock N' Jock* games on MTV.

When Seattle still had an NBA team—the SuperSonics—Ament could be spotted attending quite a few home games, and in the process befriended such players as Shawn Kemp and Frank Brickowski. But perhaps the most famous NBA player befriended by the band is Dennis Rodman. Although Rodman was constantly in the press and tabloids during his playing career and beyond, there is no denying he is one of the game's best rebounders. He also won five championships with the Detroit Pistons and Chicago Bulls. Rodman often turned up at PJ concerts, including as recently as the 2016 shows at Wrigley Field.

And a sport that both Vedder and Ament are admirers of is skateboarding. Eagle-eyed PJ fans have certainly seen a sticker on one of Vedder's Telecasters that states SKATEBOARDING IS NOT A CRIME, while there is a segment of Ament skateboarding in the *Immagine in Cornice* DVD. It turns out that Ament has been skating since 1976, after a visit to northern California, and his love for it has never diminished; he has helped open a dozen skate parks in Seattle, South Dakota, and throughout Montana. In 2014, all the members of Pearl Jam autographed a longboard for an auction to help fix up the 25-mile Ferry County Rail Trail in Washington. And in 2017, a limited-edition skateboard was manufactured by Alive and Well, which featured a classic PJ photo taken by Lance Mercer of Vedder dangling from the lighting truss at the Magnuson Park show in '92.

77 *Riot Act*

Following on the heels of the experimental *Binaural,* Pearl Jam seemed to make a conscious effort to get back to basics on their seventh studio album, *Riot Act,* which was recorded between February and May 2002 at Studio X and Space Studio in Seattle and dropped on November 12, 2002. One of the most obvious moves the band made was to replace Tchad Blake, co-producer of their previous offering, with Adam Kasper, who up to that point had worked on Soundgarden's *Down on the Upside,* the Foo Fighters' *There Is Nothing Left to Lose* and *One by One,* and Queens of the Stone Age's *Songs for the Deaf,* among other titles.

The cover of the CD version of *Riot Act* features a photo snapped by Jeff Ament of what appears to be two skeletons wearing crowns, while the cover for the vinyl version is of the same two figures photographed from a slightly different angle. By this point, PJ was fully prepared to embrace the music video medium once more—a total of five clips were shot at Seattle's Chop Suey club in September 2002. Directed by James Frost, the videos accompanied "I Am Mine," "Save You," "Love Boat Captain," "Thumbing My Way," and "½ Full." When it came to singles, four got the nod—"I Am Mine," "Bu$hleaguer," "Save You," and "Love Boat Captain."

"Can't Keep" opens the album with a composed vibe, but by this point in the PJ discography, you and I both know that by starting off the album in a restrained manner, it is only a matter of time until the

Riot Act, *Pearl Jam,*
2002. (Epic)

band cranks up the amps and lets it rip. *Riot Act* is no exception, as
the next song, "Save You," is indeed a rollicking rocker.

One of the album's most talked about tracks, "Love Boat
Captain," does a good job of highlighting the band's ability to start
slow before building momentum. The reason the tune has become
one of the most discussed over the years? The unfortunate events
that transpired at the 2000 Roskilde Festival served as an inspiration, especially in the lyrics, "Lost nine friends we'll never know
two years ago today." Also of note—it is the first PJ song for which
newest member Boom Gaspar earned a songwriting credit (the
music was co-penned by Gaspar and Vedder).

Another *Riot Act* tune that has received a fair amount of attention over the years is "Bu\$hleaguer," which focuses on Vedder's
unhappiness with the 43rd President of the United States, George
W. Bush. Other standouts include the rootsy "I Am Mine," the
stripped-down "Thumbing My Way," and the bluesy rocker
"½ Full," among others.

During the early 21st century, the booming popularity of
such file-sharing sites and software as Napster, Limewire, and
Audiogalaxy began to eat into the sales of almost all recording

artists, and Pearl Jam was not immune to those difficult times. Although there is no denying the quality of the material on *Riot Act*, it was the first album of PJ's career to not reach either of the top two spots on the U.S. charts, as it peaked at No. 5. The only country where the album went all the way the top was Australia, but it did hit No. 2 in Italy and New Zealand, and No. 3 in Norway and Portugal. *Riot Act* struck gold stateside, and secured platinum in the land down under.

78 Stone Gossard's Other Projects

The Pearl Jam member to tally the fewest number of guest appearances is Stone Gossard. That said, he is part of what is in my opinion the best PJ offshoot band: Brad.

Along with Jeff Ament, Gossard's first serious recordings were with Green River, followed by Mother Love Bone, and then Temple of the Dog. Once Pearl Jam was established, Gossard was the first to seek fun in another band, joining forces with singer/pianist Shawn Smith, bassist Jeremy Toback, and drummer Regan Hagar, in Brad.

Specializing early on in a style that alternated between piano ballads, funk, and hard rock before focusing more on their mellower side on later albums, Brad has issued a total of five studio albums thus far with a variety of bass players, including 1993's *Shame*, 1997's *Interiors*, 2002's *Welcome to Discovery Park*, 2010's *Best Friends?*, and 2012's *United We Stand*, as well as an odds-and-ends compilation with sister band Satchel, 2005's *Brad vs. Satchel*.

Additionally, Gossard has found time to issue a pair of solo efforts, the first being *Bayleaf* (which contained input from onetime

PJ drummer Matt Chamberlain and multi-instrumentalist/producer Pete Droge, but had the unfortunate luck of being released on September 11, 2001), and *Moonlander* (which again featured input from Droge and Chamberlain, as well as Matt Cameron and Barrett Martin, and was issued on June 25, 2013).

Gossard can also be spotted on Neil Young's *Mirror Ball* along with his PJ colleagues, and has reunited with two former bandmates—a few tracks on two Steve Turner solo efforts from 2004, *Searching for Melody* and *His Bad Ideas*, and Jack Irons' solo release the same year, *Attention Dimension*. He has also lent a hand to two longtime PJ mates outside of the band—Jeff Ament on the 1996 self-titled debut by Three Fish (the song "Strangers in My Head") and teaming with Mike McCready and others for a 2003 benefit album, *Live from Nowhere Near You* ("Powerless").

Finally, Gossard has been a visitor on several other artists' albums, including Thermadore's "Pushing" and "Anton" (1996's *Monkey on Rico*), Critters Buggin's "Toad Garden" (2004's *Stampede*), and a pair of solo efforts by session drummer Josh Freese, including the tracks "Men & Woman" (2000's *The Notorious One Man Orgy*) and "Who Am I to Say, Really?" (2009's *Since 1972*), among other brief explorations.

The Bu$hleaguer Controversy

Pearl Jam, and Eddie Vedder in particular, have never been shy about making their political views known. Whether taking part in Rock the Vote and Vote for Change events, performing at Ralph Nader rallies in 2000, or creating the nonprofit Vitalogy Foundation, the band tends to wear its opinions on its sleeves.

That approach was never more evident than it was in the spring of 2003, when the band was on tour supporting *Riot Act*. One of the tracks on the band's seventh full-length was titled "Bu$hleaguer," an obvious allusion to the president of the United States at that time, George W. Bush. Suffice it to say they were not fans of the president's policies, nor of the way the onetime owner of baseball's Texas Rangers had reached the White House. Don't believe me? Check out these lyrics:

A confidence man, but why so beleaguered?
He's not a leader, he's a Texas leaguer

Things came to a head on April Fools' Day in Denver, Colorado, during PJ's opening show of their tour. The country had just begun what would be known as the Iraq War. As the band began to play "Bu$hleaguer," Vedder donned a rubber Bush mask and danced across the stage. When it was time to sing, he removed the mask and placed it atop his mic stand. Vedder had used the Bush mask at previous shows in Australia and Japan without much fuss, but some fans at the Pepsi Center took offense.

"Just to clarify, we support the troops," Vedder said. "We're just confused on how wanting to bring them back safely all of a sudden becomes non-support. We love them. They're not the ones who make the foreign policy. Let's hope for the best and speak our opinions."

Some media reports, perhaps recalling the recent boycott of the Dixie Chicks after singer Natalie Maines made an anti-Bush comment, blew the event out of proportion, implying that a large part of the Pearl Jam crowd left the show in anger. Through its label, Epic Records, the band released a statement that claimed perhaps 20 or so fans left the Pepsi Center.

The group also seemed to rub the audience the wrong way at a show on April 30 at New York's Nassau Coliseum. "Bu$hleaguer" allegedly elicited boos from parts of the crowd, to which Vedder remarked, "Maybe you like him 'cause he's going to give you a tax cut." After a chant of "USA! USA!" broke out, the singer got the final word: "I'm with you: USA. I just think that all of us in this room should have a voice in how the USA is represented."

If Pearl Jam was bothered by the supposed controversy, they certainly didn't show it, continuing to play "Bu$hleaguer" numerous times over the years, both in the U.S. and around the world.

80 Influences and Favorites

Over the years, the members of Pearl Jam have been vocal about both their influences as well as contemporaries they admire. And while certain artists that left a deep impression on PJ were the lucky recipients of their own entries in this book, there just wasn't enough space to give each their own special spot. So, here is a list of five artists per PJ member that have been name-checked as a favorite at some point, a bit of info on each, plus a highly recommended recording if you're inclined to dig deep.

Eddie Vedder
The Pixies
In the late 1980s, alt-rock was rising in popularity due to support from both college radio stations and such specialty programs as MTV's *120 Minutes*. But in the pre-Nirvana landscape, the majority of artists that these outlets spun were either similar in sound and feel to R.E.M. (jangle pop), the Replacements (punk-pop), or the Wax Trax! record label roster (industrial). Thankfully, the Pixies

provided a highly original alternative to the alternative, featuring singer/guitarist Frank Black's unique vocal style (which would often alternate between yelping/barking and traditional singing... with lyrics sometimes even sung in Spanish) merged with surf guitar and noisy pop. Black even opened as a solo artist for Pearl Jam on several dates during the band's 1998 tour, and PJ covered a few Pixies songs that year.

Required Listening: *Doolittle* **(1989)**

Fugazi

After you've already been a part of Minor Threat, one of the most influential and important hardcore bands, what do you do for an encore? Somehow, Ian MacKaye found a way by forming Fugazi and helped forge another new style, post-hardcore (although I'm sure MacKaye was none too pleased that the band is often credited for influencing countless maddeningly same-sounding "emo" bands). On Vedder's 2017 solo tour, he covered the band's "I'm So Tired."

Required Listening: *Repeater* **(1990)**

Shudder to Think

A band that issued several of their early recordings via Ian MacKaye's Dischord Records, Shudder to Think started out as a part post-hardcore/part art-rock band before ultimately leaning more toward the artier side of things (and also showing off a surprising knack for pop melodicism when you least expected it). Shudder to Think was even invited by Pearl Jam to open New Zealand and Australian dates in 1998, during which Eddie Vedder would return the favor by inserting a lyrical snippet of the S2T tune, "Pebbles," in their set at the end of "Daughter."

Required Listening: *Pony Express Record* **(1994)**

The Frogs

Lo-fi rockers the Frogs were certainly one of the hippest bands to namecheck in the '90s, singled out as a favorite by the likes of Kurt Cobain, Billy Corgan, and even Eddie Vedder. And even though the Frogs opened shows for Nirvana, Smashing Pumpkins, and Pearl Jam, the Milwaukee-based group still remains quite obscure despite a three-decade-long career. Vedder certainly did his part to plug the Frogs—at Pearl Jam's radio broadcast at the Fox Theatre, Vedder changed the lyrics of "Glorified G" from "I love God" to "I love Frogs" (and also spun a Frogs tune, "I Only Play for Money," during his post-show DJ set). He asked a PJ audience a few nights later if they had "ever heard of a band called the Frogs?" at the Orpheum Theatre, and has joined the band on stage several times (locate an outstanding version of "The Longing Goes Away" with Vedder on vocals from 1994). The six-foot "bat wings" that Frogs singer/guitarist Jimmy Flemion wore onstage were given to Pearl Jam as a gift (PJ in return plopped them atop some amplifiers onstage, where they remained on display for some time).

Required Listening: *It's Only Right and Natural* **(1989)**

Zeke

Seattle did not just spawn grunge bands during the '90s, as evidenced by the arrival of hardcore punkers Zeke. Led by a man with the killer name Blind Marky Felchtone and putting out records with names like *Kicked in the Teeth* and *Dirty Sanchez*, you probably have a pretty good idea of what they might sound like. Zeke opened shows for PJ in 1998 and Vedder is an obvious admirer, teaming up with Zeke to cover two tunes, "I Believe in Miracles" and "Daytime Dilemma (Dangers of Love)" for the 2002 compilation, *We're a Happy Family: A Tribute to Ramones*.

Required Listening: *Death Alley* **(2001)**

Stone Gossard
The Stooges
Few rock bands have proven to be as influential as the Stooges (later re-billed as "Iggy & the Stooges"). The Sex Pistols, Soundgarden, the Red Hot Chili Peppers, Guns N' Roses, and Slayer have all covered a Stooges song at some point or another. And besides including one of rock's all-time great frontmen in Iggy Pop, their two guitarists, Ron Asheton and James Williamson, were incredible as well, a fact not lost on the Pearl Jam guitarist. Back in 2008, Gossard told Wired.com that he grew up on Led Zeppelin and the Stooges.
Required Listening: *Fun House* (1970)

New York Dolls
While his Johnny Thunder-isms wouldn't be all that audible by the time he was strumming his Les Paul in Pearl Jam, the New York Dolls' guitarist obviously left a mark on Stone Gossard back in the Green River days (heck, in *Grunge Is Dead*, Presidents of the United States of America guitarist Dave Dederer recalls Gossard embracing the "Thunders look" in his younger days).
Required Listening: *New York Dolls* (1973)

Led Zeppelin
It's pretty much a universally understood law of nature that Led Zeppelin's music is a mandatory teenage soundtrack. Along with the Beatles and Queen, Zeppelin was one of the most musically varied rock bands of all time, expertly taking on a variety of styles and making them their own. And guitarist Jimmy Page's groovy rhythm guitar work was an obvious influence on Gossard, especially alternate tunings and a fondness for playing sunburst Gibson Les Pauls.
Required Listening: *Physical Graffiti* (1975)

Ice Cube

The arrival of such artists as Public Enemy and N.W.A. changed the hip-hop landscape in the late '80s and early '90s. Featuring the talents of Ice Cube (real name: O'Shea Jackson Sr.) and hailing from Compton, California, N.W.A. caused a splash with lyrics that reflected what it was like growing up on the rough streets of the inner city. Gossard has been vocal about being a big-time fan of Ice Cube's early solo records, though his lyrics could certainly be categorized as misogynistic ("Givin' Up the Nappy Dugout"), racist ("Black Korea"), and homophobic ("No Vaseline")—not exactly in line with Pearl Jam's forward-thinking political stances. PJ and Cube crossed paths on the Lollapalooza '92 tour.

Required Listening: *Death Certificate* **(1991)**

Supergrass

While the Britpop movement of the '90s never truly caught on in the U.S. the same way it did in England, there were certainly exceptions—Oasis, Blur, the Verve, and Elastica, to name a few. And one band that should have also caused a splash stateside, since they certainly possessed the goods in the songwriting department, was Supergrass, who even supported Pearl Jam during the *Binaural* tour.

Required Listening: *In It for the Money* **(1997)**

Mike McCready
The Rolling Stones

It's hard to spot any recording artist after the early 1960s that was not influenced in some way by two bands—the Rolling Stones and the Beatles. Mike McCready is most certainly a "Stones man," and one of his dreams came true on New Year's 1992, when Pearl Jam was cordially invited to open for Keith Richards and the X-Pensive Winos in NYC. As a bonus, McCready got to jam with the co-founding Stones guitarist backstage (a photo indeed exists!), with PJ later opening for the actual full-on Stones in 1997.

Required Listening: *Exile on Main St.* (1972)

Jimi Hendrix

Judging from McCready's penchant early in Pearl Jam's career for playing Fender Stratocasters and alternating between a vintage distorted Marshall tone and clear-as-a-bell clean sounds, Jimi Hendrix was a humongous influence. Musically, "Yellow Ledbetter" may be the best tune Jimi never wrote—go and compare it side by side to the Hendrix classic "Little Wing," if you don't believe me.

Required Listening: *Axis: Bold as Love* (1968)

UFO

British rockers UFO recorded one of the 1970s' best live rock albums, *Strangers in the Night.* But mixed among the Englishmen was a certain German guitarist named Michael Schenker, who, along with Kiss' Ace Frehley, might be one of the most influential rock guitarists of all time. McCready is a proud member of Flight to Mars, a UFO tribute band.

Required Listening: *Strangers in the Night* (1979)

TKO

Mike McCready has never been bashful about his fondness for good old-fashioned hard rock and heavy metal. So it shouldn't come as a surprise that he has name-checked Seattle rockers TKO as an early favorite. In 2014, TKO lead singer Brad Sinsel released a single with his new project, Angels of Dresden, which featured an appearance by none other than Mike McCready.

Required Listening: *Let It Roll* (1979)

Stevie Ray Vaughan and Double Trouble

Blues music was about as close to extinct as you could get in the synth-happy early '80s. But thanks to the arrival of Stevie Ray Vaughan and Double Trouble, blues rock was given a second life. Furthermore, SRV proved that there was room for impressive technical six-string ability within the blues realm. McCready once told *Music Aficionado* that seeing SRV in Seattle was "a life-changing experience."

Required Listening: *Couldn't Stand the Weather* (1984)

Jeff Ament
Cheap Trick

Who would have thought that the merging of the Beatles' sense of pop melody with the fury of the Sex Pistols would serve as the basis for one of the best rock 'n' roll bands of the late '70s/early '80s? Of course, I'm talking about Cheap Trick—who get my vote for penning the greatest rebellious teen anthem of all time, "Surrender," a song PJ has covered on numerous occasions.

Required Listening: *Cheap Trick at Budokan* (1979)

The Clash

Certain entertainers earn the right to be known around the world by a nickname—think "The Fab Four" or "The King of Pop." Certainly, for a period of time, the one foisted upon the Clash was quite fitting—"The Only Band That Matters." One of the leaders of England's first wave of punk rock, the Clash was not afraid to overstep the genre's often strict self-imposed boundaries, fearlessly taking on a variety of styles throughout their career, nor worried about being "gobbed" on by their affectionate following. During PJ's Rock and Roll Hall of Fame induction, Ament mentioned the Clash as one of the band's heroes.

Required Listening: *London Calling* (1979)

Public Image Ltd (PiL)

For those expecting "Sex Pistols Part II" from singer John "Johnny Rotten" Lydon's first post-Pistols project, Public Image Limited, disappointment was in order. But once all the hubbub cleared, the facts came into focus—Lydon went for a different approach with PiL, and created some of the most cutting edge and uncompromising rock records of the late '70s/early '80s. Credit must also be given to guitarist Keith Levene and bassist Jah Wobble for their distinctive contributions on PiL's early recordings. During the aforementioned HOF ceremony, Ament wore a T-shirt featuring the names of artists he felt belonged in the Hall, PiL among them.

Required Listening: *First Issue* (1978)

The Police

Let's face it—gentlemen outside of Jamaica attempting to play reggae usually spells disaster. But the Police were one of the few exceptions, gloriously merging reggae rhythms with pop, rock, and even punk. It also didn't hurt that all three members were experts on their respective instruments...let alone that Sting, one of popular music's all-time greatest songwriters and lyricists, was in attendance. Ament has cited the Police as one of the biggest influences on his bass playing.

Required Listening: *Zenyatta Mondatta* (1980)

The Cult

The Cult was one of the few bands of the 1980s to appeal to both alt-rockers (tunes such as "She Sells Sanctuary" and "Love Removal Machine" were big college radio hits) and also headbangers (they took out Guns N' Roses on their first substantial tour in 1987, and opened a tour for Metallica in 1989). There is some great footage on YouTube of Mother Love Bone (and Chris Cornell) mingling backstage at a Cult concert.

Required Listening: *Electric* (1987)

Matt Cameron
The Beatles

At this point, is it really necessary to explain who the Beatles are, or the enormous, lasting impact they've had on music? In an online chat years ago, Cameron wrote that he started drumming because of musician Rick Derringer, and the Beatles.

Required Listening: The White Album (1968)

Tony Williams

For a stretch during the 1960s, it must have been difficult for jazz drummer Tony Williams to keep track of all the classic albums he was a part of, either as a bandleader (The Tony Williams Lifetime) or as a sideman (Miles Davis). And in the process, Williams helped popularize the style best known as jazz fusion (which melds together elements of jazz with rock).

Required Listening: *Life Time* (1964)

David Bowie

Few artists in the history of rock could assume different "personas," shift gears stylistically, and enjoy such a long, successful, and influential career as David Bowie did. And Bowie's knack for slithering from genre to genre obviously rubbed off on Cameron—especially evidenced in his work outside of PJ. And when Pearl Jam was inducted into the Rock and Roll Hall of Fame in 2017, Cameron mentioned that seeing Bowie on the *Station to Station* tour was a "life-changing experience."

Required Listening: *Young Americans* (1975)

Queen

Queen mastered the ability to write songs in a variety of genres, from arena rock anthems ("We Will Rock You," "We Are the Champions") to dance ("Another One Bites the Dust") to proto-thrash metal (a two-way tie between "Ogre Battle" and "Stone

Cold Crazy"). Add to it one of the greatest frontmen and vocalists in music history—the incomparable Freddie Mercury—and you have a near-perfect rock band.

Required Listening: *A Night at the Opera* **(1975)**

Monster Magnet

The early '90s gave us several bands that would eventually be considered the forefathers of "stoner rock"—Kyuss, Sleep, and especially Monster Magnet. And Soundgarden were big-time fans of MM, inviting them to open shows on the *Badmotorfinger* tour. But if you had to pick a SG member who was the biggest admirer of MM, it would probably be Matt Cameron, who is spotted wearing a MM shirt in SG's *Motorvision* home video, and collaborating with ex-MM guitarist John McBain in not one but *two* bands, Hater and Wellwater Conspiracy.

Required Listening: *Spine of God* **(1992)**

Backstage Pass

Charlie Benante
Anthrax/S.O.D.
(Stormtroopers of Death) Drummer

I remember reading an interview with Scott Ian [Anthrax's guitarist], in which he said he met Eddie Vedder once, and it turns out Vedder was a fan of the Stormtroopers of Death album, *Speak English or Die*.
I actually met Eddie at a bar, and we spoke a little bit about S.O.D., and how much he loved that record. And I think Scott may have had a conversation with him, as well. I always thought it was pretty funny that that record reached him.

Have you seen Pearl Jam live?
I've seen them many times. I saw them on the Lollapalooza thing, and numerous times after that. Back in the day, I thought they were very exciting, and young and hungry. I felt like this was something that

could probably transcend just the genre that is making waves now, you know what I mean? I thought, "You don't want to get caught up in this 'grunge bubble,' and then you're stuck in that." Which I think out of all the bands I thought would have longevity, at the time, I probably thought Nirvana would be the ones, and the least would be Pearl Jam. And it worked out in the complete opposite!

What were your thoughts on Pearl Jam's drummers?
My favorite Pearl Jam record would be *Vs.* I loved, loved, loved that record. And I think a lot of the songs on that record have a vibe...I think it's a different record than the first album, where I think it has more attitude than the first album. And I think the drumming on it is really done well, too—and that's from Dave Abbruzzese. I thought he fit the band perfectly. He just looked good in the role and played really well, too. I was like, "Wow...they got rid of him?" I thought he was like, "the guy." But to me, *Vs.* and *Yield* I thought [were] their best work.

What was it about *Yield* that makes it a favorite?
I just think the collection of songs that are on the record was really strong. And I also think that's when the band shifted in style, and maybe became a bit more in touch with themselves, and not what they think Pearl Jam should sound like. I think it was a turning point in their career.

I remember hearing a while back that Anthrax covered Pearl Jam's "Brain of J" as a B-side during the *Worship Music* era...but it never came out.
Every time we do a record, we throw around some ideas to do some B-sides of some obscure songs that some of us love. And one of my favorite songs off of *Yield* is "Brain of J." That song has this really good, punk rock feel to it, and is one of my favorite songs by them. I got the guys to do it...and we just couldn't get Joey [Belladonna, Anthrax's singer] to sing it. So, we did the track, and actually, Mike McCready played the lead on it, too.

How did Mike get involved?
I think we just reached out to him. And then we sent him the file, he did it, and then he sent it back to us.

Have you ever met Mike?
Oh yeah. I actually hung out with him after a Pearl Jam show and thought he was fuckin' awesome. A great dude.

Mike is a big fan of metal, too.
Yeah. I'd love to do a thing with him—that would come out really good, I think. Like UFO, but heavier.

So, the vocals on the "Brain of J" cover were never even attempted with Joey?
No. It's still sitting. I would like one day to complete it, just so it can be completed.

How would you compare Anthrax's version of the song to the original?
It may have a little bit more testosterone to it. For me, I always felt like the muscle in Pearl Jam came from Eddie's voice more so than anything. So, we just wanted to "metal it out" a little bit—but not go overboard.

If the opportunity ever presented itself, what about Eddie himself singing on Anthrax's version?
Oh geez…that would be fuckin' *killer.*

81 Pearl Jam's Instruments

Over the years, the members of Pearl Jam have played a wide assortment of makes, models, and brands of their respective instruments. And while it would be virtually impossible to document every instrument that PJ has been spotted with on a concert stage or heard playing in a recording studio, here's an overview of the ones each member is most closely associated with.

Eddie Vedder

While he was virtually instrument-less on stage early in Pearl Jam's career, by the *Vs.* tour and onward, Eddie Vedder developed a kinship with Fender Telecasters. Developed by Leo Fender (who would also design the Stratocaster and Precision Bass models) in 1950, the Tele was primarily associated with country players, due to the ease with which you could do clean "chicken picking" finger-style playing on it. Eventually, it became equally associated with rock 'n' roll, and especially with rhythm players. Vedder has been spotted playing several Teles over the years, the first being a black-bodied one with a sticker stating SKATEBOARDING IS NOT A CRIME, another with what is called a black "holoflake" finish with a white pickguard (that has an arrow pointing to a bullseye between the two pickups), plus an additional one with a black body and a white pickguard, with the name ZINN between the pickups on the pickguard, a shoutout to American historian and social activist Howard Zinn, who served as inspiration for the PJ song "Down."

Stone Gossard

While Stone Gossard has played a wide variety of guitars over the years, the make and model he is most closely associated with is the Gibson Les Paul. First introduced to the public in 1952, its design was a collaboration between several people, including guitarist Les Paul, Gibson president Ted McCarty, and factory manager John Huis. With two (sometimes even three) large "humbucker" pickups and a wide neck, the Les Paul proved to be ideal for rhythm playing. Although it has gone on to be one of the most instantly identifiable guitars—especially as it became so closely associated with the likes of Jimmy Page, Ace Frehley, and Slash—it hit hard times in the '60s and was discontinued for a spell before going back into production in 1968 and continuing on through today. Gossard has been seen playing Les Pauls all the way back to his Green River days, and has continued to do so in every subsequent project. In the early days of Pearl Jam, he alternated between two—one with a sunburst finish and a white pickguard that had both a "rat" sticker and the number "3" on it, and the other with what they call a "gold top" finish with "3" on the headstock). And Gossard remains primarily a "Les Paul man," although nowadays he favors them outfitted with a Bigsby tremolo bar.

Mike McCready

Like his guitar mate in Pearl Jam, Mike McCready has been spotted with a variety of guitars throughout his career. But if you were forced to select the one he is most associated with, it would be the Fender Stratocaster. As previously stated about the Telecaster, the Strat was developed by Leo Fender in 1954, and with its single coil pickups and tremolo bar (aka the whammy bar), the instrument is ideal for playing lead guitar and has been championed by such legends as Jimi Hendrix, Eric Clapton, and Stevie Ray Vaughan. Although McCready was a heavy metal shredder in the '80s, he reinvented himself as a player in the more organic vein of Jimi and Stevie at the dawn of the '90s, and hence, it made perfect sense to feature various Strats in his arsenal. He continues to play Strats today, with perhaps his most beloved one—and most played as of late—being a vintage, well-worn model from 1959.

Jeff Ament

Perhaps out of all the Pearl Jam members, bassist Jeff Ament is the one who has not been affiliated with a specific make and model for an extended period of time. Back in the *Ten* and *Vs.* eras, Ament was a Hamer man. Hamer was an Illinois-based guitar manufacturer that lasted from 1973 to 2013 (and was reintroduced in 2017), founded by Paul Hamer and Jol Dantzig, who were the owners of a vintage guitar shop, Northern Prairie Music, in the Chicago suburb of Wilmette. With Ament an admirer of the thunderous 12-string model bass that Hamer offered—which was also played by Cheap

Trick's Tom Petersson and King's X's Doug Pinnick—Ament took the plunge, and as a result we now have one of the best known bass guitar openings to a rock song: "Jeremy." Early on, Ament also utilized a fretless bass thought to be an ESP (as heard on "Black" and "Oceans"), as well as standard fretted basses (one of which featured the names of basketball players he fancied scrawled all over it in different colors). Over the years, Ament has played a variety of other basses made by Wal (Fretless MK 2), Fender (Precision bass), and Gibson (ES-335 and Thunderbird), among others. Nowadays, Ament plays primarily a guitar he has created with guitar and bass builder Mile Lull, the Jeff Ament JAXT4 Signature Model Bass Guitar (which features a very Thunderbird-looking body).

Matt Cameron
Although Matt Cameron played other drum brands early in his career, he has become a long-time endorser of Yamaha drums—founded in 1967 and a subsidiary of the Yamaha Corporation (whose factory is located in China). On Cameron's "artist page" on the Yamaha website, it lists his set as being an Oak Custom in Musashi black with vintage hoops. In a video interview for *Rhythm* magazine, Cameron's drum tech, Neil Hundt, listed his kit as "Starting with the kick, it's a 24x14. 12 and 13 tom, 16 floor, and 18 floor. The kit is a Yamaha Oak Custom. The size has been altered for Matt. The floor tom one has been shortened on the bottom so it's 16x14, and the rack one has been shaved one inch." Got it? Good.

82 The Year Pearl Jam Almost Broke Up

In the June 29, 2006, issue of *Rolling Stone*, Mike McCready was asked if Pearl Jam ever considered a breakup. McCready replied, "We came close a few times." Undoubtedly, one of these times was in 1994. Although PJ was at an all-time high both commercially and critically, things were not going as well behind the scenes. As Ament explained about that era to me in *Grunge Is Dead*, "It was a hard time. It was a time where we were all still learning how to communicate with one another. It took a couple of more records before we figured that out."

In addition to the band members still learning the fine art of communication, Pearl Jam was a perfect example of the danger of getting too much too soon. Back in the Mother Love Bone days, magazine covers and and headlining arenas might have been the principal goal of Andy Wood and company. But the sudden onslaught of MTV and media coverage of Pearl Jam was taking its toll—all you have to do is watch interview footage with Vedder from this time, and you can tell he was not at all comfortable with the scrutiny or being placed on a pedestal by millions of fans. To try and slow things down, the band did not film a single video for any of the tracks on *Vs.*, nor did they film a video for what could have quite possibly been another mega-hit from *Ten*, "Black."

Another contributing factor during this rocky period was burnout. Pearl Jam had been on the road pretty much for a solid year (September 1991 to September 1992) in support of *Ten*, then went right into the writing and recording of *Vs.* And despite *Vs.* not being released until October 19, 1993, Pearl Jam opted to spend a large chunk of the summer of '93 touring in Europe, Canada, and a handful of American cities (quite a few of these were ginormous shows opening for either Neil Young or U2). Once the album was issued, they headed out on a proper headlining tour in support of it from October to December 1993, before heading out for another trek from March to April 1994. In other words, there was not an awful lot of time spent at home during this period.

And, along with the rest of the music world, Pearl Jam was traumatized by Kurt Cobain's suicide in April 1994. Perhaps most affected was Vedder, who along with Cobain had become voices of a generation. Speaking to *Melody Maker* shortly after Cobain's death (in an article from the May 21, 1994, issue, titled "Pearl Jam's Last Stand?"), PJ's singer dropped some alarming quotes: "This could be our last show in fuckin' forever as far as I'm concerned. Kurt's death has changed everything. I don't know if I can do it anymore...I don't know where we go from here. Maybe nowhere. I think this is going to be the last thing for a long time. I'm just gonna live in a fuckin' cave with my girlfriend. I don't think I'll be showing my face for a while. I don't think I'll be making any fuckin' videos. Maybe we'll eventually do some shows or something, I just don't know...I'm having a real tough time right now. This is the last night of the tour, and I don't know how we've got through the last week. It's been so fuckin' hard, man. So hard...And tonight, you know, it's just going to be so...so weird."

And as if that weren't enough, it was also in 1994 that the band experienced a major lineup shake-up when Dave Abbruzzese was asked to exit the band. Speaking to *Spin* magazine in August 2001, Abbruzzese said, "I felt like there was a time when I had a good friendship with that guy [Vedder]. And then all of a sudden I didn't know him. But I understand—shit, if I was freaking out about stuff and having panic attacks, I can't even begin to fathom what the hell he was going through. I give it up to him just for surviving it."

Finally, you can also add the Pearl Jam vs. Ticketmaster fracas, which only added to this troubled period. But whereas many rock bands throughout history buckled under a lesser amount of pressure, Pearl Jam did not, and managed to navigate through it all and come out the other side intact. But looking back, there's no denying that 1994 was indeed the trickiest of years for the quintet.

83 *Pearl Jam*

Many notable rock bands have issued self-titled albums during the middle of their careers, including the Beatles in 1968, Metallica in 1991, and Alice in Chains in 1995. In 2006, it was Pearl Jam's turn to take the self-titled plunge. Reenlisting Adam Kasper for a second go-round as co-producer alongside the band, recording sessions lasted from November 2004 to February 2006 at Studio X in Seattle, resulting in Pearl Jam's self-titled effort being issued on May 2, 2006. The album was PJ's first to not be issued via Epic Records, but rather the short-lived J Records (the band's only recording issued via J).

The album cover art fell in line with the band's previous few releases, insomuch that it had nothing to do with the album title. This time, it was a photograph of an avocado sliced perfectly in half; it was snapped by Brad Klausen, best known for his graphic design work for PJ and other bands. Like several of PJ's past releases, if you compare the CD version's front cover art to that of the vinyl's cover art, you will detect a slight difference: the vinyl cover has the avocado and the album title perfectly centered in the middle, whereas the CD cover has the title in the upper left corner and the avocado is located in the bottom right. Two music videos from the album would be filmed ("World Wide Suicide" directed by Danny Clinch and the tremendous clip for "Life

Pearl Jam, *Pearl Jam,*
2006. (J Records)

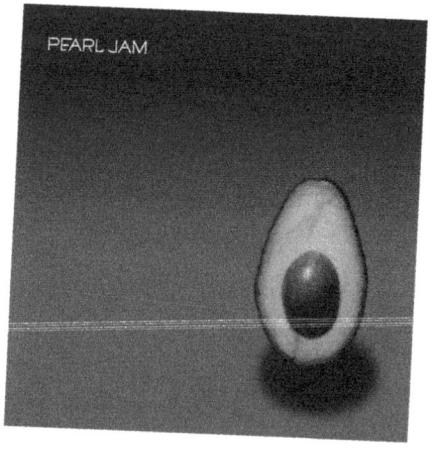

Wasted" directed by Fernando Apodaca), while a total of three singles were released ("World Wide Suicide," "Life Wasted," and "Gone").

By and large, the album leans more toward the rockier side of things, beginning with "Life Wasted" (the lyrics supposedly inspired by the passing of Vedder's close friend, Johnny Ramone), "World Wide Suicide" (one of the album's best tracks), "Comatose" (best described as an "explosive punk rocker"), "Severed Hand" (a groove-rock number), and "Marker in the Sand" (which musically sounds a bit like Mudhoney). But it's not all bash and stomp, as exemplified by "Parachutes" (which almost sounds like a lullaby), "Gone" (which starts out as a Neil Young–ish acoustic tune before working its way up to a mid-paced rocker), and the closer for the album's first half, "Inside Job." Also, one of the tunes, the mid-paced "Army Reserve," lists Vedder and Damien Echols as co-lyricists; Echols is one of the West Memphis Three, a group of young men who were convicted of the murder of three young boys, who many felt were innocent and who eventually were freed from prison.

The album saw Pearl Jam leap back up the charts, peaking at No. 2 on the Billboard 200 (and matching this feat on the Belgian, Canadian, Croatian, Czech, Dutch, New Zealand, and Swiss album charts), and topping the Italian and Portuguese charts. And PJ's self-titled offering proved to be quite satisfying when it came to the certification department—scoring silver in the UK, gold in both the U.S. and Brazil, and platinum in Australia, Canada, and New Zealand.

84 Build Your Pearl Jam Library

Among grunge artists, Kurt Cobain and Nirvana certainly take the cake for the number of books—both authorized and unauthorized—that have been written about them. But not far behind might be Pearl Jam, who have also been the focus of quite a few books over the years—in addition to the one you are currently holding in your hands or viewing on some sort of electro-gadget.

The earliest of the PJ books appeared to be mostly photo-based, since they surfaced shortly after the group's early commercial success (there wasn't much story to be told at that point), including such titles as 1993's *Pearl Jam: The Illustrated Biography* by Brad Morrell and 1995's *Pearl Jam: The Illustrated Story, A Melody Maker Book* by Allan Jones. The first books that attempted to tell the PJ story included 1994's *Pearl Jam* by Mick Wall, 1995's *Pearl Jam: Live* by Joey Lorenzo, and another book penned by Morrell, 1997's *The Story of Pearl Jam*.

But it wasn't until the late '90s that the first substantial Pearl Jam books arrived—interestingly, both surfacing in 1998—*Five Against One: The Pearl Jam Story* by Kim Neely and *Pearl Jam & Eddie Vedder: None Too Fragile* by Martin Clarke. The former is one of the better PJ bios; Neely was one of the first to write about the band for a national publication (a mini-feature in the October

A page from Pearl Jam vs Ames Bros: 13 Years of Posters. (D. Couturiaux)

31, 1991, issue of *Rolling Stone*, entitled "Pearl Jam: Right Here, Right Now"). As a bonus, the book's cover image is one of the more iconic PJ photographs ever shot: a pic by Kevin Westenberg, which sees Vedder leaning back against Ament during a daytime outdoor show in support of the *Ten* album, with steam rising off the audience.

Another pair of books that can be categorized together are photo books assembled by two cameramen who photographed the band throughout their career: Lance Mercer and Charles Peterson's *Pearl Jam: Place/Date* in 1999 and Lance Mercer's *5x1: Pearl Jam Through the Eye of Lance Mercer* in 2006. In 2007, an incredibly beautiful collection arrived: *Pearl Jam vs Ames Bros:*

13 Years of Tour Posters, which focuses on the artwork of Barry Ament (Jeff's brother) and Coby Schultz, who created some of the band's most iconic tour posters.

And now, a personal question for you, dear reader: Is it okay if I include one of my own books in this entry? Are you sure it's okay? It is? Thank you! The book I'm talking about is 2009's *Grunge Is Dead: The Oral History of Seattle Rock Music*, for which I interviewed members of all the leading grunge bands and those who were somehow connected to the great grunge uprising. In addition to interviewing PJ members Jeff Ament and Matt Cameron for the book, I was also granted an extremely extensive interview with none other than Eddie Vedder, in which he graciously discussed in great detail the early years of Pearl Jam and their subsequent whirlwind success. I recall the phone chat lasting for two hours! This was quite the accomplishment, as Vedder had just recently rejected opening up about the band's early years to *Rolling Stone* for a cover story in 2006 (explaining to interviewer Brian Hiatt, "This is the stuff I don't want to talk about, because it's bullshit, and you had to have been there"). To this day, talking with Vedder is probably the best interview I've ever conducted from a personal standpoint (right up there with the likes of David Lynch, William Shatner, Ace Frehley, Iggy Pop, Chris Cornell, John Lydon, Geddy Lee, Tony Iommi, and Ronnie James Dio, in case you were wondering who else is lucky enough to be included in the highly esteemed "Greg Prato Interview Hall of Fame List").

But in 2011, the definitive book about Pearl Jam was unveiled: *Pearl Jam Twenty*, which coincided with the outstanding Cameron Crowe–directed documentary of the same name. Authored by Jonathan Cohen and Mark Wilkerson, this hardcover, 384-page behemoth leaves not a single stone unturned, as an incredible amount of time, effort, and research was obviously put into a labor of love. It's full of rare photos and set in chronological order.

Most recently, in 2017, a pair of PJ books were issued by two people closely linked to the band: *Of Potato Heads and Polaroids: My Life Inside and Out of Pearl Jam* by none other than Mike McCready and *Pearl Jam: Art of Do the Evolution* by Joe Pearson, Brad Coombs, Jim Mitchell, Lisa Pearson, and Terry Fitzgerald. Both are quite self-explanatory; McCready's offering is a collection of Polaroid photos he snapped throughout the years, while Pearson, who was the co-producer of the Grammy-nominated animated video for "Do the Evolution," and his co-authors offer animation cells with never-before-seen storyboards and designs from said video.

Now…go get reading (once you're finished completely reading this book, of course)!

 # Stickman

Some band logos have become so well known that they've become synonymous with the bands themselves; for example, the Rolling Stones' Tongue and Lips logo or Led Zeppelin's ZoSo symbols. In this regard, Pearl Jam is no different, as most fans can easily identify the logo commonly known as Stickman.

So, how did a stick-figure doodle with long hair and out-stretched arms become the band's calling card? It turns out that it was the work of Jeff Ament, who once described its inception this way: "I drew the Stickman the night after Kelly Curtis told me that we needed artwork for the giveaway cassette for 'Alive.' The art really just represents how I was feeling at the time, playing in the best band I'd ever been in, and all of us were in such a creative zone. It didn't really have anything to do with the song."

Over the years, Stickman has become a popular figure on T-shirts and as a tattoo design. One of the first people to get the Stickman tattooed on a body part was none other than PJ drummer Dave Abbruzzese. The story goes that after his second show with the band, Abbruzzese went directly to a tattoo parlor and got the little gentleman permanently emblazoned on the bicep of his left arm.

A T-shirt featuring the Stickman logo. (G. Otsuka)

86 Boom Gaspar

Since 2002, some casual Pearl Jam fans attending their concerts may have shared the same thought: "Who the heck is that mysterious, long-haired guy playing piano, keyboard, and organ?" The answer to that question is Boom Gaspar.

Born Kenneth Gaspar on February 3, 1953, in Waimānalo, Hawaii, Gaspar began playing keyboard at the age of nine—some of his early influences include Booker T. Jones, Gregg Rolie, and Chester D. Thompson. He spent the next three decades working as a local musician, playing everything from R&B to gospel music; a stint playing with legendary blues guitarist Albert Collins during the early to mid-'70s saw Gaspar relocate to Seattle.

As with many Hawaiian natives, Gaspar is also fond of surfing, which came in handy after he befriended onetime Ramones bassist C.J. Ramone, who in turn introduced him to none other than sometime Hawaiian resident Eddie Vedder. Gaspar and Vedder hit it off after talking about their shared passions, then began jamming together, which led to the co-penning of the song "Love Boat Captain." PJ invited Gaspar to provide Hammond B3 and Fender Rhodes to "LBC," as well as other songs on their next album, 2002's *Riot Act*.

Gaspar has been a permanent touring member of Pearl Jam ever since—called the band's "unofficial sixth member" and even appearing in publicity photos with the band. He played on the subsequent PJ studio albums, 2006's *Pearl Jam* and 2013's *Lightning Bolt* (interestingly, he was not included on the sessions for 2009's *Backspacer*, as all keys were covered by Brendan O'Brien). Additionally, he has appeared on a variety of live PJ releases, plus on the tune that the band contributed to the 2003 film *Big Fish*,

Boom Gaspar stands with the crate holding his keyboards after Pearl Jam's concert in Honolulu, 2006. (AP Images)

"Man of the Hour." And as evidenced by YouTube footage—and obviously by experiencing Pearl Jam performances in the flesh—Gaspar's organ soloing skills are often showcased during live extended renditions of the tune "Crazy Mary." When not working with PJ, Gaspar has been spotted playing with a Hawaiian band, Pō and the 4Fathers.

Speaking to *Keyboard* magazine in 2014, Gaspar explained what he brings to the Pearl Jam sound: "I didn't want to take anything away from what the band had already laid down or pull songs in a completely different direction. My approach was to stay in the flow and do my best to enhance what Pearl Jam had already established. You have to find your own lane—but not go way out there—and try to be a supportive keyboard player."

87 The Ramones

Unquestionably, one of the most influential and important rock bands of all time was the Ramones. By the early-mid-'70s, mainstream rock music had become a self-indulgent, bloated beast, and with the emergence of the Ramones and other first-wave punk bands, a much-needed alternative was provided (sound familiar, grunge fans?).

Formed in 1974 in the Forest Hills neighborhood of Queens, New York, the band's original lineup was comprised of singer Joey Ramone (real name: Jeffrey Hyman), guitarist Johnny Ramone (John Cummings), bassist Dee Dee Ramone (Douglas Colvin), and drummer Tommy Ramone (Thomas Erdelyi). Always dressed in black leather biker jackets and ripped jeans, the band soon became experts at penning punk-pop gems that rarely ran longer than three minutes.

Throughout the remainder of the decade, the Ramones issued near-perfect albums such as 1976's self-titled debut, 1977's *Leave Home* and *Rocket to Russia*, plus 1978's *Road to Ruin*, which spawned such classic tunes as "Blitzkrieg Bop," "Pinhead," "Rockaway Beach," "Sheena Is a Punk Rocker," "Teenage Lobotomy," and "I Wanna Be Sedated." However, despite influencing just about every major rock band from the '80s onward, the band never scored that ever-elusive mainstream hit during their career, and were prone to inter-band bickering (be sure to view the must-see documentary, 2003's *End of the Century: The Story of the Ramones*, for the whole story).

Toward the end of their career, the Ramones crossed paths with Pearl Jam numerous times—possibly for the first time when the two toured together for a handful of U.S. dates in September

1995 (including a show on September 17, 1995, at Tad Gormley Stadium in New Orleans, which saw Joey Ramone join PJ on stage for a rendition of the Dead Boys' "Sonic Reducer"). It was right around this time that Eddie Vedder and Johnny Ramone seemingly became close friends. Vedder appeared on stage with the Ramones for a cover of the Dave Clark Five's "Anyway You Want It" during their last-ever show, at the Palace in Los Angeles on August 6, 1996 (captured for posterity on the 1997 CD/DVD, *We're Outta Here!*). In 2002, Vedder gave a remarkable speech introducing the Ramones at their Rock and Roll Hall of Fame induction, and later covered the somewhat obscure Ramones originals, "I Believe in Miracles" and "Daytime Dilemma (Dangers of Love)" (backed by Zeke), for the star-studded *We're a Happy Family: A Tribute to Ramones* compilation.

Sadly, during the 2000s, all of the original Ramones members died one by one—Joey in 2001, Dee Dee in 2002, Johnny in 2004, and Tommy in 2014. During the later years of Johnny's life, his friendship with Vedder remained very much intact; Pearl Jam is mentioned throughout Johnny's posthumously published autobiography, 2012's *Commando*. The book also includes photos of the two at a Los Angeles Dodgers baseball game, and Vedder wearing one of Johnny's wigs. But the ultimate sign of how close the two had become was Vedder's presence at Johnny's bedside when he passed away after a five-year battle with prostate cancer.

Vedder also gave a moving speech at the unveiling of a statue of Johnny at his grave in 2005, located at the Hollywood Forever Cemetery in Los Angeles (sadly, Chris Cornell, another friend of Johnny's, would be buried right next to him years later). Vedder remains friends with latter-day Ramones bassist C.J. Ramone, who introduced the singer to Boom Gaspar.

Although Johnny and most of his Ramones bandmates may be no more, their music continues to resonate with Pearl Jam: Johnny's passing was the lyrical inspiration for their popular 2006 song, "Life Wasted," and in 2014, PJ performed and dedicated a rendition of "I Believe in Miracles" to Johnny on what would have been his 66th birthday, during a show at the BOK Center in Tulsa, Oklahoma.

88 David Letterman

It seems to be universally agreed upon that one of the greatest television talk show hosts of all time is David Letterman, who as the host of two wildly popular shows—*Late Night with David Letterman* (1982–93) and *The Late Show with David Letterman* (1993–2015), became a king of late night TV programming.

Born David Michael Letterman on April 12, 1947, in Indianapolis, Indiana, Letterman first broke into television as a weatherman before relocating to Los Angeles and turning his attention to comedy. The move eventually paid off, resulting in numerous appearances on *The Tonight Show Starring Johnny Carson*.

After a morning show of his own for NBC, *The David Letterman Show*, did not work out (only running from June 23 to October 24, 1980), the folks at the network made a wise decision: instead of dropping Letterman from TV completely, they moved him to late night, to *Late Night with David Letterman* on February 1, 1982.

Up to this point, late night television seemed to appeal mostly to an older crowd, and almost completely bypassed younger audiences. Although Letterman was 35 years old, the youngsters identified with him, and in return, the show became an incredible success. When it was announced that Carson would be retiring from *The Tonight Show*, it was rumored that Letterman would inherit the gig. Letterman's old pal, Jay Leno, would get the nod instead. Understandably disappointed, Letterman fled NBC, found a new home with CBS, and launched *The Late Show with David Letterman* on August 30, 1993.

One of the things that made both of Letterman's late night shows so special was that he welcomed a wide range of musical guests on his programs; Paul McCartney, James Brown, R.E.M., the Beastie Boys, and Slayer all appeared over the years. Also appearing fairly often was, of course, Pearl Jam.

The first PJ-related appearance was made not by the full band, but rather by Eddie Vedder alone. With Letterman seemingly obsessed with the "Doo doo doo doo doo doo doo" part in "Black," Vedder appeared seemingly out of nowhere on an episode that aired on February 27, 1996, to sing the aforementioned part...and then promptly disappeared.

From that point on, PJ were regular *Late Show* musical guests, performing "Hail Hail" (1996), "Wishlist" (1998), "Grievance" (2000), "I Am Mine" (2002), "Save You" (2002), "Masters of War" (2004), and "Life Wasted" (2006). Additionally, Vedder appeared with Pete Townshend for a rendition of "Heart to Hang Onto" (1999), and offered up solo performances of "Without You" (2011) and "Better Man" (in 2015, on one of Letterman's last-ever shows).

Letterman's relationship with PJ would last beyond his final show on May 20, 2015, as he was a last-minute replacement for an ailing Neil Young, speaking when Pearl Jam entered the Rock and Roll Hall of Fame on April 7, 2017.

89 Christopher McCandless and *Into the Wild*

In the modern age, it is quite natural to feel overloaded with information, or to yearn for a simpler lifestyle, devoid of materialism. That said, it's not all that common to actually make an effort to live off the grid. But that's exactly what a young man named Christopher McCandless did, with tragic results. And when McCandless' life story was made into a major motion picture, 2007's *Into the Wild*, Eddie Vedder signed on to write and perform the musical soundtrack.

Born Christopher Johnson McCandless on February 12, 1968, in El Segundo, California, McCandless came from what seemed to be a highly respectable and successful family; his father, Walter, worked as an antenna specialist for NASA, while his mother, Wilhelmina, worked as a secretary at Hughes Aircraft. (It should be noted that McCandless' sister, Carine, wrote a tell-all book in 2014, *The Wild Truth*, which alleged that their father was both physically and verbally abusive to his wife and children.)

After graduating in May 1990 from Emory University in Atlanta, McCandless backpacked across the country. In the spring of 1992, McCandless found an abandoned and immovable bus, where he lived until his death from starvation on August 18 of that year. While it will never be known exactly what led to McCandless' starvation, the most common theory assumes he was the victim of a lethal form of food poisoning.

In 1996, author Jon Krakauer wrote a book about McCandless, *Into the Wild*, which became a national bestseller, and eventually led to a film adaptation in 2007, directed by Sean Penn and starring Emile Hirsch as McCandless. Penn eventually broached the subject of providing the film's soundtrack to Vedder, and the singer told his side of the story to *Billboard* in 2007: "I read the book and within a couple of days, he showed me the film here at the house in Seattle. In the book, what I knew immediately was, I had some insight beyond the pages of what might explain the extreme actions and reactions of Chris McCandless. We had similar upbringings and similar events in our lives. We were both young white male Americans. But I didn't have to burn my money to end up with nothing [laughs]. He took a bigger leap there. I was already off the cliff. So, I understood that much. When he showed me the film, I could see the landscapes and I could hear music in my head. But to be honest, most of it was similar to the music he had in there. Michael Brook made great choices with the way he orchestrated the score. Without even really thinking about it, I saw the film the one time and our pieces of music meshed together pretty well for not having approached it in a way of, let's make sure these puzzle pieces fit. They just did, you know?"

Released on September 18, 2007, the soundtrack was co-produced by Vedder and Adam Kasper, and features a total of 11 tracks (the iTunes version tacks on an additional four, and the vinyl version includes a two-song single). The album, which doubled as Vedder's first solo album, peaked at No. 11 on the Billboard 200 and racked up an impressive amount of awards and nominations: the song "Guaranteed" won a 2008 Golden Globe Award, and was nominated for Best Song Written for a Motion Picture, Television or Other Visual Media at the 2008 Grammy Awards and a 2008 World Soundtrack Award in the category of Best Original Song Written Directly for a Film. Additionally, Vedder was nominated for a Golden Globe Award for the material he contributed to the film's original score in 2008, while the song "Rise" received a nomination for Best Rock Vocal Performance, Solo at the 2009 Grammy Awards.

90 *Backspacer*

Might we summarize Pearl Jam's ninth studio full-length, *Backspacer*, featuring songs such as "Just Breathe" and "The End," as a kindlier, gentler Pearl Jam? While there is still plenty of rocking going on, the way the band approached their new tunes circa 2009 lacked the bite of say, "Porch" or "Animal." Of course, that's a natural maturation—after all, you can't expect an artist to stay young forever. Many of the best and most enduring artists find a way to adapt as they get older and still create captivating work. And that is what PJ was able to deliver with *Backspacer*.

Recorded between February 16 and April 30, 2009, at three studios (Henson Recording Studios in Hollywood, California, and Doppler and Southern Tracks Recording in Atlanta, Georgia), *Backspacer* was officially unveiled on September 20, 2009. Featuring album cover art supplied by artist/cartoonist Tom Tomorrow (real name: Dan Perkins), the cover features nine different seemingly random "scenes"—a flaming locomotive about to smash somebody, a transparent human body, a magician with two devils upon his shoulders, an underwater dancer, a brain, an astronaut playing drums in space, a guy dressed like Gilligan from *Gilligan's Island* and a robot, a pimp aboard a tricycle, and a shoeless woman slumbering in a purple haze.

Brendan O'Brien was back behind the mixing board, but whereas in the past he'd been listed as a co-producer, he was the sole producer on *Backspacer*. The album was the PJ studio effort to be issued via their own Monkeywrench label. On a darker note, toward the end of the album's recording, Jeff Ament and a band employee were the victims of a vicious assault and robbery outside of Southern Tracks Recording; thankfully, neither man suffered any serious injuries.

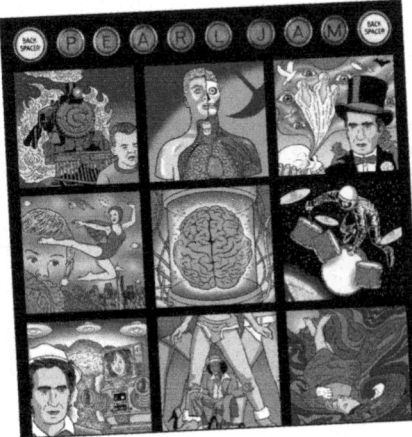

Backspacer, *Pearl Jam, 2009.*
(Monkeywrench Records)

As far as the material goes, the album-opening "Gonna See My Friend," as well as "Got Some" and "Supersonic," could classify as rowdy rock 'n' rollers, tunes such as "The Fixer," "Unknown Thought," and "Amongst the Waves" are all more moderately paced, while the aforementioned "Just Breathe" (which contains some of Eddie Vedder's best-ever lyrics) and "The End" are both in a mellower mood.

In a 2009 interview with *Billboard*, Vedder explained the genesis of "Just Breathe": "'Just Breathe'" uses the first chord from an instrumental called 'Tuolumne.' There was a lyric or something that hit me, and I picked up the guitar and played that chord. I thought, well, I'll just go with it and make something different out of it. It was a shorter song, and then I wrote a bridge to it while the other guys were working on something else. It was like our own little Brill Building at the warehouse. I ran in and wrote the bridge, which became the chorus, because [producer] Brendan O'Brien heard it that way. That's an example of letting Brendan hear things objectively and following him whatever way he wanted to take it. We weren't that malleable 10 years ago and all the years previous. You'd write something and say, 'Well, no, this is how I want it done.' One of the things as you get older is that you welcome others' input. You don't feel like you have to prove yourself."

In the good old days, a single was judged by and large by its initial release performance. But "Just Breathe" was introduced to a whole new audience when it began appearing in a variety of TV shows, films, and documentaries, including *Grey's Anatomy*, *Life as We Know It*, and *Gleason*. It was also covered by legendary singer-songwriter Willie Nelson on his 2012 album *Heroes*. As a result, Pearl Jam's version of the song has been certified platinum for digital sales in the U.S., the first PJ song to do so.

Chart performance–wise, *Backspacer* was a winner, topping the U.S. charts—the first PJ studio album since *No Code* to do so—as well as the Australian, Canadian, New Zealand, and Portuguese charts. And when it came to certifications, the album struck silver in England, gold in the U.S., New Zealand, and Portugal, and platinum in Australia, Canada, and Italy. The album's three singles were "The Fixer," a double A-side featuring "Got Some" and "Just Breathe," and "Amongst the Waves" (with "Just Breathe" being the most successful of the bunch). "The Fixer," "Just Breathe," and "Amongst the Waves" all received the video treatment.

Monkeywrench Records

After issuing their first seven albums on Epic and their eighth on J Records, few rock bands had enjoyed as successful a career as Pearl Jam. So when they became free agents after their 2006 self-titled release, they decided to start their own label, titled Monkeywrench Records, with the label's distribution being handled by Target in the United States and Universal Music Group worldwide.

While most record labels try and take on multiple acts, thus far Monkeywrench focuses solely on Pearl Jam and the side projects of its members. There remains quite a bit of mystery surrounding the label, as there has been no info posted about it on its website, monkeywrenchrecords.com, except for its logo—though fans can buy swell Monkeywrench gear via PJ's website.

So far, two PJ studio albums have been issued via Monkeywrench, 2009's *Backspacer* and 2013's *Lightning Bolt*, plus 2011's concert album, *Live on Ten Legs.* Also released via Monkeywrench are albums by Eddie Vedder (2011's *Ukulele Songs*), Stone Gossard (2013's *Moonlander*), and Mike McCready's celebrated side band, Mad Season (2015's *Seattle Symphony: Sonic Evolution/January 30, 2015/Benaroya Hall*). But by far, live recordings have the most presence on the label, as the band has issued countless titles as part of their ongoing "bootleg" series.

It will be interesting to see if Pearl Jam can "pull a Metallica" at some point in the future and regain full control of their back catalog and reissue them via Monkeywrench (as Metallica was able to do with their past records and videos, via the formation of their own Blackened label in 2012). Perhaps that was the whole idea of forming the Monkeywrench label in the first place? Keep your eyes on that Monkeywrench website!

92 Matt Cameron's Other Projects

Undoubtedly, Matt Cameron has been a member of the greatest "side band" of all his Pearl Jam mates, serving as the longtime drummer in Soundgarden. I know what you're thinking: Soundgarden, a *side band*?

Let me explain: while Cameron was a full member of SG from 1986 to 1997, once the band split, Pearl Jam became his main focus. So when SG reunited in 2010, Cameron's daily planner had to be carefully filled in; in 2014, Cameron opted out of touring with SG altogether due to his prior commitments with PJ. So, from 2010 onward, you might consider SG to be Cameron's side band…right?

Cameron may have held off on issuing a solo album until pretty late in the game, with the arrival of 2017's *Cavedweller*, but he certainly has gotten his name out elsewhere. We've already discussed Skin Yard and Temple of the Dog at length, but we have not yet touched upon Tone Dogs. Equal parts prog, jazz, and rock, the band was formed by singer/saxophonist Amy Denio and bassist Fred Chalenor during the late '80s, and when they needed a drummer to provide an off-meter pulse for their debut album, 1990's *Ankety Low Day*, Cameron was their man.

Between the *Badmotorfinger* and *Superunknown* eras of Soundgarden, both Cameron and Ben Shepherd found themselves with some free time…so why not fill it with a side band? The garage rocking Hater was soon created, also featuring Andy Wood's brother, Brian, on vocals, as well as former Monster Magnet guitarist John McBain and bassist John Waterman. The group released a pair of studio offerings, 1993's self-titled and 2005's *The 2nd*.

And while Stone Gossard's Brad is my favorite PJ side band, in second place is another collaboration between Cameron and McBain, the vintage psychedelic/space rock–loving Wellwater Conspiracy. Their 1997 debut, *Declaration of Conformity*, even saw Shepherd join the fun and provide vocals; none other than Queens of the Stone Age's Josh Homme signed on for 1999's *Brotherhood of Electric: Operational Directives*. WC's third album, 2001's *The Scroll and Its Combinations*, featured more guests, including Eddie Vedder on the tune "Felicity's Surprise" (under the alias of Wes C.

Addle... *West Seattle*, get it?), before the band issued a fourth and final recording, 2003's self-titled offering.

Additionally, Cameron has appeared on what seems to be a pair of one-off side bands—the jazzy Harrybu McCage, who issued a self-titled album in 2008, and the rocking Ten Commandos, which saw Cameron and Shepherd unite once again, this time with Eleven guitarist Alain Johannes and Off! guitarist Dimitri Coats, plus guest vocals by Mark Lanegan, for its self-titled debut in 2015.

Of all the PJ members' guest appearances, Cameron has appeared on the most by well-known musicians. Don't believe me? This list won't lie: Queens of the Stone Age's "Born to Hula" (on the 1996 single *Gamma Ray*, back when QOTSA were going by the early name of Gamma Ray), the Prodigy (on 1997's *Fat of the Land*), Smashing Pumpkins' "For Martha" and "Because You Are" (1998's *Adore* and 2001's *Judas O*, respectively), Chris Cornell's "Disappearing One" (1999's *Euphoria Morning*), and Peter Frampton's "Blowin' Smoke" and a cover of Soundgarden's "Black Hole Sun" (2006's *Fingerprints*).

And in 2000, Cameron may have outdone himself in the special appearance department when he was enlisted to perform on a pair of solo albums by two members of hard rock royalty: Black Sabbath's Tony Iommi (the tracks "Time Is Mine," "Flame On," "Just Say No to Love," and "Into the Night" on *Iommi*) and Rush's Geddy Lee (all the tracks on *My Favourite Headache* except for "Home on the Strange"). And since this is a list of Cameron's most impressive guest spots, there's no reason to include participation in Chad Kroeger's schmaltzy ballad/duet with Josey Scott, "Hero," from the *Spider-Man* soundtrack, is there?

Collect the Pearl Jam DVDs

Pearl Jam is unquestionably one of the top live rock acts of all time. So it makes perfect sense that quite a few PJ concert DVDs have been issued over the years, documenting various eras of the band.

Although the band was at their most explosive and over-the-top during their early years, particularly the tours in support of *Ten* and *Vs.*, frustratingly, there was never an official live home video documenting a complete pro-shot show from this era. In fact, the first officially released PJ home video was a documentary filmed over a three-day span of rehearsals from November 7 through November 10, 1997, when the band was gearing up to open shows for the Rolling Stones, titled *Single Video Theory*. Issued on August 4, 1998, the 45-minute long video was directed by Mark Pellington (the same man responsible for the "Jeremy" music video), and provides an absorbing fly-on-the-wall view of the band at work. And it proved highly successful, peaking at No. 2 on the Billboard Video Chart, and earning platinum certification stateside.

But with their next home video, PJ would *finally* give the fans what they wanted—a real whopper of a release titled *Touring Band 2000*. As its title clearly states, the tremendously long DVD (we're talking 28 tracks and 177 minutes in length, *plus* bonus bits) contains highlights from various performances on the band's North American tour in support of the *Binaural* album, between August 12 and November 6, 2000. And what you get is the perfect blend of classics ("Even Flow," "Daughter," "Better Man"), standout album tracks ("Corduroy," "Nothingman," "Lukin"), and then-newer tracks ("Do the Evolution," "Evacuation," "Nothing as It Seems"). The bonus features proved worthwhile, as well—several tunes utilizing the "Matt Cam," video montages, and two bonus music videos ("Oceans" and "Do the Evolution"). Once again, the release was a hit, topping the Billboard Video Chart and going platinum (while impressively going triple platinum in Australia).

While *Touring Band 2000* was certainly a winner, it was not a single full concert. That was corrected by Pearl Jam's next home video release, *Live at the Showbox*. Released on May 7, 2003, and filmed on December 6, 2002, at the famed Seattle venue, the complete DVD has been rarely seen by anyone except hardcore PJ fans; it was never commercially released, but rather sold exclusively through the band's website. Still, it is absolutely worth tracking down a copy, as it kicks off with a song rarely used as a concert opener, "Elderly Woman Behind the Counter in a Small Town," and includes such other treats as "Breakerfall," "Love Boat Captain," a surprise lyrical insertion of Edwin Starr's "War" at the end of "Daughter," "Yellow Ledbetter," and a set-closing rendition of "Don't Believe in Christmas."

As discussed earlier, Pearl Jam and Madison Square Garden have formed quite a special bond over the years, so it made sense for the first commercially available full-length DVD featuring a single concert be filmed at the famed NYC venue. Shot on the first night of a two-night engagement (July 8, 2003), the double-disc *Live at the Garden* was released on November 11, 2003, and features such standouts as a cover of John Lennon's "Gimme Some Truth," an emotional rendition of Mother Love Bone's "Crown of Thorns," Ben Harper joining in for two songs ("Daughter" and "Indifference"), and a couple of Buzzcocks appearing for a pair of covers (Tony Barber for "Sonic Reducer" and Steve Diggle for "Baba O'Riley"). In the bonus features, quite a few extra tracks are tacked on, as well as the triumphant return of the "Matt Cam," plus an Easter egg that features a performance of Temple of the Dog's "Hunger Strike," sung by Vedder and guest Corin Tucker of Sleater-Kinney. So far, *Live at the Garden* is PJ's most commercially successful DVD release, peaking at No. 2 on the Billboard Video

Chart and going triple platinum in the U.S. (and, going a whole step further in Australia…quadruple platinum).

Four years later, the next live Pearl Jam DVD was ready for unveiling, *Immagine in Cornice* (Italian for "picture in a frame"). Filmed between September 14 and September 20, 2006, in Bologna, Verona, Milan, Torino and Pistoia, Italy, the 113-minute-long film was directed by Danny Clinch, and features footage of the band behind the scenes in Italy, in addition to live performances. One particular standout among the bonus features is a performance of the Who's "A Quick One, While He's Away," which sees Eddie Vedder team up with My Morning Jacket. As far as chart performance, it topped the U.S. Billboard Video Chart and was certified gold. On November 17, 2017, Clinch and PJ released another concert DVD, *Let's Play Two*, which documents the band's performances at Wrigley Field in 2016.

Finally, we've covered the *Pearl Jam Twenty* documentary elsewhere in this book, but if you'd like to include it amongst your collection of Pearl Jam DVDs, you can go right ahead!

94 The Decline of Grunge

Although Pearl Jam remains hugely popular today, releasing albums and touring on a regular basis, there is no denying that the grunge movement as a whole was unable to sustain its success. In fact, you can pinpoint the year that it all began to unravel—1994. The most obvious reason was the suicide that year of Kurt Cobain, which ended the career of Nirvana. The band was supposedly lined up to headline Lollapalooza that summer, and were going to try a different approach on their proposed fourth studio album—either more mellow or more experimental, depending on which interview with Cobain you read, heard, or saw around that time.

While Soundgarden would go on to become one of the biggest success stories in the world of rock in 1994, thanks to their multi-platinum/chart-topping/Grammy-winning album *Superunknown*, the tour in support of the album was cut short due to Chris Cornell's vocal troubles, and friction arose within the band. As a result, Soundgarden only lasted for one more album (1996's *Down on the Upside*) before splitting in 1997 (but eventually reuniting in 2010 and continuing until Cornell's death in 2017).

Having served as one of the highlights of the 1993 edition of Lollapalooza and scoring their first No. 1 release with *Jar of Flies* in early '94, it appeared to the casual fan that Alice in Chains would continue to record and tour with a great amount of success and on a regular basis. But it turned out that Layne Staley was in the throes of a ghastly drug addiction, and after only one more album, 1995's self-titled, Alice in Chains would not issue another full-length recording with Staley, who would eventually become a hermit in his Seattle apartment before dying of a drug overdose on April 5, 2002.

Pearl Jam was affected in 1994 as well, not touring as much as they could have due to their much-publicized battle with Ticketmaster. And while they admirably refused to simply repli-cate the formula of the mega-selling *Ten* on subsequent albums, the pop fans who they picked up early on were put off by their albums post-*Vitalogy*, as each one seemed to be less accessible and successful than its predecessor (although PJ's popularity as a live act never dwindled).

Another contributing factor to grunge's decline as the '90s wore on was the inability of the Seattle's "Big 4" peers to score a break-through hit, despite the likes of Mudhoney, the Melvins, Screaming Trees, and Tad all issuing albums on major labels during that time. There was also no true "second wave" of authentic grunge, as MTV chose to embrace pretenders such as Bush, Silverchair, and Creed, rather than artists with legitimate grunge ties who were much more original, genuine, and deserving of commercial success, such as Truly, Brad, and Sunny Day Real Estate. As a result, combined with the natural changing of tastes that have occurred throughout music history, grunge was unable to sustain its initial success. But it can never be denied that it shifted the direction of rock music for an entire generation and beyond.

95 Lightning Bolt

Pearl Jam must have been quite pleased with the results of *Backspacer*, because on their following studio effort, 2013's *Lightning Bolt*, Brendan O'Brien was once again granted the sole title of producer. Unlike *Ten* and *Vs.*, which were recorded rather quickly, *Lightning Bolt* was recorded off and on over an extended period of time, between 2011 and 2013 at Henson Recording Studios in Los Angeles. Everyone in the band was simultaneously working on projects outside of Pearl Jam.

Released on October 15, 2013, *Lightning Bolt* was the second PJ studio effort issued on Monkeywrench Records. The album cover features a large eyeball, what looks like a radio tower, and several lightning bolts; it was designed by artist Don Pendleton, best known for his work in the world of skateboard graphics. The band released three singles: "Mind Your Manners," "Sirens," and the title track. "Mind Your Manners" and "Sirens" both received video treatment, thanks to Danny Clinch.

You have to give the boys credit for refusing to play it safe this far into their career. The beginning of "Mind Your Manners" is almost prog-ish, "Let the Records Play" shows PJ embracing

Lightning Bolt, *Pearl Jam,*
2013. (Monkeywrench Records)

rockabilly, while "Getaway" proves once and for all how gifted Eddie Vedder truly is at coming up with remarkable vocal melodies that add new dimensions to already strong musical compositions. That said, melody and restraint is exercised more often than not throughout the album's 12 selections, especially evidenced on such cuts as "Sirens," "Pendulum," "Sleeping by Myself," "Yellow Moon," and "Future Days."

Lightning Bolt set the charts alight worldwide, hitting No. 1 in the U.S., Australia, Belgium, Canada, Croatia, Ireland, and Portugal. The album reached gold status in both Australia and Poland, and platinum in Canada and Italy. However, *Lightning Bolt* became the first Pearl Jam studio album never to receive a single certification in the U.S., which demonstrates how off-kilter the U.S. charts and record sales are nowadays—that an album can top the charts, but not register any sort of certification. That said, I have a sneaking suspicion that not a single Pearl Jam member is losing sleep over that fact.

Visit the Rock and Roll Hall of Fame

The Rock and Roll Hall of Fame has—rightfully—drawn criticism over the years. For starters, it was unclear for many years exactly who was on the "voting committee," although the results seemed to reflect the artists *Rolling Stone* approved of. Nevertheless, Eddie Vedder has given several memorable induction speeches over the years for some of the elite names in rock music history, and eventually, even Pearl Jam found their way into the Hall.

On January 12, 1993, Vedder introduced the Doors at their induction at Century Plaza Hotel in Los Angeles, with a speech that touched upon how all four members of the group wound up avoiding the Vietnam War; later, he joined the surviving members of the group for renditions of such Doors classics as "Roadhouse Blues" and "Light My Fire."

The next time Vedder would speak at an artist's induction would be on January 12, 1995, when he welcomed in Neil Young at the Waldorf Astoria Hotel in New York. He made a humorous speech in which he pointed out that some "smartass" who arranged the tables that evening set Pearl Jam's table next to Ticketmaster's (this was just a few months after Jeff Ament and Stone Gossard stated their case against the company in front of Congress). Vedder called Young, a "great songwriter, great performer, and great Canadian." Interestingly, when it came time to perform, it was Neil Young and his longtime band, Crazy Horse, performing the tune "Act of Love," which would appear on the forthcoming album that Young and Pearl Jam recorded together, *Mirror Ball*, before PJ joined in on a version of "Fuckin' Up," a song originally done by Young and Crazy Horse on *Ragged Glory*.

But perhaps of all the speeches Vedder delivered at a Rock and Roll Hall of Fame function, the one he gave on March 18, 2002, when he introduced the Ramones at the Waldorf Astoria Hotel in New York, was his most memorable. While taking the stage sporting an unexpected Mohawk, Vedder talked about his first experience seeing the band live as a youngster, among other topics, during a speech that stretched on for 17 minutes.

To prove that Vedder is one heck of a popular HoF speaker, it was only five years later that he was once again behind the podium at the Waldorf Astoria Hotel, when he did the honors of introducing R.E.M. on March 12, 2007. Included in his speech was how

Eddie Vedder introduces the Ramones at the band's Rock and Roll Hall of Fame induction ceremony in New York, 2002. (AP Images)

Michael Stipe touched Vedder via his lyrical wisdom…without "ever being able to understand a fucking thing he was saying." And afterward, Vedder joined R.E.M. on stage for a rendition of their classic "Man on the Moon."

Ten years later, it was finally time for Pearl Jam to be inducted, as well, on April 7, 2017, at the Barclays Center in Brooklyn, New York. Neil Young was originally supposed to introduce the band, but after falling ill and being forced to bow out, David Letterman emerged out of seclusion to deliver one heck of a passionate speech; one of many highlights included discussing how Pearl Jam is responsible for so much great music and that the band would "recognize injustice and they would stand up for it." All the members had a turn at the mic, including Stone Gossard reading off a long list of people's names who helped the band over the years, Dave Krusen saying how PJ saved his life, Matt Cameron thanking his wife and family, Mike McCready also thanking family and friends, Jeff Ament talking about relocating from Montana to Seattle many years ago, and Eddie Vedder taking the opportunity to mention that we still have a lot of "evolution" to do, anything can be obtainable (by using the Chicago Cubs winning the 2016 World Series as an example), the power of music, and his family. And in case you're wondering about the other former members besides Krusen, Jack Irons was situated in the audience (as opposed to being onstage for some reason), while Dave Abbruzzese was not in the building. Afterward, three tunes were performed—"Alive," "Given to Fly," and "Better Man"—before the band took part in a "super jam" of "Rockin' the Free World," with members of Yes, Journey, Rush, and George Harrison's son, Dhani Harrison.

So, what exactly are you likely to see when you visit the Hall of Fame's exhibit for Pearl Jam? Lots of goodies. Tops on the list would be the T-shirt Vedder wore on *SNL* in 1994 with the "K" scribbled on it in tribute to Kurt Cobain and another T-shirt with the Rock for Choice logo on it, which Vedder sported on *SNL* in 1992. You'll also find a Smith-Corona Sterling typewriter that Vedder has used to compose song lyrics, and even a stuffed cow doll, which Stone Gossard utilized as a stage prop in 1991, among other odds and ends.

97 Covering Pearl Jam

Due to their immense back catalog and plethora of great songs, it's easy to understand why so many artists have covered Pearl Jam songs over the years. As it turns out, it is predominantly selections from PJ's early albums that have been the most often covered. The following is merely a sampling.

The song that everyone seems to feel should have been a single way back when, "Black," has been covered by the likes of Staind's Aaron Lewis and Tori Amos. As you might expect, Lewis' version stays quite close to the original, while Amos' version is far more interesting and bears little resemblance to the original. Others who have taken on "Black" include Chris Daughtry, Stone Sour, and, perhaps oddest of all, Major League Baseball pitcher Bronson Arroyo, who recorded it for his 2005 album, *Covering the Bases*; on August 5, 2016, Arroyo joined PJ on stage at Fenway Park to perform the tune with his musical heroes.

Ben Harper has covered or performed with Pearl Jam numerous times over the years, perhaps the most powerful being his version of "Indifference," as the focus is placed on Harper's soulful vocals. Perhaps the rarest cover of "Indifference" was performed for a very select audience: during the *Monkeywrench Radio* broadcast, Eddie Vedder recalled Jeff Buckley performing the song once upon a time, and called witnessing it "one of the most memorable moments of my life."

Another artist who has a soft spot for early PJ is O.A.R., who has covered both "Footsteps" and "Elderly Woman Behind the Counter in a Small Town," as well as singer-songwriter Charlotte Martin, who also covered "Elderly Woman" and offered up a studio version on her 2007 all-covers album, *Reproductions*.

The list of artists to pay tribute to Pearl Jam could go on and on. The members of the band Umphrey's McGee are major PJ fans, as they have covered several of their tunes over the years, including "Release," "Porch," and "Elderly Woman." Scottish rockers Biffy Clyro do a version of "Daughter." Panic! At the Disco has taken on "Jeremy." Jack Johnson has played "Soon Forget" (for which Vedder has been known to join him onstage). And one of the first bands to ever "cover" a PJ tune were old pals Soundgarden, when Chris Cornell sang a few lines from "Alive" over the extended jam part of "Slaves and Bulldozers" on their 1992 home video *Motorvision*. It wouldn't be the last time Cornell would cover a song by his friends, as he performed a solo voice/acoustic guitar version of "Better Man" as well.

A few more interesting takes: the late, great Prince offered up an instrumental version of "Even Flow" with his latter-day backing band, 3rdeyegirl, and legendary singer-songwriter Willie Nelson has covered "Just Breathe." Finally, in a case of not saving the best for last, Limp Bizkit covered a bit of "Alive" at Rock Am Ring in 2013.

98 Kelly Curtis

In some cases, the manager of an artist has taken on celebrity status in his own right. For example, Sharon Osbourne (the wife/manager of Ozzy Osbourne), Colonel Tom Parker (Elvis Presley), Brian Epstein (the Beatles), Peter Grant (Led Zeppelin), and Malcolm McLaren (the Sex Pistols) have become synonymous with the acts they managed. But then there are managers who seem averse to the spotlight and prefer to work behind the scenes with little-to-no ballyhoo. Pearl Jam's longtime manager, Kelly Curtis, would be a shining example of the latter description.

Curtis has rarely been interviewed at great length about his background or private life—even his birth date and family info remain a mystery. (There is one noteworthy nugget—a photo of his daughter adorns the cover of Pearl Jam's "Jeremy" single.) What is known is how he worked his way up the management ladder: he started out as a road manager and publicist for Heart (1976–83), before being named road manager for Japanese heavy metallists Loudness (1983–85), serving as the manager of Mother Love Bone (1989–90), and co-managing Alice in Chains along with Susan Silver (1989–91), before Silver solely assumed control. Along the way, he formed Curtis Management, and since 1990 he has been Pearl Jam's manager.

One of the things that makes Curtis (and Pearl Jam) different than the average manager and popular rock band is their willingness to turn down lucrative opportunities if they feel the band will be overexposed or damaged in the long run. In one of his rare interviews with a major publication, to *Spin* magazine, in 2001, Curtis explained, "We turned down inaugurals, TV specials, stadium tours, every kind of merchandise you could think of. I got a call from Calvin Klein, wanting Eddie to be in an ad. I learned how to say no really well. I was proud of the band, proud of their stances. We were starting to use the power for more political, more charitable-type things."

Colleen Combs, Curtis' former assistant, recalled in *Grunge Is Dead* what made him special and different when compared to other managers: "When the ball was rolling and [Kelly Curtis] could do stuff, his first thing wasn't to buy a fancy car and move his office to Los Angeles. That was one of the things that I really respected and liked about him—they stayed where they came from. And the Pearl Jam guys, I always looked at it like after the heavy metal '80s of Los Angeles, the Seattle scene was such a healthy, great place. I mean, Pearl Jam did not have strippers backstage—they had a special road case that had toys in it for the kids. And we had headphones so the kids' ears wouldn't get affected by the sound levels. That for me was a huge change."

Lastly, in addition to his PJ management duties, Curtis has also found the time to work on feature films and music documentaries (as a producer on *Pearl Jam Twenty*, an associate producer on *Singles*, a tech advisor on *Almost Famous*, and a music consultant on *Lords of Dogtown*).

99 Alice in Chains

Soundgarden and Mother Love Bone were the first two grunge bands to secure deals with major labels. Right behind them to sign on the dotted line was Alice in Chains, the first grunge band to truly break through commercially—before most people outside of the Seattle rock community had ever heard of Kurt Cobain.

Formed in 1987, the band started out looking and sounding quite similar to the likes of Mötley Crüe and Poison. In fact, an early way of spelling their name was Alice 'N Chains—a clear homage to Guns N' Roses. The first long-term lineup consisted of singer Layne Staley, guitarist Jerry Cantrell, bassist Mike Starr, and drummer Sean Kinney. They played around Seattle before being inspired by Soundgarden to shift toward the grungier side of music. Soon after, then Soundgarden manager Susan Silver and then–Mother Love Bone manager Kelly Curtis signed on to co-manage Alice in Chains. A recording contract with Columbia soon followed, and on August 21, 1990, they released their full-length debut, *Facelift*. To say that the album took a long time to build momentum is an understatement, but the band stayed busy by playing with just about any rock act that would take them on tour, opening for everyone from Extreme to Iggy Pop.

It was around this time that Alice in Chains first connected with the band known as Mookie Blaylock, when the pair played the Moore Theater in Seattle together on December 22 (a concert that was filmed for both bands, resulting in footage eventually surfacing in *Live Facelift* and *PJ 20*, respectively). Alice in Chains would take the then-renamed Pearl Jam out on tour outside of Seattle, their first dates outside of their hometown, throughout February 1991.

However, it would not be until late spring of 1991 that MTV had taken notice of the black-and-white video for the *Facelift* standout "Man in the Box." By the time the band had wrapped up arena tours supporting a thrash metal package comprised of Slayer, Megadeth, and Anthrax (dubbed the Clash of the Titans) and Van Halen, *Facelift* had been certified gold. However, it was also around this time that the band members got bitten by the drug bug, something that would eventually lead to the original lineup's undoing.

Despite not being as clear-headed as they once were, Alice in Chains benefitted greatly from the success of *Nevermind, Ten,* and *Badmotorfinger* in late 1991 and early 1992, as they were mentioned in just about every article penned about the burgeoning Seattle scene. An acoustic EP, *Sap* (released February 2, 1992), helped bridge the gap between albums, and fans' appetites were whetted further when a killer track, "Would?" (inspired by Andy Wood's death), turned out to be one of the standouts on the *Singles* motion picture soundtrack (alongside a pair of PJ songs). AiC and a rather drunken PJ would again cross paths at the taping of the *Singles Movie Premiere Party* for MTV, on September 10, 1992, in Los Angeles.

Just 19 days later, Alice in Chains' highly anticipated sophomore full-length, *Dirt,* would be unveiled; it could be fittingly described as a dark masterpiece. In addition to Cantrell fast becoming a master at creating monster guitar riffs, it was Staley's seemingly brutally honest lyrics about drug addiction that made the album stand out from the rest of the grunge, alt-rock, and metal releases at the time. That is especially true of a trio of tracks in the middle, "Junkhead," the title track, and "God Smack." It also catapulted the band to arena-sized status, with the album peaking at No. 6 on the Billboard 200.

The first sign that not all was hunky dory in the AiC camp, aside from rumors and interpretations of song lyrics, was when Starr was abruptly excused from the group mid-tour, with former

Ozzy Osbourne bassist Mike Inez taking his spot in time for the 1993 edition of Lollapalooza. But unbeknownst to fans, the dates in support of *Dirt* would be the last time the Staley version of the band would launch a substantial tour together. An all-acoustic EP would be issued, *Jar of Flies*, which topped the Billboard 200 chart upon its release on January 25, 1994. However, around this time rumors gained momentum about the depths of Staley's drug addiction and its effects on him, especially after a planned performance at Woodstock '94 and an entire run of summer dates with Metallica were nixed.

It was around this time that Mike McCready had successfully completed a rehab stint, which ultimately resulted in the formation of the band Mad Season—fronted by none other than Staley—that resulted in their classic self-titled album, which was issued on March 14, 1995, and peaked at No. 24. McCready's main goal in forming the band was to try and help Staley get serious about sobriety, which unfortunately did not go according to plan.

Alice in Chains was able to squeeze out one more studio full-length with Staley behind the mic—a self-titled album, released on November 7, 1995, which became the band's second consecutive chart-topper. However, the album was not as focused nor inspired as its predecessors, and a *Rolling Stone* cover feature about the band on February 8, 1996, entitled ALICE IN CHAINS: TO HELL AND BACK, painted a grim picture, especially with such quotes from Staley as this one: "I wrote about drugs, and I didn't think I was being unsafe or careless by writing about them. Here's how my thinking pattern went: when I tried drugs, they were fucking great, and they worked for me for years, and now they're turning against me—and now I'm walking through hell, and this sucks. I didn't want my fans to think that heroin was cool. But then I've had fans come up to me and give me the thumbs up, telling me they're high. That's exactly what I didn't want to happen."

A now-classic *Unplugged* filming took place on April 10, 1996 (and was subsequently issued on CD and DVD), but the last public appearance by the singer would be several shows that Alice in Chains would open for Kiss on their highly successful reunion tour during the summer. Then…*nothing.* No sign of the singer, and little was heard from the band, as everything seemed to grind to a halt, aside from a 1999 box set (which included two new tracks, "Get Born Again" and "Died"), a concert set (2000's *Live*), and a best-of compilation (2001's *Greatest Hits*). Then, the inevitable: Staley's body was found on April 19, 2002, having overdosed on drugs on approximately April 5 (in a strange quirk, the same day as Kurt Cobain's death eight years earlier).

Even prior to his passing, Staley—along with Vedder—had become one of the most copied singers in all of rock, as a seemingly endless parade of new vocalists aped his trademark style and the way he and Cantrell would vocal harmonize together (namely Days of the New, Staind, Puddle of Mudd, Cold, and most obviously, a band that took their name from an AiC tune—Godsmack). As a response to these copycats, Pearl Jam would pen a song entitled "4/20/02," which would appear on the *Lost Dogs* compilation in 2003. The song's title represents the day after the date that Staley's body was discovered, and includes clear jabs at all the imposters: "So sing just like him, fuckers / It won't offend him, just me / Because he's dead."

Cantrell, Inez, and Kinney would rekindle Alice in Chains in 2005, with William DuVall taking Staley's spot, resulting in the arrival of 2009's *Black Gives Way to Blue* (No. 5) and 2013's *The Devil Put Dinosaurs Here* (No. 2). Unfortunately, there was one more sad chapter to add to the Alice in Chains story—the death of Starr on March 8, 2011, also from a drug overdose.

100 The PJ20 Festival

No one can ever say Pearl Jam did not go all out to celebrate the band's 20ᵗʰ anniversary.

In addition to the *Pearl Jam Twenty* book, Cameron Crowe documentary, and soundtrack released in 2011, the ambitious members of Pearl Jam figured, why not throw a two-day concert festival with a bunch of other bands? And so was born the PJ20 Festival.

Scheduled to take place over Labor Day weekend, September 3 and 4, 2011, at the Alpine Valley Music Theatre in East Troy, Wisconsin, the two-day concert offered fans an embarrassment of riches: sets by Glen Hansard, Joseph Arthur, Liam Finn, John Doe, and thenewno2 to get the crowd going, then performances by Mudhoney, Queens of the Stone Age, and the Strokes, before Pearl Jam hit the stage to headline each night.

Surrounded by thousands of their most die-hard fans from around the world, the band knew that even the deepest album tracks would be well received; at one point, Eddie Vedder told the crowd, "We feel like we could play just about anything and you fuckers would know it." He was right: over the two nights, PJ played songs rarely heard in concert, such as "Pilate," "Wash," and "Push Me, Pull Me."

As you might imagine, there were numerous guest appearances in both directions: the Strokes' Julian Casablancas joining PJ on "Not For You," Josh Homme appearing for "In the Moonlight," and Mudhoney playing "Kick Out the Jams," while Vedder joined Hansard on "Falling Slowly" and the Strokes for "Juicebox." Casablancas said, "This is great, 'cause he sings it so much better than I do."

But undoubtedly the highlight of each night occurred midway through PJ's three-hour set: a full Temple of the Dog reunion with Chris Cornell. They ran through all the band's classics—"Hunger Strike," "Say Hello 2 Heaven," "Call Me a Dog," and "Reach Down"—to a euphoric crowd that could hardly believe what it was seeing and hearing.

"This doesn't make us feel older at all," Vedder said toward the end of the weekend. "It's given us some sense of rebirth. It feels like a new beginning."

About the Author

Greg Prato is a writer based in Long Island, New York, whose work has appeared in *Rolling Stone*, *Songfacts*, and *Vintage Guitar*, among others. He is also the author of numerous popular books, including *Grunge Is Dead: The Oral History of Seattle Rock Music*, *A Devil on One Shoulder and an Angel on the Other: The Story of Shannon Hoon and Blind Melon*, and *Too High to Die: Meet the Meat Puppets*. He has been interviewed numerous times on radio and television, including on *The Howard Stern Wrap-Up Show*, *Eddie Trunk Live*, and *Electric Ballroom*, as well as for the DVD *Pearl Jam: Under Review*. You can follow him on Twitter @gregpratowriter.

Other Books by Greg Prato

Music

A Devil on One Shoulder and an Angel on the Other: The Story of Shannon Hoon and Blind Melon

German Metal Machine: Scorpions in the '70s

Grunge Is Dead: The Oral History of Seattle Rock Music

Iron Maiden: '80, '81

MTV Ruled the World: The Early Years of Music Video

No Schlock...Just Rock!: A Journalistic Journey, 2003–2008

Overlooked/Underappreciated: 354 Recordings That Demand Your Attention

Primus, Over the Electric Grapevine: Insight into Primus and the World of Les Claypool

Punk! Hardcore! Reggae! PMA! Bad Brains!

Scott Weiland: Memories of a Rock Star

Shredders!: The Oral History of Speed Guitar (and More)

Survival of the Fittest: Heavy Metal in the 1990s

The Eric Carr Story

The Faith No More & Mr. Bungle Companion

The Other Side of Rainbow

The Yacht Rock Book: The Oral History of the Soft, Smooth Sounds of the '70s and '80s

Too High to Die: Meet the Meat Puppets

Touched by Magic: The Tommy Bolin Story

Sports

Dynasty: The Oral History of the New York Islanders, 1972–1984

Just Out of Reach: The 1980s New York Yankees

Sack Exchange: The Definitive Oral History of the 1980s New York Jets

The Seventh Year Stretch: New York Mets, 1977–1983